ENGLAND 1553

A Turbulent Year in Tudor History

Chris Leuchars

Copyright © 2021 Chris Leuchars

All rights reserved

Chris Leuchars obtained his D.Phil at Oxford University, and has since worked as a History teacher and museum educator. He has written books on such diverse subjects as the Paraguayan War, the Donner Party, and John Snow and Cholera.

Contents

List of Illustrations	2
Introduction	3
Preamble – Northumberland Comes to Power	11
1. 1553: A Year of Promise?	26
2. The Problem with Mary	41
3. 'My devise for the Succession'	65
4. Preparing the Ground	90
5. The Rebellion against Mary	113
6. Mary the Queen	143
7. Establishing the New Regime	167
8. The Wooing of Mary	183
9. Revolt and Resolution	206
10. Aftermath	238
Conclusion	244
References	256
Bibliography	265
Index	273

Illustrations

Cover photograph: *John Dudley, duke of Northumberland*, unknown artist. *Mary I*, by Antonis Mor

Edward Seymour, duke of Somerset (unknown artist)	15
'4 Suns', Charles Wriothesley	25
Charles V, by Titian	49
Edward VI, after William Scrots	60
Edward's 'devise'	66
The Tudor Family Tree in 1553	69
Henri II, studio of François Clouet	96
William Cecil, attributed to Marcus Gheeraerts the Younger	105
East Anglia	120
Presumed portrait of Lady Jane Grey, unknown artist	124
Henry Fitzalan, 12th earl of Arundel, unknown artist	137
Stephen Gardiner, unknown artist	153
William Paget, attributed to Jan Vermeyen	154
Thomas Cranmer, unknown artist	170
Philip of Spain, copy of original by Titian	202
Thomas Wyatt, by Hans Holbein	213
Kent	215
Wyatt's advance on London	221
The Execution of Lady Jane Grey, by Paul Delaroche	240

(The images in this book are taken from Wikimedia Commons, and are understood to be copyright free)

Introduction

A quick glance at a timeline of the monarchs of Tudor England appears to reveal a picture of serene continuity. Henry begets Henry, who begets, more or less in turn, Edward, Mary and Elizabeth. No unexplained Edwards or Richards to cloud the picture, nor even yet an Oliver. Tudor England; an apparent oasis of tranquillity amid the turmoil of centuries past and future.

Yet look more closely, and certain anomalies start to show. Somewhere, in the midst of this calm, a Jane briefly appears, and then a Philip – fleeting visits, easily overlooked, and leaving little mark on the broad historical record, but there, nonetheless. Perhaps Tudor England is not such a model of seamless progression after all.

1553, temporally close to the middle of the Tudor era, certainly seems to contradict the image. It saw three monarchs – one dying before his time, with vague suspicions of poisoning; one ending up sentenced to die on the scaffold; and one – the least likely – surviving, despite being illegitimate and thus possibly not deserving to be there at all. Among them were England's first two reigning queens. It also saw the execution of a chief minister, a coup, two revolts, a complete change in religion, and the decision to appoint a foreigner as king.

There would seem to be enough here to justify a book simply on the basis of these extraordinary events, but to focus a study on one particular year demands something more - a context, and an explanation for why this year was so significant. Yet we must be careful. Despite a natural desire to make sense of events, and to find in them some sort of explanation, or pattern, this can become a somewhat artificial exercise. Sometimes, things just happen. It is hard to imagine that anyone, in January 1553, could have foretold a single one of the events mentioned above, so to try and find a context that explains them runs the risk of ignoring the way life unfolds. Nevertheless, the duty of the historian is to interpret, as well as to relate, and there are some background threads that this year can be set against.

*

On the surface, 1553 fits in – both temporally and thematically – with the much-discussed 'mid-Tudor crisis'. This is generally taken to cover the reigns of Edward VI and Mary, when an apparent lack of effective leadership, severe economic problems, uncertainties over religion, and a decline in England's international prestige are supposed to have led to a sense of malaise and stagnation, and a general loss of direction. The events of 1553 can be seen as a symptom of these issues, and it will not be hard to find evidence of them throughout this book.

However, it is somewhat unfair to tar this period – this year, even – with a brush that can be used to paint a much larger timespan. Economic problems were the backdrop to the whole early modern period and have remained so to this day. Religion became a divisive national issue as early as the fourteenth century, if not before, and continued for the next five, and as for issues of leadership, the Tudor period really was an oasis of calm compared with the centuries either side of it. Perhaps the crisis is not so much one that affected the Tudors themselves, as one that has bedevilled historians, anxious to know how to categorise this hard-to-define gap between the glittering reigns of Henry VIII and Elizabeth I. It has not been helped by the fact that each reign was discredited, and almost surgically removed, by its successor, so that we are left with an impression of stagnation and insignificance, neither of which can be so easily justified on closer examination.

Yet, if we are to adopt this interpretation as a template, it might be more instructive to see the events of 1553 not so much as a *symptom* of this malaise, but as a *refutation* of it. Northumberland's coup was evidence of too much leadership, not too little. Rather than let events take their natural course, he actively intervened to pre-empt them. He posed a serious challenge to the survival of the Tudor dynasty, but the significance is not so much in the challenge, but in the *defeat* of that challenge. The same can be said of Wyatt's revolt; Mary survived it and ended up stronger. Her triumph was to allow for a seamless and unchallenged succession for Elizabeth. If there is a lesson to be learnt from this one year it is more about the survival and strength of the dynasty, not its weakness.

Introduction

*

Ask an average English person to think about the Tudors, and the likelihood is that two images will swim first into their mind. One, of a vastly overweight, heavily-jowled, powerfully-dressed, man staring threateningly towards them; the other, a woman, with wisps of orange hair over a face alarmingly white with layers of make-up, above a high ruff and a billowing dress dripping with jewellery. Henry and Elizabeth – the two icons of the Tudor Age – the symbols of the dynasty and of the century in which they ruled.

The Tudors have long been popular. Many history teachers will tell you that the two favourite lessons for their students in the entire curriculum are those that deal with the wives of Henry VIII, and the confrontation between Elizabeth and her cousin, Mary Queen of Scots. The number of books, films and television 'histories' dealing with these personalities is a reminder of the enduring fascination, and almost limitless appetite, for recycled information about them. Perhaps this is because women played such an unusually prominent role in these national events, or maybe it is simply that these incidents are such good and easily relatable stories.

About the other Tudor monarchs little is known. Mary is just 'Bloody Mary', Edward is the sickly child who never made it, while Henry VII – arguably the most laudable of the lot – is to many people a complete blank. Similarly, with the periods on either side. There might be a few incidents from Medieval times – the Black Death, the Peasants Revolt, the Wars of the Roses – that are dimly remembered, and from the Stuarts most are aware that Charles I had his head cut off - by Oliver Cromwell, possibly - but who could tell you much about the monarchs between him and Victoria?

So why is it that these two, and by extension the Tudors as a whole, have so captured the popular imagination? Other periods have their fair share of spectacular and/or unhinged rulers. Is it just because of the paintings that these particular monarchs have become so well-known, and if so, do they reveal something about the Tudor Age that lay behind them, and which provides the explanation – perhaps encouraged, if not instigated by them – for their enduring celebrity?

The answer is, quite simply, yes. The sixteenth century – almost the entirety of the Tudor period – has to be seen as one of the most extraordinarily dynamic and transformative periods in the whole history of the English/British nation, rivalling, if not even surpassing, that of the Victorians. The England of 1485 was similar in so many respects to that of 1066, but the England of 1603 was in as many ways unrecognizable from that of 1485.

Two Europe-wide movements fortuitously underpinned this transformation – the Renaissance and the Reformation – neither beginning in England, but each being enthusiastically adopted and given a peculiar national flavour that contributed significantly to the development of the country. Neither came accidentally to England; both were enabled by the unparalleled period of peace and stability that was the gift of the Tudor monarchs.

Nothing symbolizes this so well as the development of country houses, many of which still proudly stand some five centuries later, and which give people nowadays a more intimate understanding of the Tudor period. They are clear evidence that no longer were nobles locking themselves up in draughty, forbidding and heavily-defended castles, and behaving like warlords. They were now civil administrators, spending their money on elaborate and comfortable homes filled with Renaissance luxuries such as paintings, sculptures, tapestries and objects of beauty, listening, perhaps, to the gorgeous music of English composers such as Byrd and Tallis, their libraries bulging with printed books and poems and plays from internationally-recognised writers, their suits of armour safely stowed away in the basement. By the end of the Tudor century, the measure of such men lay less in their skill at arms than in their taste in interior décor.

The sons of these nobles were educated not for war, but in the liberal arts, and sent away to the new schools which were opening up around the country. Then they might become JP's and help with keeping their local areas well-governed and peaceful, the same areas that a generation or two before they might have been trained to repress or terrorise. The younger sons might even stand as members of Parliament and take part in the growing influence of that organization in the running of the country. Even the daughters were educated – in languages, the classics, poetry and music. In the towns, merchants thrived in the time of peace and prosperity, and the enormous surge in court cases, and in the number of lawyers, showed that here was a gentler way of securing justice than the traditional resort to arms.

Then there was the Reformation in religion, a movement that released people from the limiting hold of the Catholic Church in so many areas of life – education, medicine, scientific discovery, thought – and a movement which in England was not a protest against the government and Church, as it was in other European countries, but instead ordained and promoted by the government itself. Protestantism, like Humanism, was a belief that celebrated the importance of the individual, encouraging enterprise and self-reliance, and giving stimulus to those who wanted to better themselves. It also, by removing the power of the Roman papacy, strengthened the nationalist identity of the country and gave Englishmen an enhanced pride in their uniqueness.

This, then, was the age of the Tudors, and they, with their glittering courts and ostentatious lifestyles, put themselves at the forefront of such changes, enthusiastically adopting the Renaissance and beginning the process of Reformation. The changes reached their apogee in the court of Elizabeth, when England transformed itself into an international power, and when the opportunities for exploration, discovery, progress and growth seemed limitless, until the coming of the Stuarts and the unpleasant realization that all this somehow had to be paid for.

1553 – the year that Mary, against the odds, came to the throne, and managed to hold onto it - was an exceptional year, full of extraordinary events, but its significance lies less in the events themselves than in the light it throws on the context of the Tudors and their century. As we shall see, it is the very limited impact of these events, which at any previous time may have led to disastrous conflict and loss of life, and which during the Wars of the Roses a century before did exactly that, that showed the full achievements of the dynasty. The fact that they are little remembered, even by devotees of the Tudors, is evidence of the strength and permanence of the changes that had been made.

*

It may seem a bit of a let-down to introduce a book by suggesting that what it contains is not terribly important, but this would miss the point. The events of 1553 are not unimportant in themselves. Indeed, they held two possibilities for turning points, one of which might have taken the country in a very different direction, and seen the end of the Tudor dynasty. They might very easily have resulted in a foreign invasion, and even occupation. It is well worth taking the time to consider why such consequences did not happen. And it is also important to consider why there should have been such upheaval during this one year, and why the coming to power of England's first female ruler should have been so difficult, and so contested.

These events are not completely unknown to the modern historian, or to the general reader. Over the centuries, numerous books have been written about Northumberland's plot and the brief reign of Lady Jane Grey, and a number of recent biographies of Mary Tudor have also covered the period. There have also been studies of Wyatt's rebellion. Where this book can offer a different perspective is by investigating both the plot and the rebellion and seeing them as part of the same issue; namely the fear aroused by the accession of Mary.

Almost every English person knows about Henry's obsessive desire for a male heir, so the tortuous process by which he went about securing one hardly needs to be repeated here. Not so well understood, however, is exactly *why* this should have been so important to him. It is commonly assumed that this was down to a misogynistic belief, common at the time - or so it is supposed - that women were incapable of being rulers. While there is some truth in this assumption, and in the understanding that producing a male heir was a matter of personal pride to Henry that would enhance his credentials as a physically powerful ruler, the explanation is far too simplistic. After all, Henry was quite happy to leave the realm in the hands of his sixth wife, Katherine Parr, while he went off on his expedition to France in 1544, and he still placed his daughters firmly in the line of succession after Edward.

There were undoubtedly problems with a female succession, but most of these were mere legal details, and with a little imagination and goodwill they could be resolved, as indeed they later were by both Mary and Elizabeth. A slightly greater problem was in the status of both daughters as illegitimate, a designation that had its roots in the way Henry had gone about disposing of former wives in his search for one who would give him a male child. In 1553, this nearly resulted in the exclusion of Mary, yet with careful manipulation of Parliament, it later managed to be overcome with comparatively little difficulty. But the greatest problem of all, and one that was felt to be particularly acute for Henry and the Tudor dynasty, is revealed by the clause in the 1536 Act of Succession which stipulated that neither daughter could marry without the consent of the Privy Council.

For this was the heart of the issue. Common law dictated that a wife and all her possessions were under the control of her husband, and thus whoever either of the daughters married would effectively have dominance over her and, if she were to succeed as queen, over the whole country. He would effectively, if not actually in name, become king. This thought provoked nightmare scenarios. If she were to marry within the realm, would her choice provoke jealousy and conflict and lead to resumption of the strife witnessed just a few generations before in the Wars of the Roses? If she were to marry abroad, would this mean the end of England's independent status and it becoming a satellite of a more powerful entity and maybe forced into wars against its will, its riches plundered, and maybe its princes spirited away and raised as foreigners?

Elizabeth, of course, was to solve this particular issue by not marrying at all, and Mary partly resolved it by being unable to conceive an heir. But both solutions were to mean the end of the Tudor dynasty. Despite all his efforts, Henry had, effectively, been checkmated both by the lack of males in his family, and by Edward's early death. The issue was so important that Mary faced two rebellions within six months of her accession; one to deny her the throne in the first place, and the second to try and get her off it. And on both occasions her choice of partner – potential in the first case, actual in the second – was a principal cause. Usually, these have been seen as discrete events, but they were not, and evidence from the time clearly demonstrates this. The ambition of the duke of Northumberland was certainly a factor in the former, and was a handy explanation both then and since, but it misses the main point, which is that he didn't, and couldn't have, acted alone.

1553 was not, as this book will suggest, just an interesting year with lots of eventful stuff going on; it was no less than the setting for a battle for the survival of the Tudor dynasty, and for the continuing independence of the English nation.

Preamble

Northumberland Comes to Power

Perhaps we should begin with an execution...

They beheaded Edward Seymour, duke of Somerset, former lord protector of England, shortly after 8 o'clock on the morning of Friday 22 January 1552, on the patch of trampled grass and mud, known as Tower Hill, which lay between the eastern edge of the city, and the Tower itself. This was in keeping with the strict protocol for such events: royalty would meet their end privately, within the confines of the Tower; nobles on Tower Hill; and commoners at Tyburn, or wherever it pleased the authorities to erect a gallows.

They – the authorities – were clearly nervous about this one. Although executions were public – for the edification and education of the masses – they made last-minute efforts to try and limit the numbers attending. The Privy Council had ordered constables in every ward in the city to go round the streets earlier that morning to forbid anyone to leave their house before 10 o'clock. Perhaps they were worried about the safety of so many people crammed into such a relatively small space; after all, this was an extremely high-profile killing – Somerset had enjoyed the status of a regent, almost of a king – but more likely they feared a riot. The victim's popularity among the common people was well known, and feared.

The injunction did little good. By 7 o'clock there was already a crowd estimated in the tens of thousands, and people continued to stream in from the suburbs, and from the city itself, curious, perhaps, at why they should have been banned from attending. There, if they could get close enough, they would have seen the wooden scaffold – a platform raised above the ground for better visibility – and the panoply of death – the block, the axe, the straw and sawdust, and the masked headsman, or hangman as he was often known. Surrounding the scaffold, on this occasion, was a tight circle of armed pikemen.

There were many reasons why people flocked to public executions in Tudor times, not all of them reprehensible. Many came from simple curiosity, either to see a killing, or because it was a spectacle, a must-see occasion, and the more important the victim, the more impressive the 'I was there' stories. Others undoubtedly found a ghoulish enjoyment in the proceedings, and were *habitués* of all such events. Some came to sell refreshments – the wait, especially for those who wanted a space close to the platform, could be a long one – some to cut the purses of spectators crammed together and inattentive to the causes of the pushing around them, and some to pick up and be picked up – the atmosphere at these events was often sexually charged.

But many came with a sense of solidarity with the victim, and a desire to be with him and support him on his final journey, and this was particularly true of this one, which doubtless explains the unease of the authorities. Somerset was a figure who divided opinion, but by now the idea, or myth, was firmly established among the poor that he was on *their* side, and that his conviction for felony was both unfair, trumped up, and a result of envy on the part of the ruling classes. The presence of so many soldiers indicated that something was not quite right, as did the feeble attempts of the authorities to ban attendance. The atmosphere around the scaffold was tense, and potentially explosive.

Those who had come long before dawn to secure the best places had to wait until 8 o'clock for the duke to appear. By now, some would have had to relieve themselves where they stood, and the ground would have become muddy and churned-up, and the smells from so many people might have caused many a pomander to be raised to the nose, if, indeed, there was enough room to lift an arm. At least the presence of so many people would have kept them warm, for this was a late January morning, and temperatures were sure to have been low. Those pushing in from the back would have created an unpleasant crush near the front, where the pikemen would have been forced up against the scaffold, and jostling, swearing and scuffles would have broken out among the nervous and impatient spectators.

According to contemporary accounts, the duke was 'nothing at all abashed' at the sight of the ghastly paraphernalia of death, and showed 'alacrity and cheerfulness' as he climbed the steps to the platform and prepared to address the crowd.[1] Tudor executions were a highly-ritualised affair, and those about to suffer death were expected to perform according to a well-established, though unwritten, set of guidelines. These included the expected show of nonchalance, the distribution of alms to the needy – the cash provided out of council funds - and also the formality of the final speech. The latter was important, both for the victim and the authorities. It was a chance for the government to have the truth admitted, and advertised in public, and for the accused to clear his conscience – after all, his next conversation would be with his maker, and he did not want to greet Him with a lie on his lips.

Somerset did not disappoint. Bidding the crowd to be silent, he addressed them solemnly. He made no attempt to proclaim his innocence of the charge, but simply stated that he had never acted against king or country, and that as he was condemned by the law so he must die by the law. He then went on to exhort those listening to continue with the changes in religion that he had begun, a process which had brought the Church back closer to the aims of the early fathers. And then, suddenly, there was chaos.

At the back, a group of pikemen from a nearby village, ordered to be present to help with controlling the crowd, suddenly appeared. Noticing the duke already there, and realizing that they were late, they began to push through to get to the front. Those around them, seeing armed men rushing towards the scaffold, became convinced that this was an attempt to rescue the duke and, fearing being caught in the crush, began to panic. Calling out 'Away, away', they began to rush in all directions. As in any crowd, fear quickly spread and soon people were pushing and shoving, and running anywhere for safety. The noise of so many feet sounded like an explosion of gunpowder, or the trampling of horses, or thunder, or even an earthquake, and some swore the earth actually moved.[2]

Many fell into the Tower moat, others into puddles, and some ran for safety to nearby houses. Some, including the historian, John Foxe, stood frozen to the spot in fear.[3] Even some of the soldiers fell grovelling to the ground, and calling out in terror 'Jesus save us'. In the middle of the tumult, people saw a rider forcing his way towards the platform and became convinced that he was carrying a pardon from Somerset's own nephew, the fourteen-year-old monarch, and they threw up their caps, calling out 'God save the King'. But they were wrong.

Gradually, calm was restored, and people shuffled back around the platform, the tension broken. The only man who seemed unruffled by events then resumed his speech, from time to time asking the crowd to remain calm, and in a moving and dignified manner calling on all those present to show obedience to their rulers, and asking forgiveness of any whom he might, in life, have offended. The only sign of nerves was when he reminded them that their continued quietness would help him face his fate with similar calm, and without 'trouble'.

Then it was time for the main event, which, after the excitement that preceded it, must have seemed almost an anti-climax. Somerset knelt down and handed a scroll to Dr. Cox, his spiritual advisor, containing a 'confession to God', which was then read out. He stood up and said farewell to the sheriffs, the lieutenant of the Tower, and others on the platform, before tipping a few coins to the executioner, whom he forgave his onerous task. He then took off his gown and knelt down again in the straw, loosening his shirt strings, while the headsman turned down his collar. Somerset tied his own handkerchief around his eyes, and lifted his face a last time to the sky, showing no sign of nerves, though those nearer the front remarked at a faint blush on his cheeks.

But the ordeal was not yet over. His doublet still partly covered his neck, and the headsman, worried that he might not be able to deliver a clean cut, asked him to stand and take it off. Still showing remarkable patience, Somerset complied, and then lay down again, fully prone, his neck resting on the block, calling three times 'Lord Jesu save me', the axe mercifully ending his torment halfway through the third. The powerful spurts of blood gradually gave way to gentler trickles as the executioner held up the head to show the crowd, and then to face the body that lay still twitching in its death throes. Those closest to the scaffold had handkerchiefs ready to dip in the gore, but the row of pikemen, whose uniforms must have been well-bespattered, made this task difficult. The hush gradually gave way to awed murmuring, and then more raucous conversation as the crowd slowly began to disperse.

And so Somerset died, and so the legend of the 'good duke' was born, a legend that persisted for centuries without contradiction until, towards the end of the twentieth, historians began to look more closely, and with a greater degree of analysis, at how deserved it really was.

They began to discover that behind the 'courteous, wise and gentle'[4] image, there lurked an ambitious, vain, weak, selfish, arrogant and vacillating individual, who overthrew the dictates of Henry VIII's will, showered honours on himself and his friends, enriched himself shamelessly from the royal treasury, ignored the advice of those he was supposed to rule alongside, and followed disastrous policies that virtually bankrupted the kingdom, leading to one of the most serious outbreaks of civil unrest in the sixteenth century with thousands of needless deaths. His so-called love for the poor seemed to have been simply an affectation that he adopted to increase his own popularity, and which resulted only in more suffering for those same people.

Edward Seymour, duke of Somerset (unknown artist)

But legends persist, and this one was enhanced by the presence of another: that of the 'bad duke'. For what else could explain the fate of such a paragon, but evil doing? And the duke of Northumberland perfectly fitted the bill. Cunningly plotting the downfall of Somerset, so the story went, he then set up his own dictatorship, ruling the council and the country with an iron hand, meekly surrendering the hard-won fort of Boulogne to the French, and land and castles in the north to the Scots, and then, as if this was not enough, plotting the disinheritance of the rightful heir to the throne, Mary Tudor, in favour of his own daughter-in-law, Lady Jane Grey, in a clear attempt to subsequently acquire the throne for himself.

Twentieth-century historians have a lot to answer for, for they began to debunk this legend, too. From the ashes of one of the most apparently - and delightfully - evil men in English history, there began to emerge an image of a capable and intelligent ruler, who restored the finances of the kingdom, reformed its religion, ended pointless wars in favour of peace and trade, and… well, the disinheriting of Mary Tudor was more of a problem: there's only so much rehabilitation that can be done in the face of evidence.

The story of John Dudley, later duke of Northumberland, is central to the events of 1553, and to the problems surrounding the accession of Mary, regardless of which interpretation you choose, but the explanation for what later happened may partly be found in the very same spot we have just visited. For there, on 17 August 1510, his father, Edmund, suffered the same fate as the duke of Somerset. And with perhaps the same degree of justification.

Edmund had risen to power under the first of the Tudors, the usurper Henry VII, and become a trusted and loyal advisor, and probably second in the realm only to the king himself. He had made himself useful by being the instrument by which Henry maintained order, namely by taxing the rebellious nobility, who had subjected the country to a quarter-century of internecine warfare, into submission. Naturally, this made him extremely unpopular with powerful people, and when the new king, Henry VIII, succeeded in 1509, it was easy enough to convince him of the need to dispense with Edmund. A charge of treason was concocted, which resulted in his demise, and an immediate popularity boost for the new monarch.

At the time of his father's death, John was six years old. We do not know what lessons, if any, he extracted from this episode, and how much it contributed to his later ambition, but it seemed to instil in him a need for caution, and the recognition that whatever position he reached in later life he would always be subject to the whim of the monarch. As his father had been attainted by Parliament, the wealth he had accumulated was returned to the Crown, and John, effectively penniless, was farmed out as a ward to a minor noble, Sir Edward Guilford, a fortunate choice as it turned out, for he inherited his estate, married – very happily and fruitfully – his daughter, and was introduced by his guardian to Cardinal Wolsey, the lord chancellor.

Patiently, and without drawing unnecessary attention to himself, he benefitted from Wolsey's patronage to begin his rise through the ranks, taking part in military and diplomatic expeditions, as well as winning a seat in Parliament and on the Privy Council. Although he is usually described as a soldier, it is hard to find many precise details of his accomplishments, but we know he took part in Henry's invasion of France in 1543, for which he was knighted on the battlefield – usually a sign of some significant behaviour – and in the 'rough wooing' against the Scots in 1544, and the later Battle of Pinkie Cleugh in 1547. Perhaps his most significant contribution was as lord admiral, in which role he is credited with creating a formal bureaucracy for the management of the navy, as well as tactical innovations, which made that service the most effective arm of England's military.

He also followed his father in quietly amassing estates and titles. From merely Sir John Dudley he became Viscount Lisle in 1542, and earl of Warwick in the general share-out of honours following the death of Henry VIII in 1547. Each advancement brought him lands, and he indulged in the general aristocratic practice of selling and buying estates to improve his portfolio and personal wealth. By modern standards, such behaviour might be seen as simple corruption, but although over-reaching oneself could bring down such charges, it was the accepted practice, and with the perennial need for money to survive at the highly costly Tudor court, not to have done so would have effectively stymied his career.

Although some did this as much for greed as any other reason – and Somerset could well be accused of this – there was another factor at play, for despite the efforts of Tudor governments to modernize, below the surface the feudal system still effectively held sway. Patronage was at the heart of the system – the conferring of gifts of lands and titles to secure support and loyalty. The king, naturally, was at the hub of this, but any of the leading nobles would have enough lands to play the same game. These lands contained tenants, and tenants could be persuaded to support the lord, with arms if necessary. Anyone seeking high office would use this system of patronage, and might, at times, even be obliged to raise an armed force of such retainers, either in the service of the king, or for their own ends. Land, therefore, still meant power, and Dudley was as aware of this as any.

In the later years of Henry VIII's reign, he began to play a more overt role in politics, particularly in the factional struggles within the court. One of the more obvious fault lines was over religion. After Henry's divorce from Katherine of Aragon, and renunciation of papal authority, it seemed that England might become a fully Protestant country, but Henry dithered. He wanted the power and the wealth that the Church offered, but in liturgical matters he remained, at heart, a Catholic. This ambiguity led to divisions among his advisors into reformers and conservatives, each group's influence ebbing and flowing according to the whims of the monarch. Dudley, carefully assessing the situation, allied himself to the evangelical, reforming, wing led by Somerset - the earl of Hertford as he then was - and the queen, Katherine Parr. He was fortunate to have survived a late attempted coup by the conservatives in 1546, who tried to win over the confused and changeable mind of the ailing monarch, but at the time of the king's death his faction was in the ascendant, and he was named one of the executors of Henry's will.

In an extraordinary - and some have suggested, highly suspicious - break from convention, Henry named not a regent to rule during the nine-year old Edward's minority, but the executors themselves. England would effectively be governed by committee. There is much historical debate over not just this decision but even the legitimacy of the will itself.

At any rate, the king's body was scarcely cold before Hertford/Somerset subverted it, managing to secure the agreement of the others that he should be the regent, or protector, a negotiation made easier by the prompt, and unwholesome, distribution of titles among the executors. And so the stage was set: Somerset was to rule, and Dudley/Warwick, now one of the most powerful men on the council, would be effectively his number two.

This may have been, to all intents and purposes, a coup, though it seemed a more sensible option. It was not, however, a success. Somerset showed no inclination towards conciliar government, and only consulted the Privy Council when he chose. This caused resentment and frustration, and resulted in some poor decision-making. Through his determination to continue with Henry's active foreign policy he led the country to the edge of bankruptcy. His war with France in defence of Boulogne may have been temporarily successful, but it was costly, and its worth debatable. He may have massacred much of the Scottish army at Pinkie Cleugh, but he failed to prevent the infant queen, Mary, from escaping to France and forming a dangerous bond between those two countries, and his garrisons established to keep the Scots at bay soon proved indefensible and had to be abandoned.

His worst mistakes, however, came with his social policy, which led to serious outbreaks of rebellion. Posing as the people's champion, he set up commissions to investigate the controversial practice of landlords enclosing their fields and, more particularly, the common land, which denied commoners the right to farm or graze there. These commissions, led by the reformist-minded lawyer, John Hales, openly criticized the practice and gave local people the belief that the government would support them in tearing down the hedges. This led to a full-scale rebellion in Norfolk, in 1549, led by Robert Kett, which Dudley was sent to deal with. The latter had no difficulties disposing of the rebel army at the 'battle' of Dussindale, since despite the peasants having more men, he had trained mercenaries and cannon. Thousands died and, although he was not nearly as brutal in the aftermath as local landowners desired, he won a gruesome reputation in the region, and a degree of hatred that was later to prove significant.

Somerset also faced revolts the same year from another quarter, and although he could be blamed less for their outbreak, his handling of the crisis proved disastrous. His religious policy, which involved a radical reformation and a move towards European-style Protestantism, had otherwise attracted surprisingly little opposition. Nevertheless, in the West Country, in 1549, there was an armed uprising which had hatred of the religious changes as its focus. Somerset dispatched armies to deal with it, but then insisted on interfering and producing a series of contradictory instructions – one moment ordering negotiation, the next suppression – which drove his commanders to distraction, and caused the outbreak to spread and the ultimate victory to be more painful than it need have been.

Dudley was not the only one to feel frustration at Somerset, both for his incompetence and the fact that he was bypassing the council. The council secretary, and Somerset's closest confidant, William Paget, frequently tried to point this out, and even produced written guidelines on how the protector should behave. But when the coup came, it was not specifically from these two, but from the conservative faction led by the earls of Arundel and Southampton. Faced with opposition, Somerset reacted impetuously and kidnapped the young king, moving him by night to Windsor where he intended to use him as a hostage. His calls for armed help from the armies returning from the West Country fell on deaf ears, and he was obliged to resign. He was sent to the Tower to await his fate.

Far from immediately benefitting from Somerset's fall, Dudley now found himself in a position of some danger, as it quickly became clear that the conservative faction wanted to get rid of him, too. Matters came to a head when the conservatives proposed having Somerset tried for treason. Aware that his fate was linked to the former protector, he now seized the opportunity to defend Somerset, and challenged others in the council to support him. Unwilling to have the blood of two of their colleagues on their hands, a majority of councillors agreed, and the way was open for Dudley to complete his move.

The difference between the two men could be seen in the way he now went about consolidating his power. While Somerset had paid little heed to the formalities, and had relied on the advantages of his position as protector to help him rule, Dudley was determined to do everything by the book. He had already shown his respect for the council by assiduously attending meetings, unlike his predecessor, and now that he was effectively in charge he was going to keep it close to him. He did not want the title of protector, which he felt had been tarnished by Somerset, but he needed a role that formalised his control. And he was astute enough to see how to get it.

Somerset had paid scant attention to the young king. He had surrounded him with tutors and a household, but otherwise seemed to take little interest. Thanks to the dry stamp, which enabled the king's signature to be appended whenever needed, and without specific royal assent, he felt he did not need to take Edward into his confidence. So neglectful was he that he even failed to give the king pocket money, which provided an opportunity for his brother, Thomas, to wheedle his way into Edward's affections as part of his efforts to gain power for himself. Nor did he even bother to guard him properly, which enabled the same Thomas, one night, to attempt to kidnap Edward, in a harebrained scheme that resulted in him shooting dead the king's dog.

While Edward was a mere boy such neglect may not have mattered, but by 1550 he was a teenager, and maturing fast, and Dudley was well aware that the king's moral authority could be used to back him in his designs. Consequently, he took great care to move his own supporters into Edward's household, to surround him and ensure that he was kept away from rogue opinions. Chief among these 'special men' was Sir John Gates, who was appointed the king's vice-chamberlain, and who became Dudley's eyes and ears at the court, keeping a close watch over Edward's every movement.

Dudley was also aware of a constitutional link between the court and the council, which meant that whoever held the title of great master of the royal household, was also *ipso facto* president of the council. This position was currently held by William Paulet, but it had had little relevance while Somerset was virtually ruling on his own. Paulet had played an ambiguous role during Dudley's coup but seemed happy enough to accept a marquisate, and promotion to high treasurer, in return for vacating his position, which Dudley promptly filled himself. Now he was master of the two centres of power – the court and the council – and had the added security of operating *within* those two bases, rather than outside as Somerset had preferred to do.

These moves say much about his political guile. Though neither appointment was the most prestigious, both gave him the greatest access to power. The ranks of president of the council and great master, for example, were inferior in precedence to the chancellor and high treasurer, but, as president, Dudley had the right to chair meetings of the council, set agendas, decide on the regularity of sessions, determine which councillors should attend, and select and disbar councillors at will. Interestingly, following his coup, and even later when it seemed his power was unchallenged, he still allowed certain members of the conservative faction to remain, albeit ensuring that they were in a minority. This may be evidence of his confidence that he could allow some alternative opinions to be heard, or else he wanted a token opposition as a fig leaf to cover the extent of his dominance. Or it may show that he was never as completely in control as his detractors have suggested. Even more surprisingly, in April 1550, he allowed back onto the council the duke of Somerset.

There may have been a completely innocent explanation for this. Somerset appeared to hold the same views on religion as him, and they had worked together both on the council and on the battlefield. Here was a man of some ability, and hopefully a supporter of his policies, and, moreover, one who was popular with the people, which Dudley conspicuously was not. Also, Somerset owed him a favour for saving his head. What harm could it do to take him out of the Tower, where he might still pose a threat, and include him in the government where he could share responsibility for (Dudley's) decisions, and where he could be under some sort of control?

But there may have been another explanation, one more in keeping with the skill and cunning that Dudley was beginning to demonstrate: that he needed an excuse to get rid of him. He had tried before, but had had to backtrack in order to save his own life. He knew Somerset's character. He knew he could only accept a position of subordinacy up to a point. Sooner or later, the duke would overreach himself, and then Dudley could be done with him. In the event, he seems to have become bored of waiting and decided to speed things up himself. After a campaign of deliberate demeaning of his rival, and open opposition between the pair in council, Dudley acted.

The plot, of which Somerset was finally accused, owed more to the Arabian Nights than to the relatively ordered conduct of Tudor England. Rumours were spread of a peasant revolt involving thousands, a rising among the northern, conservative, earls, and another in London among the apprentices, and then, most bizarre of all, an invitation to a banquet at which Dudley and the earl of Northampton were to be decapitated. Much of this came from the fertile imagination of Sir Thomas Palmer, a Dudley supporter, who later admitted he had made most of it up, though there does appear to be evidence that Somerset was plotting something.

This was the excuse that Dudley needed. Having made himself duke of Northumberland, and raised his supporters - Henry Grey to duke of Suffolk, and William Herbert to earl of Pembroke - he now reckoned he had enough backing for a showdown. In October 1551, Somerset and his allies, including the earl of Arundel and William Paget, were arrested and interrogated. From the information gathered there appeared enough evidence to justify a trial for treason.

The hearing duly took place on 1 December, and lasted only one day. Like most such trials it was not designed to establish the truth, but to establish guilt. Even so, there was still not enough evidence to convict Somerset of treason, and he was acquitted. Westminster Hall had been surrounded by a huge crowd who had come in support of the former protector, and when the verdict was announced the cheers were loud enough to be heard by Edward in his palace. Even bonfires were lit. However, there was a sting in the tail. Amid the noise of celebration, it was hard to hear the secondary verdict: that Somerset was guilty of a felony - of encouraging unlawful assembly - a law that had been passed shortly before and which, conveniently, also carried the death penalty.

And so to the events, two months later, on Tower Hill. This was an unusually long time between trial and execution. Northumberland is said to have visited Somerset on several occasions in the meantime, though it is not known what they talked about. He had shown a significant degree of callousness and subterfuge in framing Somerset, even though it is perfectly possible that if he had not it might have been him awaiting execution, but probably he still lacked that ultimate spark of ruthlessness.

He may have dispatched the Scottish nobility at Pinkie, and the Norfolk peasants at Dussindale, but now he was being asked to sanction the cold-blooded murder of one who used to be the *de facto* ruler of England, and his friend. This was a big step.

Of course, if he had wished it, and if his control over the king was so secure, then he could have persuaded Edward to pardon his uncle. But he did not. Edward's attitude towards the affair is curious. It is said that he was upset and heavy-hearted about the whole business, though, in truth, he had little reason to mourn Somerset, who had held him hostage once, and who now seemed to be plotting against a man whom he personally respected. His laconic diary entry 'The Duke of Somerset had his head cut off upon Tower Hill between eight and nine o'clock in the morning'[5] has been taken to show his indifference, though, in truth, Edward seldom revealed his personal feelings in his diary. He seems to have believed the facts of the conspiracy – as previously mentioned, he had had enough experience of the waywardness of the Seymour brothers - and his regret was mainly that his uncle could ever have considered such a thing.

So, while spectators waited around the bloodstained scaffold, pushing through to dip handkerchiefs in the dead duke's blood, Northumberland could reflect that he had finally crossed his Rubicon: he had become a 'man of blood'. A little regretfully, perhaps, he could congratulate himself in having disposed of the last serious opposition to his power, and he could now look forward to bringing the kingdom to a better state, according to his own designs.

We know enough about John Dudley as a political figure, but remarkably little about him as a *person*. He was undeniably ambitious, and occasionally ruthless – that much can be gleaned from his career – but at times so self-effacing as to talk himself out of promotions that he was offered. In 1545 he succeeded in denying himself the post of president of the council, and in 1549 asked for William Parr, earl of Northampton, to lead troops against Kett, rather than himself. Such behaviour could be attributed to courtly modesty, or perhaps political purpose, but it could equally be an indication of a genuine inferiority complex, a trait that he was to show further signs of later. He also spent long periods – months at a time – away from government, claiming, or feigning, illness. This may have been due to some genuine, undisclosed, malady, or hypochondria or, more likely, stress. We have examples of his sensitivity and over-reaction to situations – already he had been banned from the council for a time for striking a fellow councillor at the table – all part of a picture of someone unusually highly-strung. As to whether he was loyal, or treacherous, later events would provide more clues.

He may have been satisfied with the situation he had created, but Somerset's death was not viewed with relief by everyone. Charles Wriothesley, among other chroniclers, noted several disturbing events that closely followed the execution. In February, in Antwerp, four suns and two rainbows were seen simultaneously in the sky, and the same apparition appeared in Bucklebury in Berkshire a month later. Wriothesley thought it significant enough even to draw the extraordinary sight.[6] Before that, a lamb with two bodies had been born, an event notable enough to be mentioned in other chronicles, too. In May, in Holland, a terrible hailstorm, with stones weighing half a pound, and some in the shape of the crown of thorns, and accompanied by a dreadful stench, laid waste to houses,[7] while in London, on Whitsun eve, the rain lay on the grass as red as wine,[8] or blood.

'4 Suns', Charles Wriothesley, *Chronicle*, p.67

To compound the unease, in August, in Oxfordshire, a woman gave birth to twin girls, joined at the navel and sharing an anus, who lived a fortnight, and shortly after, in the same county, a chicken with two heads was born. That same month, dolphins were caught in the Thames, and a few days later three whales just off Gravesend. Some thought these marvels might presage the coming of something terrible; others thought they might portend the death of a king…[9]

1

1553: A Year of Promise?

Despite the ominous signs of the previous year, the start of 1553 looked, for some, to be a time of hope. The king had apparently recovered from the worst of the health problems that had plagued him the previous autumn, and had enjoyed an entertaining Christmas at Greenwich. The country was still at peace, both internally and with its neighbours; the reform of religion was proceeding remarkably smoothly; and the dreadful financial situation was beginning to come under some sort of control. There were no obvious clouds on the horizon to trouble the minds of Northumberland and the council.

In fact, so calm and uneventful were the first two months that the chronicler, Charles Wriothesley, had little to impart, other than the doings of the lord mayor, Sir George Barne, who set about punishing coalmen for selling underweight sacks, sentencing bawds and whores to be driven around in carts as a mark of shame (though probably equally effective for the ladies as a means of advertising their wares), and whipping vagabonds out of the city. Even better, he reported that the price of wheat had fallen, and that the penny loaf would now be measured at 34 ounces, rather than 20.[1] Things could hardly look more promising.

Edward's recuperation seems to have been helped by the antics of the lord of misrule, one Sir George Ferrers, who had laid on an action-packed round of banquets and masques - the Triumph of Cupid being a highlight - some of which Edward had taken part in. Early in the New Year, Ferrers took his players into the city, with a great procession of lavishly-clothed figures winding through the streets, amid feasts and plays at various points, to the delight of the watching crowds.

It was a good start to the year also for an unnamed felon who was taken on 3 January from the Marshalsea prison to be hanged. While dangling from the gallows, the rope that was slowly strangling him snapped, and he fell to the ground. After a wait, a new rope was found and he was strung up again, and a second time the rope snapped. And so, in the words of the chronicler, Henry Machyn, 'he skapyd with ys lyffe'.[2]

The Privy Council met early that year, on 4 January, at Greenwich. Given that the year technically still began in March, the record of that meeting carried the date of 1552. Eleven councillors were present, including two secretaries, but not the duke of Northumberland who had been absent since the previous October with a long bout of the undisclosed illness with which he periodically suffered. Not that he seems to have missed much. Business, at least that much that was recorded, was limited to the sending of letters asking for various experienced representatives of the Staplers and Merchant Adventurers guilds to appear next Monday; for the king's agent in Antwerp to send over cloth for His Majesty; and for the lord admiral to start proceedings against pirates apprehended in the West Country.

It became a little more varied three days later, when records mentioned an order for a man to be sent to the Marshalsea for using seditious words against the king's coinage, and for two suspected murderers to be brought to the Tower and tortured. All was part and parcel of the tasks assumed by the council in running the country, the minutiae of business sometimes appearing overwhelming when considered alongside the serious discussions of matters of state, about which there is, regrettably, no mention.

The Privy Council, which was to play a highly significant role in the events of the year, was a relatively new organization in English government – in fact, little more than fifteen years old. The king, it was recognized, could not deal with all the detailed business of running the country by himself, and so he needed help. Traditionally, there had been an unofficial 'Great Council' of nobles, who advised the king on general matters of policy, but this had been called on an *ad hoc* basis – both in terms of timings and personnel – more or less at the whim of the monarch. There had also been a 'continual council',[3] which carried out the mundane functions of running the kingdom, and behaved much like a civil service. However, the task of administration had become more complex, especially the financial aspects, and Thomas Cromwell, secretary, and effectively chief minister, to Henry VIII, had introduced reforms which combined the two into a permanent Privy Council, and made this organization the centre of government. It would sit regularly, its meetings be recorded (though nowhere near as thoroughly as modern minutes require), and its personnel, who were almost all office holders of state, be limited, and sworn in officially. It also acted as a court of law and, while at Westminster, it sat in one of the rooms in the palace which had a ceiling bedecked with painted stars. This was known as the Little Star Chamber, not to be confused with the Court of Star Chamber which had a similar ceiling next door.

Henry, generally so mindful of the need to secure a seamless succession, had muddied the waters by bequeathing power during his son's minority not to this Privy Council, but to the named executors of his will. As we have seen, the duke of Somerset had already decided that England would be better governed by a single figure, and that that figure should be him, and with the connivance of Henry's secretary, William Paget, he named himself protector, and appointed 12 new councillors to add to 14 of the executors to form his new Privy Council. His autocratic behaviour ensured that this body operated more or less as a rubber stamp for his policies.

But since Somerset's downfall, things had reverted to what Henry had originally intended, with no protector, but with leadership coming from *within* the council. Despite all the criticisms of his behaviour over this affair, Northumberland had actually restored, rather than subverted, legitimacy. The new duke was anxious to ensure that issues should be discussed and decisions taken around the table, and that however much he might be able to dominate the council, he could always fall back behind the cloak of shared responsibility. That much he had learnt from the death of his father. This, then, was the organization that was now ruling England during Edward's minority.

And it wasn't doing a bad job of it. This was the first time that England had been without either a regent or protector: the first time that it had been ruled by a committee. Some historians have delighted in describing these years as the 'mid-Tudor crisis', but this seems unfair. In the six and a half years of Edward's reign, there was only one period of revolt – serious, admittedly, but this was mainly down to the failure of Somerset to nip it in the bud. By contrast, every other Tudor monarch experienced at least one major uprising. The long-drawn out business of getting rid of Somerset could, unarguably, have been handled better by a monarch, but this issue was one that affected only the apex of power and had little immediate impact on the country as a whole.

By contrast, this committee had succeeded in carrying out one of the most radical transformations in English life since the Norman Conquest – the religious Reformation – and with surprisingly little opposition. Although Mary would hardly be grateful for that achievement, the council would still be able to pass on to her a country in immeasurably better financial state than Henry had left it, and arguably more secure internationally. Not bad for an organization that had not even existed a generation before.

All this involved a significant workload. There were secretaries, and clerks, to write the despatches and transmit written orders, but, as has been seen from the examples already given, the council had to deal with the type of minutiae which modern cabinets would not concern themselves with. Added to this, there were its legal functions which meant that it often had to settle disputes, deal with pleas, and even involve itself in criminal cases. Of course, the breadth of its functions was less in the sense that matters such as transport, health, education, social care were not then the business of government, but there was enough to be getting on with during this period that the frequency of meetings rose to over four per week, and these often lasted the whole day.

This put a heavy burden on councillors who also had vital roles as JP's and lords lieutenant within their counties to fulfil, not to mention the effective management of their own estates. These were certainly not men who wasted time looking good around court; they can justifiably be regarded as professional politicians and bureaucrats. Not all attended every council meeting, but some attended most. Between April 1552 and June 1553, eleven of them attended at least 50% of the meetings[4] - not bad considering that many lived several days journey from London, and that for some of this time the council was away from the capital, accompanying the king on his progress around the south of England.

The period of Edward's minority, particularly the years after the downfall of Somerset, saw a significant step in the evolution of government in England. Although there was a king, he had limited power, and so the council was effectively ruling the country on its own, with no higher authority to oversee it. In terms of actual management, it had established itself as a permanent and effective fixture, one that could survive a change in regime, and one that offered a degree of stability and continuity that could make the job of any incoming monarch so much easier. Provided, of course, that he, or she, could trust its members, for this council would shortly take onto itself powers that went far beyond what was intended: the power even to choose the next monarch.

What is irritating for historians is how little we know of what actually went on behind the closed doors of the council chamber. The *Acts of the Privy Council* really only record actions to be taken, and presumably not even all of these. We have no idea of the discussions and arguments that took place, and who was on which side. It was said at the time, and has been repeated often since, that Northumberland ruled the council with an iron hand, but it is hard to find direct evidence of this. Certainly, from his position as lord president, he controlled the personnel and the agenda, but how much he dominated the discussion we have no way of knowing.

One interesting point is the amount of time he was not even present at council meetings. For example, between 25 October 1552 and 29 January 1553, he was not there at all. Also, in the late summer of 1552 he left to do an inspection of the Northern Marches, and so was nowhere near London for long months. His absence could have given the opportunity for any amount of mischief if councillors had been so inclined. Either he was such a dictator that none of them dared raise a hand against him, or else they were quite happy with the way he was running things. Although the Imperial ambassador was convinced of, or chose to report, the former version, somehow, given that plotting was almost a way of life in Tudor courts, and the opportunity beckoned, it doesn't quite ring true.

After all, this was Tudor England, not a twentieth century dictatorship where communication could be instantaneous, and leaders kept in touch wherever they were. If councillors had decided to create trouble it would be weeks before Northumberland, on the Scottish border, could have done anything about it. Nor could it be said that his two most trusted supporters – the duke of Suffolk and earl of Northampton – would have been particularly effective at quelling any conspiracy. Robert Cecil, council secretary and close confidant, would have been more useful, but he was also away during much of this time with his own health issues.

*

One of the reasons that councillors may have been prepared to tolerate Northumberland was that he had been making clear and realistic efforts to solve the perennial background issue of the royal finances, an issue that affected everyone in the kingdom, including themselves, both directly in terms of their own wealth, and indirectly in keeping the people contented and peaceful. On 20 January 1553, the Imperial ambassador reported that large quantities of money were being amassed, and that these were going not to the Treasury, but to the Tower.[5] He suspected an attempt to meddle with the value of the coinage – yet another debasement – and later he was to assume that the purpose was to build up Northumberland's war chest for his attempt to seize power, but he was almost certainly wrong. This was more likely part of an on-going attempt to steady the nation's finances.

And there was a real problem. In the sixteenth century, as indeed previously, national finance meant *royal* finance. With the money collected in taxes, rents, fines, the selling of lands, and any other means, the king was expected to pay for his household administration, the defence of the nation - which could also mean wars of aggression - and the collection of taxes. The king was not responsible for education, health, transport, or all the other spending responsibilities of modern governments; they were the burden for local administrations, or charitable individuals and foundations. Unfortunately, the areas of responsibility for which monarchs were responsible were increasingly expensive, and if they were not managed correctly, everyone suffered.

The accepted belief during the Middle Ages, which theoretically still endured, was that the king should 'live of his own'. In other words, his income should be enough to deal with the needs of administration. Of course, war was an additional expenditure, and if the nation was threatened the king could legitimately ask Parliament for extra help – a subsidy, or tax, on most or all of the people to tide him over in the hour of the country's need. It was accepted that this recourse was exceptional, and its request gave Parliament its unique power over the king, a power that later monarchs were to toy with at their peril.

In 1540, just 13 years previously, Henry VIII's income from crown lands was measured at roughly £200,000, while his expenditure was about £145,000.[6] Although Henry was notoriously extravagant, this was evidence that the king could quite happily carry out his obligations without resorting to extra measures or bankrupting the country. However, 1540 was a year of peace. In 1542 and 1543 he embarked on wars against Scotland and France which, by 1546, had cost c.£2.1million,[7] which demonstrated, quite clearly, that the king could no longer live of his own *and* conduct an ambitious foreign policy, which, as a Renaissance, European monarch, he felt duty-bound to do.

To solve the problem, Henry had resorted to a variety of methods. In the last five years of his reign he collected four forced loans – taxes for which he did not need the consent of Parliament – and three subsidies. But this was money coming from the pockets of ordinary people, and it was not popular. In the short term he got away with it, but he was storing up problems for his successors.

His other methods of raising money were even worse for the country, and for the future. The process of dissolving the monasteries, which was in full swing at this time, meant that the Crown inherited large amounts of valuable land, the rent from which could bring in a steady income well into the future. But Henry needed money, and he needed it fast, so he sold off much of this valuable asset, for short-term gain at the expense of long-term stability.

But this was still not enough, and he was forced to raise huge loans with Antwerp bankers, usually at 14% interest - not particularly high by the standards of the time, but nevertheless money which would have to be paid off - and, arguably even worse, devalue the coinage. The latter meant calling in old silver and gold coins, re-minting them with lower levels of the precious metals, and then releasing them under their former values. Naturally, merchants understood exactly what was going on, and simply raised their prices to compensate, causing inflation and more misery for buyers. Foreign merchants and governments consequently re-calibrated their exchange rates so that exports and imports became more expensive, and the price of English cloth – the country's major money-earner – declined. These were all short-term expedients, and at this moment Henry died, leaving his executors to pick up the pieces.

Somerset appears either not to have understood, or not to have cared, about such matters, since he continued the wars, and the selling off of lands, and further depreciations of the coinage. Even without the strain of extra wars, Henry had left expensive legacies – the outpost of Berwick on the Scottish border, and the town of Boulogne in northern France – which had to be defended and paid for, ensuring a continuous drain on finances even when things were peaceful. Somerset's Scottish expedition of 1546 had been unnecessary, and had resulted in more forts and outposts that had to be maintained. He didn't improve matters with one of his first actions in office which was to reward himself and his friends with titles, lands, annuities and pensions, all of which came out of royal revenues.

Between 1547 and 1551, the cost of protecting English assets against the French and Scots could be estimated at c. £1.35million.[8] Somerset raised money for this by selling off chantries – religious buildings – further debasing the coinage, a tax on sheep, and securing further ruinous loans. The debasement is reckoned to have brought in c.£500,000[9] in ready cash, admittedly a significant sum, but one which does not begin to calculate for the harm resulting from it in trade, confidence or in human misery.

For the crown, this might mean the frustration of reduced military and diplomatic capabilities; for ordinary people the issue was more existential. Between 1546 and 1551 - the period of the debasements - the price of cereals rose 86%. Over the whole of the sixteenth century, the cost of rye – the cheapest cereal – rose almost sevenfold; wages by comparison, merely doubled.[10] Debasement also led to a consequent raising of rents. If this is considered alongside the growing practice of enclosing common land, of replacing agriculture with sheep farming, frequent bad harvests – particularly from 1549 to 1551 - and a significant (for the time) population increase causing pressure on remaining land, then it can be seen that the Tudor age was not so glittering for all.

There can be no doubt that this was a terrible time to be poor. The above statistics were bad enough, but considerable hardship had also resulted from the dissolution of the monasteries. For Henry they may have been a source of easy money, but to others they were an essential part of the fabric of society. They provided employment, alms, medical care, shelter, and with the loss of this support structure many people became homeless and were forced to wander the country from parish to parish seeking help. Lawlessness was an inevitable concomitant, with bands of vagrants stalking the towns and countryside. The revolts of 1549 were undoubtedly connected to such social and economic hardship, and the nervousness of the government towards any hint of criticism or discontent showed in the number of hangings authorized by the council for simply expressing contrary opinions.

Somerset had tried to address the problem with force, and his Vagrancy Act of 1547 had banned begging and permitted the enslavement of vagrants for up to two years. Northumberland had reversed this with his Poor Act of 1552, in which the provision of poor relief in towns and parishes would be systematized, though the money would come not from the government but from local ratepayers. It was a start, and its provisions would later be deemed solid enough to be adopted in a fresh act by Mary, despite her inclination to erase just about everything that Northumberland had stood for.

Even the young king himself became involved. It appears that he was so impressed after hearing a sermon on charity given by Nicholas Ridley, bishop of London, that he invited him to Whitehall that same evening and asked him to contact immediately the City authorities to see what could be done. The result was that within months the old Grey Friars abbey and Christ's hospital had opened as orphanages, the hospitals of St Thomas and St Bartholomew had been built for the care of the poor, the impotent, the lame and the sick, and in April 1553 the royal palace of Bridewell was donated by the king for the chastisement and rehabilitation of bawds and vagabonds and other ne'er-do-wells. Elsewhere in the country, local authorities were encouraged to follow suit, and the number of foundations still bearing Edward's name testify to the example he had shown. While, admittedly, it only started to tackle the problem, this flurry of activity perhaps merits the description of 'the greatest experiment in social welfare in Tudor England'.[11]

In part, English rulers had been victims of a situation prevailing throughout Europe – a general price revolution. There are many theories as to what caused this – more expensive military equipment, such as cannon and firearms; inflation caused by the influx of gold from the Indies; harvest failures; a rise in population – but the result was an unforeseen and unprecedented limitation on royal power. Previously, a king could pay for his own foreign policy, with a little help from time to time: now, the resources of the whole nation would be needed, and that required a fundamental shift in governance and the whole philosophy of the state.

Northumberland doubtless was not fully aware of the background factors – such ideas would only develop with hindsight – but he did recognize the crisis. He saw the importance of financial stability, even though he was honest enough to admit he didn't understand the details. The overriding aim and purpose of his regime became stability and retrenchment. All areas of government had to be devoted to the target of restoring the nation's finances, both to rescue the country from the real possibility of defaulting on its loans and becoming technically bankrupt, and from a repetition of the dangerous revolts of 1549, which he correctly attributed to economic hardship. He had hardly completed his initial coup against Somerset when, in January 1550, he and Paget, England's top diplomatic negotiator, travelled to France to negotiate the handing back of Boulogne to Henri II.

The continuing ownership of Boulogne was indefensible on just about every level. It had been won by Henry VIII in 1543, and in a subsequent treaty of 1546 France agreed not to take it back for a further five years. It was a typical dynastic conquest – won during a campaigning season that earned a bit of glory and one-upmanship for the king. But as a national asset, it was expensive, vulnerable, and of almost no strategic value, given the presence of the better-defended garrison of Calais a short distance away. Boulogne had cost almost £100,000 a year to maintain,[12] at a time when it was never even under direct threat. A king would never have consented to give it back, but Dudley was not hampered by royal credibility. He could see that its value to the nation was negligible, and he was encouraged by Henri's offer to pay a significant sum in restitution. Northumberland was heavily criticized for his supposed weakness but, possibly without appreciating the significance, he had just taken an important step towards a national, rather than a purely dynastic, foreign policy.

He followed this with a raft of further money-saving, and money-generating initiatives. His focus was on ending debasement and restoring the credibility of the coinage; paying off the foreign debt; reducing expenditure wherever possible; earning money from selling church plate and silver; investigating suspected corruption at the royal mints; and calling in debts owed to the crown. Realising his personal inadequacies in such matters, he put William Cecil, secretary to the council, in overall charge, ably assisted by the marquess of Winchester at the Treasury, and Thomas Gresham as agent on the Antwerp money markets.

Not everything ran smoothly. Even he had to resort to one further debasement, before calling in the bad coinage in July 1551, and replacing it in September with a new, improved version. Unfortunately, the delay caused merchants to stockpile meat and other foodstuffs, which caused yet more temporary hardship. So great was the need for quick money that he couldn't avoid continuing to sell off crown lands, though he did look at how these had been come by, which spelled the temporary end to several political careers, including that of Paget, who was imprisoned for embezzlement. His scheme to make Ireland pay for its own defence failed, and the colony continued to be a drain on England's finances. Another scheme to pay off the Antwerp debt with bullion also foundered.

Yet, overall, he did manage to stem the tide, and build some stability for the future, though the concept of the king living of his own was unachieved, and by now probably lost forever. He reduced expenditure on the navy, dissolved the *gendarmes* – a type of standing army made up mainly of those discharged from the Boulogne garrison – withdrew from the indefensible and economically ruinous outposts in Scotland, and paid off the Antwerp loans through a deal made with the Merchant Adventurers by which they provided the necessary sum in return for the government abolishing the monopoly rights of the Hanseatic (Baltic) merchants. He also launched commissions to investigate what had happened to the church goods 'lost' during the Reformation, and succeeded in getting some of them returned.

Throughout 1552, he embarked on his most significant scheme to tackle the root of England's finances – the so-called Revenue

Commission. This was a thorough-going investigation into the main organisations involved in the collection and disbursement of monies – the courts of the Exchequer (ordinary tax collection), First Fruits and Tenths (taxes owed by the clergy), Wards and Liveries (income from estates of under-aged heirs), Augmentations (money from former monastic lands), and the Duchy of Lancaster. The aim was to get a clear view of income and expenditure in each court, to check on abuses, and to see if the system could be improved. The recommendations, which were under consideration at the start of 1553, included amalgamating Augmentations with the Exchequer, a proposal that Northumberland did not find time to implement, though it was to be one of the early changes put into effect by Mary.

By 1553, he had reduced the crown debt from £260,000 to £180,000.[13] He had made sure that accurate accounts of income and expenditure were shown to the Privy Council so that all should be aware of the situation. He had established a separate fund of £40,000 per annum to deal with royal household expenses, thus extracting it from the national budget - possibly the first time that such a distinction had been made between royal and national finances. In short, the country, although still drastically short of money, was in a vastly improved situation from the one he had inherited, and, moreover, with a basis from which it could develop in a more sustainable way. His activities even aroused the interest of the young king, who produced his own memorandum on how to make the country financially stronger. Although guilty himself of lavish spending on luxuries and rewards, Edward's concern should have been a positive sign for the future. For now, Northumberland turned his mind to the tricky task of further helping the situation by securing a subsidy from Parliament, which was due to meet in March.

*

Parliament sat throughout the month of March 1553. This was a notably short time, but Northumberland, who had called it, had only one significant item of business. Many countries looked at this English institution with amazement, wondering how a modern monarch could tolerate such a thing, not fully understanding that, if used correctly, it could actually increase the power and authority of the king. A clever ruler would work with Parliament, persuade it to grant him the money he needed, and then collect taxes with the moral force of consent behind him. This, potentially, made him so much stronger than continental rulers who relied on force. The problem came with gaining that consent. Parliament could not be relied upon to do automatically what the king wanted; it had to be carefully managed.

Northumberland was well aware of this. Henry VIII had only called it nine times throughout the 39 years of his reign, but under Edward it was called every year except 1551. The reason that Parliament was summoned at all was almost always money, and this was inevitably the case in 1553. Northumberland still needed to balance the books, and for this he needed extra help: a subsidy. Normally, subsidies were only requested in time of war, to cope with the expensive demands of 'defending' the country. However, 1553 was not a time of war; in fact, things had seldom looked less like war; he was going to have to be clever.

The House of Lords was seen as the main problem, since it held most of the conservatives who disliked him for his religious policies. In January, he had put forward a proposal to allow even the heirs apparent of noble families to sit in the Lords, and possibly to vote – an obvious attempt to overcome with numbers the conservative opposition.[14] It is not clear whether this actually came to fruition, but it showed his intent.

But the Commons, in 1553 still very much the junior partner, could also be fractious, especially when it came to money. There is evidence from letters sent officially by the council that deliberate attempts were made to influence which members should be returned. Of 14 individuals named in these letters, 11 were eventually voted in[15] – a figure which could equally show the strength of central government's hold over the country, or the independence of the (admittedly tiny) electorate.

Maths was important. Most of the privy councillors, of whom there were 31, sat in the Lords, and this bloc, which would hopefully be united in the case of finance, could be a formidable influence. In the Commons, he had fewer guaranteed supporters – perhaps only 17 out of a total of some 350 members[16] – but even this small number could be a loud and influential minority. He had the right to select the speaker, who determined the order of business, length of debate, and who should be called to speak. The speaker could also decide whether a vote was to be made by acclamation – loud shouting, allowing an opportunity for selective hearing - or division, which enabled numbers to be accurately counted.

In practice, a small coterie of government supporters, strategically placed within earshot of the chair, and able to cast beady eyes over opposition elements, could prove a significant influence. No-one forgot that advancement came through patronage, and annoying those who dispensed it was not a good career move. Northumberland also had favours to call in, particularly from those newly-enfranchised boroughs – some 50 over the last six years – who owed their attendance to him.

Worryingly, it was opened, and closed, at Whitehall, rather than Westminster, due to the king being sick with a cold. He was able to participate in a shortened ceremony, but those present would have noticed his alarming cough. On 14 March, after two days of debate, the Commons granted a subsidy and two fifteenths and tenths, as requested. Unfortunately, the *Commons Journal* gives no details of debates, simply the end result, so we have no idea of how much opposition, if any, the bill faced. Four days later, the tax was formally passed by the upper house. No votes were recorded. Sitting in the Lords that day were 22 members of the reformed clergy, who might be expected to support him, and 49 lay peers, of whom over half were councillors. It sounds like it was a shoe-in, but Northumberland had taken no chances. Aware that many might point to the way that councillors had been busy enriching themselves, he laid down strict instructions as to how the bill should be presented, emphasising that it was the king who needed the money, for the payment of debts rather than for his own pleasure, and that it was the fault of Somerset that the royal finances were in such dire straits.

We cannot be sure what the money was that Jean Scheyfve, the Imperial ambassador, reported going into the Tower at the start of January 1553, or if he was even correct in his information. It may have been remnants of old coinage due to be melted down, or even church plate, or perhaps the special fund for the king's expenditure. Its entry into the Tower was, by itself, hardly suspicious, for this was the location of the principal mint. The details of Northumberland's estate do not suggest it was destined for him personally, and if this was part of a plot to seize the throne, this seems to have existed, at this stage, purely in the imagination of the envoy.

By the end of March 1553, Northumberland still seemed in a strong position. He had his money from Parliament, which would help with the payment of outstanding debts; the country was peaceful; and he had shaken off his own illness. There had been no challenges to his authority from within the council during his lengthy absences the previous year, and maybe with the good harvests and lower prices in the markets even his own unpopularity might start to diminish. Some, though, may have been aware that the stability of the kingdom was not as solid as it could have been. Edward's recovery seemed to have stalled. He was unable to shake off a cough, and some of his doctors suspected tuberculosis, a potentially fatal condition. If he were to die, and it was forbidden to talk aloud of such a possibility, then the next in line to the throne, assuming that he did not live long enough to have children, would be his half-sister, Mary.

2

The Problem with Mary

By spring 1553, Mary had become a problem. Not that there was anything new in this: Mary had always been a problem, ever since her birth. She was the girl who should have been a boy – an heir for Henry to parade as both a sign of his manliness, and as a guarantee for the continuation of the Tudor dynasty. And, as time went on, and the hoped-for son did not appear, she grew to be an even greater problem. She did not, in truth, always help the situation with her often contrary and petulant behaviour, but closer examination of her early years is likely to provoke more sympathy than scorn.

Put simply, for most of her life Mary was surrounded by people who would have preferred that she wasn't there at all. And since her death, much of historical writing has tried to pretend that she never really was. With the exception of some recent biographies, which have taken a more balanced view, if she is dealt with at all she is simply the aberration, the one who tried to turn the clock back, who lost Calais and was a failure; let's move on to Elizabeth. Even now, she is just 'Bloody Mary'; remembered most for the burnings that punctuated her rule, and, more jocularly, as a cocktail.

Her early years might be summed up as ones of gilded neglect. As a princess, she was entitled to all the luxuries that could be bestowed on a Tudor girl, save one: the attention and love of her parents. Not that she was uncared for, just that those who surrounded her daily, and were responsible for her upbringing, were seldom those whose attention she most craved. She had more contact with her mother, Katherine of Aragon, but her father, who she clearly adored, and who she desperately wanted to please – and who, in his own curious way, seems to have had a genuine affection for her - was a distant figure, appearing rarely, and whose fleeting 'duty' visits must have been, given his character, unsettling.

She had received a privileged education, benefitting from the new ideas stimulated by the Renaissance, which taught that women, too, were worthy of instruction in the liberal arts. Her mother even commissioned Juan Vives, a noted scholar, to write a book especially aimed at her upbringing. She did not excel at her studies, but was well spoken of, and achieved a mastery in French, with some Latin, which turned out to be useful when she became queen. However, this education was very much geared towards women, and lacked the practicality of the training that Edward was later to enjoy. There was certainly little else that would be helpful to a future ruler.

Her status and worth became clear from an early age. She may have had no importance as a future monarch, but as a future spouse of a monarch she was a valuable bargaining chip. She was just two years old when, in 1518, she was betrothed to the dauphin of France as one of the terms of the Treaty of London. Two years later, due to changing international circumstances – or, more probably, the changing whims of her temperamental father - this was broken off and she was temporarily betrothed to the Holy Roman Emperor, Charles V. This might be seen as a step up the European pecking order for the four-year-old, who doubtless knew little about it, but it simply established her true significance – just a counter to be tossed onto the table by players, rather than a sentient being whose needs and future happiness were worthy of consideration.

At least, in this case, she was actually to meet and become acquainted with her proposed husband, when Charles paid a visit to the English court in 1522, and she must have been aware of the circumstances for she formed a bond – romantic, in the terms of a six-year-old - with the young man which was to remain for the rest of her life. However, the actual union with Charles was to last only until 1526, when he married the infanta of Portugal and, in the following year, she was betrothed to the younger son of the French king. How much this cynical merry-go-round had any emotional effect on Mary we do not know, but we can be sure that her father's subsequent marital behaviour severely damaged her, and both of these factors must have coloured her attitudes towards marriage.

For, by this time, relations between her parents had turned sour, and Henry was engaged in the drawn-out process of attempting to divorce Katherine. It is sometimes forgotten that, for Mary, this drama, which horrified Europe, intrigued the court and country, and has since fascinated generations of students of Tudor history, was the very personal and painful break-up of her family. And it was demanded of her, later on pain of death, that she take sides.

The wider consequences of the split are well-known, but for Mary they boiled down to two: the need to accept her father as head of the English Church, in contravention of everything she had been brought up to believe; and the acceptance of her own illegitimacy, and loss of her status as princess. It is not known how devoutly religious she was at this stage. It is possible that she could, like untold others, have taken the Oath of Supremacy, and made whatever peace with her conscience she deemed necessary, but she refused, most probably to spite her father. We know that she was outraged by her loss of status – petulantly demanding to be referred to by the now-forbidden title of princess – and by the treatment of her mother.

Wisely – unusually for him – Henry did not publicly demand compliance from Mary, as he had from others. The divorce was unpopular enough; he did not need the execution of his, widely-liked, daughter as well. And so, for three years there was a stand-off – Katherine and Mary being effectively imprisoned in separate houses, forbidden to see each other, and then, even more humiliatingly, after her mother's death, Mary being attached to the household of the newly-born Elizabeth, daughter of the hated Anne Boleyn.

During these years, Mary's health declined, and she became prone to bouts of illness, either real or imagined. She was listless and lonely, longing for the approval of her father, but determined not to be the one to relent – traits of character that were to become embedded, and which would account for aspects of her later behaviour. More significantly, she became reliant on the Imperial ambassador, Eustace Chapuys, who met her frequently, and who acted as a conduit with both Katherine and Charles V. He was the first in a succession of Imperial envoys on whom she was to depend for the rest of her life.

Katherine's death, in January 1536, brought matters to a head. Anxious to be reconciled with his daughter, Henry made clear that this would depend on her fulfilling the two obligations. Mary refused. Thomas Cromwell, the chief minister, put his reputation, and life, on the line in his efforts to mend the fracture, and became exasperated at her stubbornness. It may have been Chapuys, not slow to claim credit, who resolved the impasse by convincing Mary that she could serve the Catholic cause more effectively alive than dead. The faith already had its high-profile martyrs – More and Fisher – it did not need another. For whatever reason, Mary signed the ultimatum that Henry presented – an action she is said to have bitterly regretted.

Suddenly, all was sweetness and light again. Mary was welcomed back at court – crowds turned up in the hope of catching a glimpse of her – and she was given her own household and treated on the same level as Elizabeth. For the rest of the reign, she adopted a low profile, accepting her father's bewildering succession of marriages, and apparently at ease with the birth of Edward and her consequent relegation down the line of succession. Her health improved, and she took up hunting, hawking and gambling, and became a popular member of the royal household. She stayed clear of politics, and managed to avoid the embarrassment of the rebels of the Pilgrimage of Grace demanding that she be restored to the succession, and Henry Courtenay's doomed attempt to declare her the rightful heir ahead of Edward.

By 1553, Mary's situation was, in constitutional terms, temporary. She was next in line to the throne, by dint of Henry's will, but only until such time as Edward produced an heir. Then she would suffer a gradual slide down the order of precedence as Edward's line bypassed her. She was content, for the time being, to live quietly. She had made no fuss at Edward's accession, even though many in the kingdom, and most in Catholic Europe, believed that she, as Henry's firstborn, had a better claim, since the legitimacy of Henry's divorce from her mother was still disputed. Yet, when occasion allowed it, she took the opportunity to raise her profile, and remind people of her position.

On 10 February 1553, Mary came to London to see Edward. This was a rare visit. She had been invited every Christmas, but matters of religion had caused division between them both and, fearing an unpleasant argument, or even possible arrest, she had declined. But with Edward's worsening health, the situation had changed. There was the distinct possibility that she might soon become queen, which lent her a certain measure of security, and opportunity.

This was no low-key affair. She was escorted through the streets of the capital by over 100 horsemen and women. The king was too unwell to see her at first, but three days later she rode out to the court at Westminster, escorted by another huge procession, and was welcomed by Northumberland himself, and privy councillors, before being taken in to see her half-brother. The Imperial ambassador reported, presciently, that the lords 'did duty and obeisance to her as if she had been Queen of England'.[1]

For once, the ambassador did not draw conclusions, though he might well have been suspicious at Northumberland's gracious behaviour since relations between the council and Mary had been at rock bottom during the previous few years. The issue was over religion, or so it appeared. Put simply, Mary was Catholic, and determined, as were unknown numbers in the kingdom, to hang onto her faith. She heard Mass, and used all the old rituals, despite the laws that were coming in forbidding such practices.

Somerset had decided, probably wisely, to let sleeping dogs lie. If Mary was content to hear Mass in the privacy of her house, then let her carry on. As long as she didn't make an issue out of it, then no harm would be done. Besides, her links with her cousin, Emperor Charles V, made it wise not to push the issue, and remind outsiders that England was a heretical country that Catholic rulers were duty-bound to bring back to the true faith. The English ambassador, Nicholas Wotton, had assured Charles that Mary would be left alone and, for a time, that seemed to work.

However, Northumberland had taken a different view, and determined to bring Mary to order. It is not immediately clear why. Although he appeared to be one of the main movers behind the rapid changes in religion, he was not particularly interested in such issues himself, and was certainly not personally fanatic or devout. Mary was not causing trouble, and the progress of the Reformation did not seem to be held up by her, quiet, opposition. Nor was there any sort of ideological reign of terror in progress, such as was later to be released by Elizabeth against the Catholics. No Catholic was burnt by Northumberland's order. There were fines for those not attending church, and possible imprisonment for open opposition, but this stage of the Reformation was, otherwise, remarkably relaxed.

It is possible that the issue was one of dominance and conformity, and that religion was merely the issue over which this was fought. Certainly, Northumberland liked to be in control of every situation, and Mary's disobedience must have rankled, yet he was a clever politician, and he must have been aware that deliberately picking a fight with the heir to the throne was not a particularly intelligent move.

There is another explanation, however; that it was not Northumberland's idea, but Edward's. In 1550, the king was 14, and well able to know his own mind. He was religiously devout, with the borderline fanaticism that teenagers are often prone to. The idea of his older half-sister defying his orders, and her tactic of continuously reminding him that he was not yet old enough to make decisions for himself, must have been extremely annoying. It is perfectly possible that he made it clear to Northumberland that he wanted something done about it, and that the latter, not wishing at this comparatively delicate stage to lose the king's favour, complied.

Not that relations had always been bad. In August 1549, during the first coup against Somerset, Dudley had tried to get Mary's support against the protector, even suggesting that she become regent, though on the advice of Charles V she had declined. However, by January 1550, Mary had made her true feelings clear, declaring to the then Imperial ambassador, François van der Delft, 'The Earl of Warwick is the most unstable man in England. The conspiracy against the Protector has envy and ambition as its only motive...For this reason I wish myself out of the kingdom'.[2]

It is not clear what had upset her, as there had, as yet, been no specific threats against her personally, but an instruction by the council to bishops the previous December to root out Catholic practices throughout their sees was possibly the cause of her alarm. At any rate, the idea of fleeing the kingdom took root in her mind, and, despite the initial opposition of van der Delft, who feared that 'the good lady through her own incompetence might fall into a worse evil',[3] a daring plot was hatched by Charles V and the head of Mary's household, Robert Rochester, to spirit her out of the country in a fishing vessel.

However, when the time came, Mary, so often the vacillator, could not make up her mind. Van der Delft had suggested to her that if she were to leave that would be the end of any hope of becoming queen, though she had denied this, saying 'I feel certain that the whole country would be favourable to me'.[4] When the rescue party arrived at her house in the evening of 31 June 1550, they found her only half ready, and hysterical. Rochester pointed out the danger of attempting the escape, possibly hoping that she might stay – for he had heard that Edward's horoscope predicted he would not survive the year - and Mary asked for more time to decide. The opportunity was lost.

Northumberland and the council became aware of the plot, and now decided to move against her. In late July, they forbade Mass to be said in her house, overturning their previous policy of turning a blind eye. They argued that Mary was welcoming all comers into her house to hear the service – she was reputed to have as many as six chaplains - whereas Somerset's 'agreement' was that it should just be for her and a few servants. Next, the council summoned her to see Edward to explain her conduct, to which she refused, pleading ill health. Two of her chaplains were then arrested.

Over Christmas 1550, Mary did consent to come to court, where she had an angry discussion with Edward that left them both in tears. In the New Year, the council again wrote to Mary forbidding her to hear Mass, and Edward followed up with a personal rebuke: 'It appears to us… that you, our nearest sister, in whom by nature we should place reliance and our highest esteem, wish to break our laws and set them aside deliberately and of your own free will, and moreover sustain and encourage others to commit a like offence'.[5] Part of the letter was written in the king's own hand. However much Northumberland may have dictated it, this was a clear sign of royal frustration and disapproval.

On 15 March 1551, Mary came again to London, ostensibly to patch things up, though the manner of her entrance was hardly that of a supplicant. She rode through crowded streets with 50 knights before her and 80 ladies and gentlemen behind, all ostentatiously displaying banned rosary beads, in an evident show of defiance. Both she and Edward said their pieces - Mary alone in the chamber, surrounded by the king and his council, and refusing to back down. The council asked her to remain in London, though not specifically under arrest, but then inexplicably allowed her to leave a few days later, with nothing further resolved.

By now, the matter had become a full-scale diplomatic incident. Perhaps with nothing better to discuss, or perhaps because Charles was taking an unhealthy interest in matters in England, the situation regarding Mary became the main topic in despatches between the emperor and his ambassador. The situation was compounded by the undiplomatic behaviour of Richard Morison, the English envoy to the Imperial court who, rather than simply gloss over the religious differences between the two sides, insisted on engaging the emperor in religious debate and haranguing him for his views.[6]

At the same time, the English ambassador to the Low Countries, part of the Empire, requested the right to hear the Anglican communion in his house. Charles refused, citing the council's treatment of Mary, even though he demanded that Scheyfve, his new envoy, should still be allowed to hear Mass in his residence in London, arguing that it was the 'true' religion.[7] On 19 March, Edward noted in his diary that the Imperial ambassador had given him a message from Charles threatening 'warre' if Mary was not allowed to hear Mass.[8] This was obviously an exaggeration, even though there was some sort of veiled threat to break off diplomatic relations,[9] but it may have jolted the council into action. They promptly allowed Mary to leave London, and replaced Morison.

Yet the harassment continued, though for the time being more subtly than before. In May, the council condemned Francis Malet, one of Mary's chaplains, for saying Mass, and, on the express orders of Edward himself, threw him into the Tower. Shortly afterwards, three of her gentlemen were imprisoned for hearing Mass in her house. Mary, however, was not directly challenged. In July, England and France signed a treaty, which included the future marriage of Edward to Henri II's daughter. With French backing behind them, in case Charles should be tempted to take matters further, or even follow up the advice of Mary, Regent of the Netherlands, to seize an English port,[10] the council felt more secure in taking on Mary again.

Charles V, by Titian

On 9 August, they decided they would 'wink at sin'[11] no longer, and ordered Mary to stop hearing Mass, even in secret, even alone. So serious was their intent that they even swore the Catholic-leaning earls of Arundel and Derby onto the board just to sign the letter, which was then endorsed by the king. They summoned Rochester to London, and demanded that he persuade the princess to obey. She refused even to listen to him. When he returned to London with Mary's message, he and two other household servants were promptly imprisoned. The council then sent members to confront Mary in her home, and succeeded in extracting a promise from her chaplains that they would desist from saying Mass. Security was tightened around her; ships were sent to guard the coast to forestall any further attempt to escape; but almost no further mention was made of the whole business.

The decision of the council to lay off Mary, and Charles to suspend his demands on her behalf, may have been helped by other matters. In October, the plot against Somerset was beginning to come to fruition, which gave Northumberland more important issues to deal with, while in the same month Henri declared war on Charles, and the Habsburg-Valois struggle resumed. Charles was not going to provoke England unnecessarily, especially considering the recent Anglo-French alliance – he needed English neutrality – and Scheyfve's reports made few references to Mary during 1552.

On the face of it, it looked as though Mary had won, but in March 1553 she wrote to Charles asking him to intervene again with the council to allow her to hear Mass in secret, stating that this had been denied her for almost two years. Considering Mary's personality, and the importance her faith held for her, it seems scarcely credible that within the confines of her own household she had not had the Mass said for her. It is also interesting that she should have chosen this moment to bring the matter up, while preparing for her visit to Edward, and at a moment when the king's health was in the balance. Could she have been reminding Charles of the stakes, and subtly asking for his support?

Mary's 'state' visit to Edward in March 1553 marked something of a rehabilitation, though there is more than one way of looking at it. We have no record of a formal invitation by the Privy Council, though there must have been some correspondence as Mary was, effectively, under house arrest. Nor do we know how many of the hundreds of lords and ladies who accompanied her through London were her own people, rather than laid on by the council. Both sides clearly had their own agenda for the visit.

Less fashionable, for it has seldom been the practice to credit Mary with any degree of political skill, is the suggestion that she was behind the whole episode, choosing to come to London at a moment when Edward's illness made the succession very much a topic in people's thoughts, if not on their tongues, and to show herself to her future subjects not as a virtual outlaw, but as the unashamed and confident heir to the throne. Although talk of the king's illness was banned, and punished severely, this did no more than encourage rumours to fly around the streets. Those watching would have suspected that they were looking at their next ruler, and Mary, always considerate of the power of personal appearance, was not going to disappoint them.

Northumberland's motives are more clouded. It may be that the initiative for the visit was his, in which case he may have been trying to curry favour with Mary, whom he, better than any, must have suspected would shortly be his next boss. Ever mindful of the circumstances of his father's death, he had every reason for patching things up with her, whatever the outcome of Edward's illness. Others, less charitably, have suggested that this was already an attempt to lull Mary into a false sense of security, the easier to apprehend her later. This would assume that he was already plotting to disinherit her, a suggestion for which there is, at this early stage, no reliable evidence.

*

The fight between Mary and the council was a symptom of that mighty struggle of faith that was endemic in most European countries at this time, which, in truth, had been occurring for centuries past. England had come late to the lists, and almost reluctantly. Henry VIII had viewed the rebelliousness of continental Protestantism with horror, particularly in the apparent attacks on established authority, but there was one aspect that he did like: the supplanting of the pope as head of the church in Protestant countries with the lay ruler.

That meant, if handled correctly, and from the top, a significant increase in his own authority. No more church courts deciding on matters outside his concern, no more appeals to Rome over his head, no more foreign interference in English affairs, and, more positively, he in complete control of his own country, with the ability to take over and use the riches of the Catholic Church for his own and his country's benefit, and, perhaps most important of all, the opportunity to permit himself a divorce from his barren wife.

Which was about as far as he was prepared to go. He had little stomach for the new doctrinal ideas, which was why the English Reformation was, at least in the early days, always more political than spiritual. In his later years, fearing he had gone too far, he returned his country, with the Six Articles, to a more orthodox Catholicism. For him, the key issue had always been his supremacy over the English Church, which was why, whatever else they might believe, Englishmen had to swear this particular oath.

His executors, however, had different ideas. Somerset was intent on launching a full-scale religious Reformation, both of belief and practice, and Dudley seemed more than happy to go along with him. Again, politics reared its head, and the council was split between religious reformers – the evangelicals – and the traditionalists, most of whom were not prepared to go beyond the situation at the end of Henry's reign. But there was always a feeling that religion wasn't really the issue; that it was more a means of identifying fellow travellers in the continual struggle for survival and advancement within the council. These fault lines, however, were to fester, and they were still much in evidence in 1553. Edward, significantly, was very much on the side of the reformers, a stand that was made more likely given his humanist education, and the beliefs of those most close to him, and which was to become an individually-held passion.

In six years, the reformers had changed the country from a quasi-Catholic into an almost wholly Protestant nation, and with astonishingly little opposition. Henry had perhaps done the difficult part with the Act of Supremacy and the dissolution of the monasteries, two measures which did result in significant protests, and which, in their effects on belief and daily life, were possibly the most uncomfortable. Yet the doctrinal basis of the Anglican Church was laid during Edward's minority, and not even the reactionary reign of Mary could significantly alter the course it had set for English history.

Naturally, there were disputes over doctrine, and radicals and conservatives fought over exact interpretations, and there were some victims – high-profile bishops such as Gardiner, Tunstal and Bonner, among others, were sent to the Tower for refusing to accept the changes - though the only execution was of a woman from an extreme Protestant sect. There were some revolts, though only one major one – in the West Country in 1549 - and there are doubts as to how much religion was the real reason behind it. Ordinary people may have disliked the reduction in saints' days and holidays, and religious processions and ceremonies, and regretted the loss of paintings and ornaments in the churches that would have enlivened many a dull sermon, but most seem to have taken it in their stride, and accepted the new rules and practices with equanimity.

There were also issues over control. Bishops of any stamp did not like their powers being removed, and Northumberland and the archbishop of Canterbury, Thomas Cranmer - former allies - had fallen out over this, especially over the duke's insistence that bishops be chosen by Edward, and that their stipends and the size of their sees be reduced. In the case of the bishopric of Durham, Northumberland was prepared to put its elderly bishop, Cuthbert Tunstal, in the Tower in his failed efforts to secure half of its lands for himself. He also overplayed his hand by bringing down the radical firebrand preacher, John Knox, from Scotland to speed up the process of change. Knox, proved too unruly and unmanageable, and had to be quickly dismissed.

Yet it would be wrong to think that the Reformation was forced on a reluctant population. Many were pleased by the English version of the bible - perhaps, along with printing, one of the most significant steps in the progress of literacy - and the fact that they could now understand what the priest was saying during the service. They also enjoyed being able to take part in the communion, rather than watching it from afar, or, in the case of many churches, not seeing it at all. As to what they thought they were actually consuming – Christ's body, or a symbol thereof – we cannot say, as such beliefs could be privately held. The law may have said it was a symbol, but who would know if you felt otherwise?

And this may shed an interesting light on the Reformation, and its significance in ordinary lives. Certainly, the people of England had had a confusing time lately. Within a lifetime, religion had gone from the orthodox Catholicism of Henry VIII's early reign, through the break with Rome and adoption of royal supremacy, back to the more conventional Catholicism of the Six Articles, and now the radical Reformation of Edward. Given the presumed importance of religion within ordinary people's lives, these changes might be assumed to have put a significant burden on their consciences.

But perhaps we need to make a distinction between religion and faith. People in sixteenth-century England were undoubtedly God-fearing. Life was so uncertain, and usually short, that they had little alternative. But how much care did they really give to 'religion', as defined by the pronouncements of the Church and government? Given that Catholic services were conducted in Latin, and some essential parts hidden from ordinary view, much of what went on in churches would have been little understood anyway. People developed their own narrative and explanation, despite the catechisms that they had to learn by heart. Any changes by those in power would have sailed over the heads of many of them, who would have continued with their faith in their own way. A later Imperial ambassador, Simon Renard, summed this up succinctly: 'the common people who know nothing of religion or doctrine, partly because of their simplicity, and partly because these things have never been properly explained to them'.[12]

Likewise, the fact that there were so many changes may have weakened their respect for the Church and 'religion', but it would not have affected their own, personal, faith, and their own interpretation of the mysteries. The Reformation was always as much political as religious, and most people appear to have obeyed the laws, kept their heads down, and kept what was important to themselves. This may explain the absence of any war of religion in England, like those that afflicted continental countries, though it shouldn't hide the fact that, at times, loyalties and behaviour were determined by this religious divide.

Outwardly, though, there was to be no objection. The use of the new Prayer Book was enforced by the Act of Uniformity; attendance at church was compulsory, and fines could result for non-compliance; and churches were stripped of their valuables by force of law. Yet, although some might disagree, there was no systematic persecution of recalcitrants such as would be evident during the reigns of Mary and Elizabeth. Only those who were particularly outspoken, and these were mainly on the Protestant side, were pursued. Which makes it all the more surprising that the council should have stirred up a hornet's nest in its dealings with Mary.

In November 1552, Cranmer had presented his second Prayer Book, which was ordered to be used in all churches, and which was much more radical than his first in 1548. This new version shook off all the Catholic influences that he had not been able to remove previously, and effectively established the spiritual basis of the Anglican Church. However, his attempt to follow it with the Forty-Two Articles of doctrine proved too extreme and caused problems between the bishops and council over where power should reside. Parliament would not agree to them, and when they were finally promulgated by the council in June 1553, they would lapse a month later with the accession of Mary.

Nevertheless, the Reformation, incomplete though it still was, had changed much of the religious and social landscape. Monastic buildings were in ruins, and newcomers owned their lands; chantries in their physical and charitable form had been abolished - education, alms and hospitals were now the responsibility of individuals and lay foundations; new bishops were in place, and priests could take wives. Within churches, Latin was nowhere to be heard, altars were replaced by communion tables, vestments and plate were largely gone – even the lead from the roofs of churches in some over-enthusiastic cases – the walls were bare, and there was a new set of rules to be followed. The thought that if Edward's health gave out, and Mary came to the throne, all this might revert back was a chilling prospect, particularly for those who had helped bring it about.

*

The worry over what Mary might do if she came to power was not limited to religion; it was also connected to the identity of her future husband. This would be of vital importance. It was taken for granted that she would marry, for how else would she be able to rule without a husband's firm hand to guide her? More concerned by this than most, Henry had specified in his will that the Privy Council should have the last word in who this should be, but Henry's will had been easy enough to get around, as Northumberland knew only too well. Supposing Mary *did* become queen, and resolved to marry a Catholic? And more alarming, and more likely, a *foreign* Catholic. Would the council then be in a position to defy her?

There had been an effort, in early 1550, to marry her off to Dom Luis, the son of the king of Portugal, but this had apparently been an initiative of Somerset, and with his fall the idea lapsed. Mary remained resolutely uninterested in marriage for now, but this could change, and now that

Edward's health was showing signs of serious concern, the matter was becoming more urgent. Northumberland, perhaps realising that his, and the council's, reputation with Mary was at a low, had refrained from broaching this delicate subject. There was, of course, another option, which would solve the problem of religion and marriage...

For one foreign power, however, the matter was one of great interest. Mary was half Spanish, and Spain was part of the Habsburg dominions, that mighty and ill-matched agglomeration of nations and races that made up the inheritance of Charles V, Holy Roman Emperor, archduke of Austria, king of Spain, duke of Burgundy, and a host of other titles. Moreover, she was cousin to the emperor, and had, admittedly while still a child, even been betrothed to him. On 2 April 1553, Charles wrote to his widowed son, Philip, suggesting he take another wife. He put forward the name of Maria, daughter of the King of Portugal. Surprisingly, perhaps, although he named other possibilities, Mary was not among them.

Yet England held a position of considerable importance to Charles at this time, particularly with the resumption, in October 1551, of the Habsburg-Valois struggle. Ever since the French king, Charles VIII's, invasion of northern Italy in 1498, the battle for dominance between these two great powers of western Europe had provided the backdrop to diplomacy and the foreign affairs of most, if not all, the lesser powers. Although Henry VIII had done his best to raise England out of this category and establish it as a major player, in terms of resources and territorial size it could not compete. Henry's actions, aimed primarily against France, had been pinpricks - irritating, but ultimately insignificant.

If England had any sort of importance, it was in its geographical position, and the threat to the Empire from France rendered this more immediate. For Charles to get Spanish troops to the Low Countries, and Spanish bullion to pay them, he needed unhindered passage up the English Channel. If England was to stray onto the side of France, then this route could be effectively sealed. For the moment, England was neutral, and its ships would not actually prevent a Spanish fleet from sailing through. If Mary was to come to the throne, then the outlook might be even more positive.

As far back as 1522, Henry VIII had signed a mutual assistance agreement with Charles – The Treaty of Utrecht - pledging help if either were attacked by France. Given that England's main trading partner was the Low Countries, under Imperial control, and that France was a traditional enemy that could attack either across the narrow width of the Channel, or down from its close ally, Scotland, this seemed a sensible option. England also owned the outpost of Calais, perpetually vulnerable, and Charles could be helpful in protecting it.

Henry's idea of foreign policy, however, was essentially dynastic. He believed in showing off, with short campaigns that he would lead, and which would hopefully win something that could then be touted as a triumph. Typical of this was his war of 1542 in which he acquired Boulogne, subsequently protected by a five-year treaty. This was presented as a great victory, but really it was nothing more than a costly white elephant. France could have taken it back whenever it chose, but it was prepared to pay the price to satisfy Henry's ego so that he would not intervene on Charles's side in any more meaningful way.

Northumberland, free of dynastic baggage, recognised that it was hardly in the national interest to have two, basically indefensible, outposts on the north coast of France, and negotiated the treaty which handed it back. He then took advantage of the situation to agree a non-aggression pact with France, which included the betrothal of Edward to Henri's daughter. This effectively forestalled the danger of any attack coming from, or through, Scotland - another potentially hostile power - whose infant queen, Mary, was already betrothed to the French dauphin.

By modern standards this might seem a neat piece of business. England had protected itself from involvement in a European war, in which its weakness would have prevented it playing any significant part, and reduced the possibility of any hostile moves from Charles in favour of Mary, which might include the restoration of Catholicism. Not everyone agreed, either at the time or later. One historian has concluded that this policy was 'disastrous' and made England 'the laughing-stock of Europe',[13] but this is akin to a sixteenth-century, dynastic, view in which success is measured by territory won, rather than territory upheld. Recognising one's limitations, and working within them, is not always a sign of weakness.

But in June 1552, Mary of Hungary, regent of the Netherlands, challenged this policy of protected neutrality by writing to Edward invoking the 1522 Treaty of Utrecht, and asking for men or money. She was not hopeful about the response, noting privately that the English would probably try to argue their way out of it by claiming doubts over who attacked first.[14] She was right. Scheyfve followed this up in person, but Edward, evidently well-schooled by his council, apologised that, as Northumberland was currently away in the north, nothing could be decided immediately.

In July, Charles V wrote to Edward personally, reminding him of his obligations. The ambassador was advised by two councillors that, because of his age, it was necessary to proceed 'deliberately' with the king. Scheyfve retorted that although Edward 'was young he was very able, and quite capable of understanding',[15] a point that somewhat contradicted his frequently-expressed assertion that Edward was merely the puppet of the duke. In August, the council informed Scheyfve that England could not afford to offer aid as it was still recuperating from its last war with France. This was, at least in financial terms, partly true. Buoyed by agreements with both sides, Northumberland now felt strong enough not to be lured into conflicts in which he and the country had little interest.

*

However, at the start of 1553, foreign affairs were not the most important of Northumberland's concerns. Although matters in the kingdom were generally proceeding satisfactorily, there was a cloud beginning to loom on the horizon: the health of the young king. As early as February, Scheyfve reported that Edward's life could be in danger, and that doctors were beginning to decline responsibility for what might happen. He suggested that the problem might be something congenital – that his right shoulder was higher than his left, causing compression of the organs leading to breathing difficulties.[16] This aspect is not borne out by Edward's portraits, but then it doubtless wouldn't be. However, the ambassador had a well-placed mole within Edward's medical team, so his observations cannot be ruled out.

With the benefit of hindsight, it is easy to characterise Edward as a sickly child, doomed to an early end, yet this was not the perception at the time, at least not until 1552. However, the Tudor era was not a healthy one, and life was always precarious. Plague occurred at such frequent intervals that it could almost be termed endemic. Along with this, and all the other diseases which, given the rudimentary state of medical knowledge, could easily turn fatal, there was a new and deadly infection - sweating sickness, otherwise known as the English sweat - which periodically visited the country throughout the first half of the sixteenth century.

In July 1551, another serious outbreak began in London, and spread beyond. Two close friends and fellow pupils of Edward's - the duke of Suffolk and his brother - were carried away one night as they slept together in the same bed. Hundreds died, and Scheyfve reported that Londoners were 'terror-stricken'.[17] The king was removed to Hampton Court for added safety. A year later, it struck again, and the duke of Northumberland, in a surprisingly moving letter to Cecil, described how he sat at the bedside of his stricken daughter-in-law and watched her pass away only hours after showing the first symptoms. The disease which, after a few outbreaks, disappeared as mysteriously as it arrived, and has eluded attempts of modern doctors to identify it, was a symbol of just how random survival was in these days. Nothing could be taken for granted.

Yet, for most of his life, Edward had avoided such horrors. He appeared a healthy, fit young boy, and the odds looked good for his survival to manhood. However, the obsessive care shown to him in his infancy, and the extraordinary regime of diet and hygiene that Henry prescribed for his hope for the immortality of the Tudor dynasty – the walls and floors of his rooms had to be scrubbed three times daily - awarded him little opportunity to build up the defences needed for any later assaults on his health. Edward was, quite simply, cocooned inside a bubble, a stranger to dirt, and allowed none of the risky pursuits of young boys that would have enabled him to build up a physical toughness.

All seemed to be going well, however, until, in March 1552, he contracted, almost simultaneously, smallpox and measles, two eminently fatal diseases. These laid him low to the extent that he was unable to preside at the closing of Parliament in April, though by the end of that

Edward VI, after William Scrots

month a special envoy of the emperor succeeded in getting an audience and found him 'very cheerful'.[18] Recovery might have been complete if not for the supremely unwise decision, two months later, to allow him to undertake a progress through the south of the kingdom to show himself to his people.

Given the problems of communication in sixteenth-century England, the only way that most of the king's subjects would have personal contact with their monarch was for him to visit them. The purpose of the royal progress was various. There was an obvious propaganda value in the king showing himself – it made him less distant - and it had an important psychological effect; rebellion would be more difficult against someone seen personally. For the king, it would enable him to keep local officials on their toes, see for himself the state of the realm, and listen to the complaints of the people and promise to do something about them.

This was Edward's first major progress, and it was a long one. It took him as far away as Portsmouth, visiting Guildford, Southampton, Winchester, Salisbury, Reading and Windsor - not far, admittedly, by modern standards, but a significant distance then. Roads barely existed, and if they did, they would have been in a terrible condition, the winter mud having been baked into iron-hard ruts. Long hours would have been spent on horseback, or in a litter drawn by horses, either of which would have provided a jolting, bruising and desperately uncomfortable ride. And this was in mid-summer, with all the issues of heat and dust, and with the king not yet fully recovered from two extremely serious illnesses.

We do not know how much of an effect this had on Edward's health, but it is unlikely that it helped much. One of the chroniclers, Thomas Cooper, claimed that he became exhausted with too much hunting and hawking,[19] as those with whom he lodged fell over themselves in efforts to entertain him, but the journey by itself would have been enough. He was obliged, in mid-September, to cut short the progress, ostensibly due to 'maladies prevalent in the country'.[20] He didn't mention any health worries in his diary, yet two months later his journal abruptly stopped for good, and he became ill again with the onset of another affliction, probably tuberculosis.

From then on, by degrees, it was all downhill. From February 1553, Scheyfve was holding out the likelihood that he might soon die. Partly, this was wishful thinking – he had given Northumberland, who was also absent due to poor health, the same prognosis the previous December – as he, of course, couldn't wait to see Mary on the throne. Given his propensity for over-reaction, and the lack of other sources of inside information, it is hard to get a balanced view of how serious Edward's illness was at any stage, but it seems that, with odd patches of remission, the king had been in a terminal decline since the previous November, and possibly even before.

Northumberland had invested a lot of time and energy in Edward, and this situation was highly concerning. Throughout his career he had shown awareness that the goodwill of the monarch was the key to his political advancement, and survival, and he had always been conspicuously loyal. This new prospect threw him into confusion. Not least because he might lose someone with whom he had forged a solid understanding, but also, if Edward were to die, his successor would almost certainly not be willing to work with him.

It is often supposed that the 'evil' duke kept his 'puppet', Edward, surrounded by his henchmen as a virtual prisoner within the royal court. In fact, ever since the coup of 1550, Northumberland had been engaged in a gradual process of liberating the king from his bubble. Somerset had continued the policy of wrapping Edward in proverbial cotton wool. Partly this was to protect him, but it was also down to an exaggerated belief in the new humanist ideal of education – that princes should no longer be brought up to be leaders in war, but to be cultured, literate, knowledgeable, and skilful in debate. Erasmus even recommended, in his *Education of a Christian Prince*, that training-at-arms, hunting, riding and chivalric literature should be removed from a royal curriculum.

This was all well and good in theory, but Edward was a boy, and like all boys he thought of little else but war and chivalric deeds – his diary is full of minute descriptions of the battles that were taking place on the continent, garnered from the diplomatic reports that he was allowed to read – and he chafed under this regime.

It might have been just to secure the young prince's approval, or because he felt Edward needed a more rounded education, that Northumberland permitted him to take part in more conventionally manly pursuits. Edward's delight was clear, in June 1550, when he was invited to watch a mock battle on the Thames, in which a fort, built on a boat, was stormed by naval boats and marines. In March 1551, he issued a challenge to 17 gentlemen of the court from himself and 16 of his chamber to contests of running and shooting. He won his first race, and as he confessed in his diary to losing the shooting, and the running at the ring (quintain), it clearly wasn't just a case of letting the king win. We can presume that he must have been allowed to practise these skills beforehand so that he could hold his own in competition, and it may have been the strength derived from this exercise that enabled him to fight off two of his illnesses in 1552.

Not that he was uninterested in formal education. Far from it; he seems to have excelled at his studies. He had two noted teachers - the severe disciplinarian, Dr. Cox, and the younger, more liberal, Roger Ascham, as well as French and music tutors, all overseen by the royal tutor, the distinguished Cambridge graduate, John Cheke.

Edward appears to have been a receptive and intelligent pupil. Whether he was quite as gifted a prodigy as Ascham described him in a letter in April 1550 - 'Our illustrious King Edward surpasses all men, as well as his own years, and everyone's expectation, in talent, industry, perseverance and learning'[21] – we cannot know, but the contents of his schoolbooks, which do survive, appear to our modern eyes as exceptionally precocious. Even at the age of 13 he was capable of expressing, if not even formulating, ideas for the progress of religion and the better running of the state, in remarkably erudite language.

In July 1551, Edward was allowed to take part in his first major diplomatic engagement, when he entertained the French delegate, Marshal St André, who had come to sign the treaty of friendship between the two countries. The young king's pride is evident in his diary, writing of how he dined with the older man, inviting him to be present at the royal dressing the next morning, and how he showed off his skills at shooting and lute playing. Edward gave him a ring from his finger – worth £150, he confided to his diary – and took him hunting and coursing in Hyde Park.

From 1551, Northumberland began to train Edward in the processes of government, allowing him to see despatches from diplomats, and, more importantly, to be present at certain meetings involving the Privy Council. For this purpose, a 'Council for the State' was formed, in March 1552, consisting of over 21 existing privy councillors. As no records of these meetings exist, there is some doubt among historians as to whether they involved the king in real policy discussions, or whether they were laid on solely for the purpose of educating Edward – a pretend council - particularly since protocol dictated that he should not attend meetings of the regular council. If so, that would have been a waste of everybody's time.

The point was that, as he reached maturity, Edward's approval was becoming ever more important. Certainly, there was still the dry stamp, by which the king's signature could be appended to any document without him necessarily being aware, but it would have been increasingly unwise not to have sought his opinion, and perhaps even acted on it. It is far more likely that these meetings involved semi-formal discussion of government policy, in which Edward was briefed, and his opinion sought. They would, therefore, have been an education for both sides, and their very existence shows that Northumberland was more interested in producing a well-rounded monarch, capable of understanding and reasoning matters of state, than an ignorant and easily-manipulated puppet.

By 1553, with Edward now in his sixteenth year, there was every hope for England's future king. Northumberland, and the tutors, had helped produce a person who was well-versed in humanist thought, modern-looking in terms of religion, interested in manly pursuits, and with a good grasp of government institutions and processes. True, he was showing signs of the same extravagance, and generosity with rewards, as his father, but caps had been placed on royal spending, and he had been shown the need to at least try to balance the books. Edward looked set to be a brilliant monarch, and with the country at peace and in economic recovery, he would soon inherit a kingdom that could support his ambitions.

If only he could shake off that cough…

3

'My devise for the Succession'

But the cough did not get better. In fact, it became more persistent, and at some stage Edward, and Northumberland too, decided to resolve the problem of Mary, and protect the work they had done, by amending the succession.

That they did it, there is no doubt, but how, when and why they took such a dangerous, and arguably illegal, step is more open to question. The traditional story is that the 'evil' duke, spurred by ambition, forced Edward to draw up letters patent removing Mary as heir and replacing her with his daughter-in-law, Lady Jane Grey. This was the version put forward by commentators at the time, successive governments, and the majority of historians in the following centuries. It has the benefit of being simple, supported, at least partly, by evidence, and absolves Edward of any blame for what occurred. And it makes for a good story. It does not, however, adequately answer any of the above questions.

The principal documentary evidence that might help with these questions is limited to three surviving items: Edward's 'devise for the succession'; his letters patent, often regarded as his will; and a later account by Sir Edward Montagu, chief justice of the common pleas. The last two will be dealt with more fully in the next chapter.

No-one can be quite sure when Edward decided to take matters into his own hands and pen his, now infamous, 'devise'. This single sheet, written in his own hand, with numerous additions and crossings out, has become one of the most pored-over documents from his reign, and remains one of the most enigmatic, giving rise, over subsequent centuries, to numerous interpretations in scholarly books and articles. Its significance cannot be understated, for it would, if followed through successfully, have cut short the Tudor dynasty, deprived us of the reign of the 'Gloriana' Elizabeth, and sent English history on a new trajectory. For these reasons, at least, it is well worth further investigation.

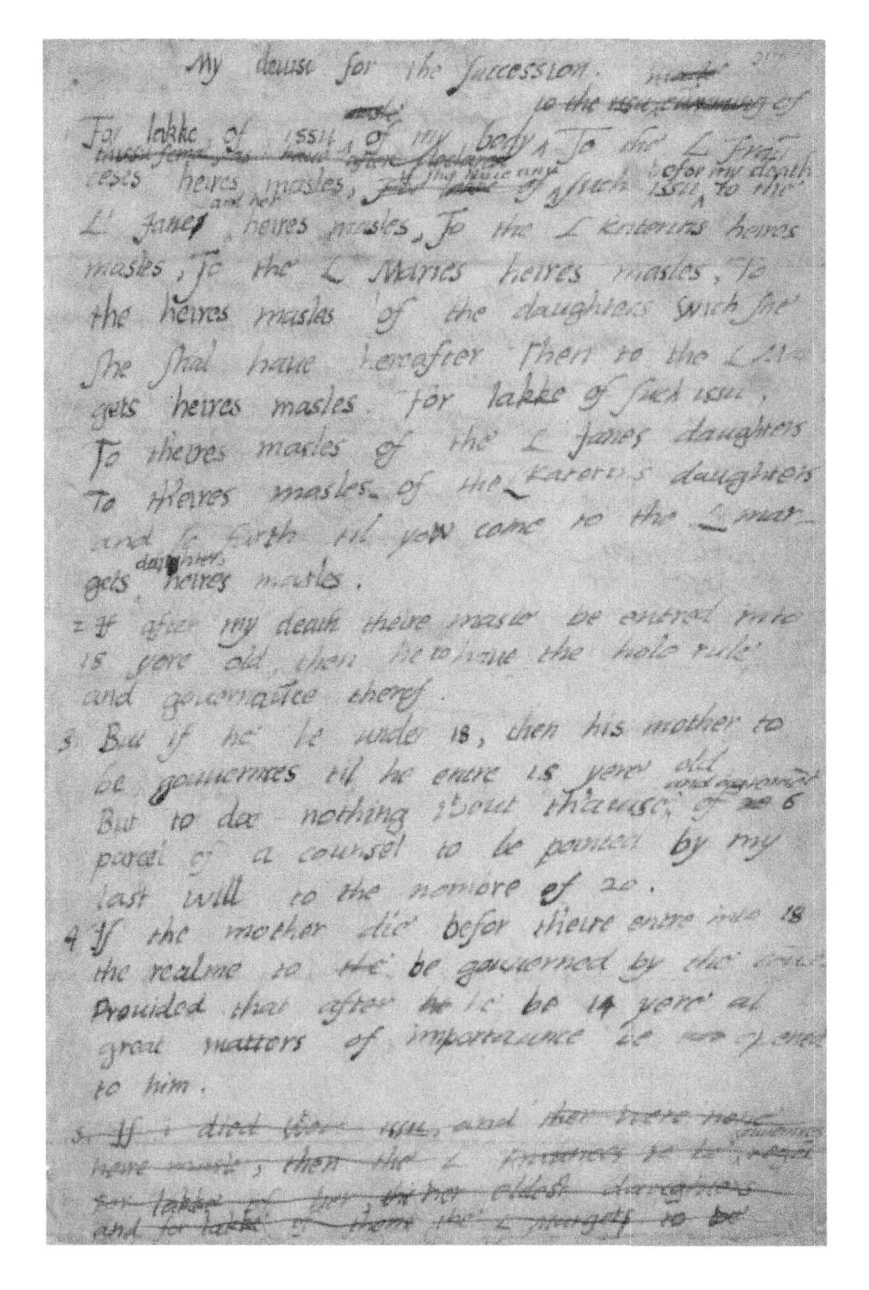

Edward's 'devise'

It was, put simply, a new plan for the succession if he should die without heirs. The question of what it says should, in theory, be the easiest to answer. The document survives intact; it is clearly legible, even to those not used to Tudor spelling and style; and it is easily, and freely, accessible to view. Yet this remains possibly the most difficult question of all. This is due to the numerous alterations, particularly in paragraph one, each of which can give a significantly different meaning to the intention of the writer.

What is clear is that there are at least two, and possibly more, different versions of the text within the same document. If we ignore all the alterations, and simply read the text without any additions or crossings out, we have a version. But is it a complete one? Were the changes made as Edward wrote his first draft, and can therefore be considered a part of version one, or were they inserted later? And how many changes and stages of re-writing were there? This matters because the document is almost the only clue as to what Edward, himself, was trying to do, and why.

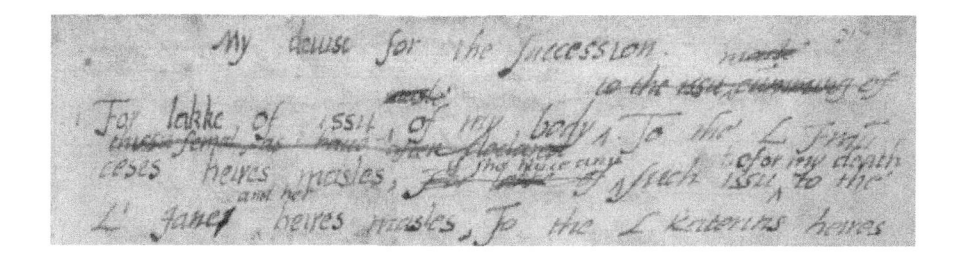

The first sentence is a good example of the problem. It begins 'For lack of issue of my body.' This seems clear enough; if Edward is to die childless, then the following will apply. Putting aside any revisions, it carries on to name male heirs of particular females, all outside his immediate family. This suggests that Edward's purpose at this stage was to ensure a male succession. The insertion, and then removal, of more words to the first sentence doesn't change this aspect, but it does add an extra consideration. Before the full stop, Edward has inserted 'to the issue coming of the issue female as I have after declared', and then he has inserted the word 'male' to read 'to the issue *male* ...'. This follows the revision in the first part of the opening sentence, where he has inserted the word 'male' to make it read 'For lack of issue male ...'. What this shows is a change of heart for, rather than going immediately outside the Tudor family in order to find a male, he is now allowing the son of any *daughter* of his to succeed. But, of course, as can be seen from the above extract, he has then crossed out this whole insert, including the word 'male', and so has returned to the idea that he may have no heirs.

There would appear to be two possible explanations for these changes, changes which are highly significant because the version we are left with effectively ends the Tudor dynasty. One is that Edward was trying to balance ensuring a male succession with keeping the crown within his own family. That is why, at one stage, he has allowed the son of a potential daughter to be in the succession. The other is that it is a question of timing. There seems to be two, or maybe three, versions. The original, in which Edward concentrates solely on securing a male heir, irrespective of whether this removes the Tudors from the succession; the second in which he considers there might be time to rescue the situation by having a daughter; and a third in which he has given up hope and has reverted to the original text. These changes could mirror the developing course of his illness.

On one level this this could be viewed as a fairly typical process undergone while drafting a document – Edward was simply working his ideas out on paper as he wrote - and possibly of no great significance, but on another it begs some fairly important questions: at what stage were the changes made, and who inspired them? It is perfectly possible that the three versions were separated by only seconds or minutes, and should therefore be classed as a single version, indicating the developmental thought process of the writer as he considered the task. Another possibility - more sinister, perhaps - is that the changes came later, and as a result of advice from someone else.

Things become a little clearer as he runs through his desired line of succession. The next in line, assuming he had no children, would be the male heirs of his father's cousin, Frances Grey, duchess of Suffolk, and, failing that, the male heirs of her daughters - in turn, Jane (Grey, or Dudley, depending on when the 'devise' was written), Katherine and Mary. This was significantly different from the existing line of succession as laid down in Henry's will, in that it removed the daughters themselves in favour of their (potential) sons.

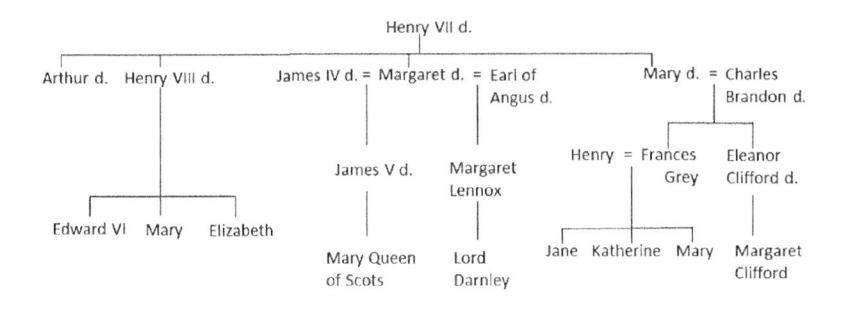

```
                              Henry VII d.
    ┌──────────┬──────────────────┼──────────────────────────┐
Arthur d.  Henry VIII d.   James IV d. = Margaret d. = Earl of      Mary d. = Charles
                                                 Angus d.                    Brandon d.
                                  │           │
                              James V d.   Margaret           Henry = Frances    Eleanor
                                  │        Lennox                    Grey       Clifford d.
    ┌──────┬──────┐               │           │             ┌──────┬──────┐         │
Edward VI Mary Elizabeth      Mary Queen    Lord         Jane  Katherine Mary   Margaret
                              of Scots    Darnley                                Clifford
```

The Tudor Family Tree in 1553

However, he then muddies the waters with another insertion. Following on from the 'Lady Frances' heirs males', the original text goes on to say 'for lack of such issue to the L. Jane's heirs males', which is clear enough – the succession goes to Jane's sons if Frances doesn't have any - but he has then altered this to read 'if she have any such issue before my death to the L. Jane's heirs males'. Not only is it unclear whether this stipulation refers to Frances, or Jane, but it is also hard to understand what Edward intended by it. Why should it make any difference whether Frances (or Jane) had sons before, or after, Edward's death, especially since none of the females mentioned had sons, anyway, whenever the 'devise' may have been written? However, this alteration might make more sense in the light of another, more critical, change that we shall come to shortly.

Following on, the next in line would be the sons of Margaret Clifford, Frances's niece. So far, then, a certain logic in that all those in the line of succession should be male. However, here the logic falls a bit flat since not one of those males actually existed. As if aware of this rather significant omission, he then relents and names next the male heirs of the *daughters* of Jane and her sisters and Margaret Clifford. Not that this made the position on the ground much easier. Given that Frances was probably past the age of child-bearing, and that Jane was only 17 in 1553, and her sisters even younger, England might have to wait until the birth of their grandsons, and another 18 years beyond that, to get its next adult monarch.

Having sorted out who was where in the pecking order, in the next paragraphs Edward explains how England should be governed if the appropriate male was under 18 at the time of his (Edward's) death. Here, at least, things make slightly more sense. England would be ruled by the boy's mother as 'governess', an interesting and unusual choice of word – in paragraph five the term 'regent' is used, but then substituted with 'governess' – but she could not act without the agreement of a 'parcel' of 20 (later changed to six) councillors to be appointed by Edward in his will. This mirrored the system laid down by Henry VIII in his will with his 18 executors. If the governess were to die before the prince reached the age of 18, then the council should govern, allowing the prince to have revealed to him 'great matters of importance' after the age of 14 (as had been allowed to Edward himself).

Paragraph five, which is later crossed out completely, then deals with the issue of what would happen if Edward died without any of these males appearing. In that case, Frances should be governess, and if she died then Jane, followed by her sisters and Margaret Clifford. If, at any moment, a male appeared, then that child's mother would automatically become governess. There is something slightly endearing, and pathetic, about this instruction that the governess of the kingdom should be the child's mother, irrespective of her age or competence. Edward, of course, never knew his own mother, and here perhaps is evidence of a subliminal regret. It is also further evidence, although not accepted by all, that Edward really was the author of this document.

The final paragraph deals with how the governess should arrange for more councillors to be chosen if four of them should die, and, interestingly, how after the age of 14 (originally 18) the prince should do the choosing. Edward was obviously enjoying being given greater responsibility in executive decisions, and wanted this benefit passed on to his successor. As with the will of Henry VIII, though, there is confusion over the word 'council' - whether he is referring to the Privy Council or his 20 executors.

From a reading of this document, various observations spring to mind. The first is that it is a complete nonsense. If this was written in spring

1553, as many historians seem to believe, at the time of his terminal illness, when his survival was in the balance, then in no way does it provide for a seamless succession. As Eric Ives has explained, it would result in an unseemly competition among various women to produce an heir, and thus rise or fall in the established order of seniority accordingly. It also explodes his apparent wish to have a male successor by ensuring that, for some considerable time, the ruler would effectively be a woman. A better recipe for dissension and strife it would be hard to imagine. If, however, Edward did not consider that he was at death's door, then it would make better sense. But then why write it at all?

The next observation is that it takes the succession away from the core of the Tudor family. True, Henry VIII had also nominated the Greys, but only after his son and daughters. If one thinks of the lengths he had gone to during his reign, upsetting the religious beliefs of his people and the social fabric of the country, challenging the emperor and pope, just so he could secure the continuation of the Tudor dynasty, then it seems remarkable that Edward should hand it over so easily, particularly since there were apparently plausible, and existing, alternatives that would keep the succession within the family.

And this brings us to the most important feature – what the 'devise' does *not* say. For nowhere in the text is there a single reference to those who Henry had nominated as successors to Edward should he die childless – his own daughters, and Edward's half-sisters, Mary and Elizabeth. Since, so far as we can tell, the majority of the country naturally expected Mary to be Edward's heir if he should die childless, and since by act of Parliament she was the legally-designated successor, then her omission is extraordinary. It can be argued that if his intention was simply to have a male successor – a belief he may have inherited from his father - then ignoring Mary and Elizabeth would have a certain logic, but why could he not allow *their* male heirs to succeed? Because that would entitle Mary to be 'governess'? Without much further thought, it soon becomes clear that the real point of the 'devise' was to exclude Mary from the succession.

This is backed up by the simple observation that, otherwise, the whole exercise seems completely pointless. There already was a 'devise for the succession': Henry's will. This was supported by act of Parliament, and so was, apparently, legally watertight. Edward did not have to do anything to enable a smooth succession. The glaring difference between the 'devise' and Henry's will was the exclusion of Mary and Elizabeth, and so this must have been the reason for it. The question then arises: what was so wrong with his two sisters that meant Edward felt compelled to go against the existing lawful arrangements?

Given the almost obsessive way that Henry VIII had set about trying to exclude Mary from the succession, before ultimately reinstating her, it is sometimes taken for granted that a female monarch was not a practical consideration in Tudor England. However, this may not have been such a concern at the time. Certainly, the prevailing view of women was that they were the weaker sex, ruled by emotion rather than logic, and therefore not ideal as monarchs, but this need not necessarily rule them out completely. For a princess would, naturally enough, find a husband and it would be he who would guide her in all the important decisions, as would the, exclusively male, Privy Council.

There was no Salic Law in England, as there was in France, which forbade female rulers, or even those males inheriting the throne through the female line. Back in the thirteenth century, during the rule of Edward III, Parliament had passed the Statute of Merton, which laid down that the succession should pass to the oldest male child, but if there were no males available there was nothing in law that precluded a female ruler.

But it was still not an ideal situation, especially if, as already suggested, that female was unmarried. Henry's decision to include Mary in the succession was more an act of desperation than genuine will. Keeping the crown within the family was his most important consideration, and since he only had one son, he had little option but to name her as a back-up. His insistence that she should not marry without the consent of the council was a fail-safe mechanism, in case the worst happened and she actually did come to the throne.

Not that there was anything especially wrong with Mary as a person. The elements of her character which emerged during the period in which she was *persona non grata* at Henry's court, due to her refusal to acknowledge him as supreme head of the English Church – stubbornness, excessive devotion to the unreformed religion, disobedience – could equally be construed as determination, courage, and loyalty (to her religion and her mother). However, by spring 1553, she had become, to some, a major problem.

For with Edward's illness, and possible death, it was clear that she was now the rightful heir to the throne. Since there was no immediate possibility of a male ruler, the fact that she was a woman became less significant; it was *who* she was that was now important. Judging by the course of subsequent events, the majority of the country had no problem with her, but for two people in particular she was a very real danger. And those two people just happened to be the most powerful in the land.

If we accept that Edward composed the first version of the 'devise' on his own (and this issue will be discussed later), then we must accept that for him Mary's accession was not at all welcome, for why else would he make no mention of her. Other than an, already-stated, wish for a male heir, there are perhaps three explanations for this.

Firstly, and perhaps most importantly for him, was the fact that Mary remained a Catholic. There was every sign that, if she were to succeed, she would impose her will on others and turn England back to the days of her father, and possibly even to before the break with Rome. This would mean the undoing of all Edward's work - his personal project; his legacy. Mary was committed and highly devout. She had continued to hear Mass in her household, and had put up with threats to desist from the Privy Council and Edward, himself, including the arrest of her priests and closest advisors, to the point where she had very nearly fled the country. And she firmly believed that those who followed the new religion were misguided and sinful. The one thing that Edward could pride himself on was the change in religion, a process that he was deeply committed to, for he was every bit as devout as Mary. How could he stand back and allow it to be destroyed? How would people and, more importantly, God, judge him if he allowed Mary to gain the throne?

And then there was the personal issue. Mary was only Edward's half-sister, but still close enough, perhaps, for sibling rivalry. Admittedly, there was a twenty-year age difference between them which would have diluted this aspect as Edward was growing up. Indeed, Mary had helped look after him when he was younger, and what little evidence we have suggests that there was genuine affection between them, and that Mary always treated him with kindness and respect.

But the relationship changed when Edward became king, and when the new religion began to be imposed. Throughout his reign, Mary was always kept at arms' length, and treated with suspicion. Only occasionally did she come to court, and usually only when summoned, and sometimes not even then as she was equally suspicious of him. Her refusal to obey the council's orders to stop hearing Mass must have rankled, and the occasion – at Christmas 1550 – when he personally tried to browbeat her, and ended up in tears at her refusal, must have been a humiliation. And her argument that she would accept his orders only when he was properly grown up would have hurt even more. A young teenager, reminded daily that he was king and the most powerful person in the land, defied by his own sister, and seen to be powerless over her, and then to have to accept her succeeding him and ruining all he had done... how could he allow that?

The third possible reason was perhaps the most compelling, though we have no way of knowing whether it was one that went through Edward's mind as he wrote the 'devise', or even if he fully understood its significance. For, things being as they were, Mary could probably not, according to the laws of the land, actually become queen.

The problem had been created by Henry VIII who, during his attempts to secure a male heir, had worked himself, and the country, into a legalistic mess. Unable to secure the pope's blessing for a divorce from Katherine, he had adopted the conceit that the marriage had been invalid in the first place, due to her having consummated her previous marriage to his brother, Arthur. If the marriage had been invalid, then, naturally, any offspring must be illegitimate, and so Mary was declared, by act of Parliament in 1533, a bastard. And under English common law bastards could not inherit, though whether they could inherit the *role* of monarch was less clear-cut. The same thing happened when Henry's marriage to Anne Boleyn ended, and their daughter, Elizabeth, was also declared a bastard, thus ruling her out of the succession, too.

When Henry came to write his will in 1546, this situation remained, but as no further male heirs were forthcoming, the back-up to his nine-year old son, in the possible event of him not surviving to father his own heir, had to be Mary, followed by Elizabeth. Otherwise, the Tudor line, which he had made his life's focus to preserve, would die out.

Unfortunately, in this will, his daughters were still confirmed as bastards, for to legitimise them would be to threaten the validity of his separation from Katherine, put in doubt the legality of his subsequent marriages, and possibly deprive Edward of the throne. Therefore, by statute law, Mary and Elizabeth were successors to Edward, but by common law they could never succeed.

Of course, this situation could easily have been resolved as, indeed, it later was. Parliament could have been asked to legitimise Mary, and with a bit of persuasion this could doubtless have been arranged. However, no-one saw a reason to do this until Edward was clearly dying and, although Parliament did sit throughout March 1553, this was before his illness was judged to be terminal, and no-one considered, or dared (for interfering in any way with the succession as laid down in the parliamentary statute of 1543 was treason, a matter reinforced by Edward's own Treason Act of 1547), to take the opportunity.

Mary's situation, therefore, created a legal battleground that has exercised historians to this day. Arguments over the primacy of statute law, that is acts of Parliament, which the 1544 Act of Succession represented, over common law, which dealt with bastardy and laws of general inheritance, have divided historical opinion and, if the succession had ever been put to a court of law, it would have kept Tudor lawyers very busy, and, presumably, very happy, for many years. But it was not, and the succession would be determined by more old-fashioned methods. How much this all played a part in Edward's initial thinking is not known, and he did not refer to it in his 'devise'. Later, however, lawyers, tasked with making legal sense of the document, did use this argument in the letters patent as a justification for ignoring the princesses.

But Edward was not alone in fearing the accession of Mary; the duke of Northumberland also had reasons to be dismayed. The discussion over whether, and how much, Northumberland was involved in the 'devise' will be dealt with shortly, but subsequent changes to the document, and his use of it thereafter, show that he was at least on board with some of its intentions. For if Mary was to succeed, that would surely signal the end for him, politically and maybe even literally.

Mary had very little reason for liking Northumberland. He was the one who she saw as mainly responsible for the changes in religion which she so detested, and he seemed to be the one who after 1550 increased the pressure on her to conform. He was also the head of the government that was creating a rift between her and Edward. Given her anguish at the time of her considered flight from the country in 1550, it is clear that she even feared for her life, a concern that was not entirely unjustified. Her dislike of him was assiduously fed by successive Imperial envoys, who saw Mary as the only hope of restoring Catholicism, and Northumberland as the main obstacle to this end.

This gave Northumberland good reason to dread Mary's accession. Though he was never particularly religious himself, he, too, would have been unwilling to see all his work introducing the new religion wasted. He may also have feared a possible outbreak of civil strife if Mary attempted to turn back the clock. And he may, of course, as many of his detractors claimed, have seen in the uncertainties an opportunity to improve his own power and standing in the country. But there was another, more immediate consideration. Ever present in his mind was the memory of what had happened to his father; the unpopular chief minister sacrificed for the benefit of a quick boost for the new regime. He had disposed of Somerset easily enough; it would not be hard for others to find evidence against him, and there would be no shortage of those willing to bring it. Northumberland has been accused of many things over his behaviour during the spring and summer of 1553, but it is possible that his primary motivation was simply self-preservation.

The belief that Northumberland was involved in the drawing up of the 'devise', either personally, or through one of his 'special friends' who surrounded Edward daily, was fostered by changes subsequently made to the document, as well as by his determination to see it carried into law. As the first version stood, it was not a practical consideration for ensuring a seamless succession in the immediate future. In fact, it foresaw no adult monarch on the English throne for at least a further 18 years. This was unthinkable.

Someone, at some stage, realized that it could be amended very simply, and to great advantage. As already written, the next in line to Frances's male heirs were her daughter, Jane's, male heirs. The sentence currently read: 'to the L. Janes heirs males', but with the crossing out of a single letter, and the insertion of two small words, the text could now be made to read 'to the L. Jane *and her* heirs males'. So, with just a few strokes of a pen, done, it appears, in Edward's own hand, Lady Jane Grey had suddenly become the next queen of England.

This was a perfect solution to the problem, at least for some. Jane was a devout Protestant, and so could be relied upon to carry on the Reformation. This would suit both Edward and Northumberland, and, hopefully, would bring continuity and stability to the country. She was the daughter of the duke of Suffolk, Northumberland's ally on the council, and so he would be able to influence her as easily as he had Edward. It nominated a living person, and therefore avoided the potential turmoil of a long regency, or the accession of Mary, and there may even have been another advantage, either already realized, or in the pipeline: for at some stage, Lady Jane Grey had been married to his son, which would make him, Northumberland, the father-in-law of the new queen, and, if things turned out right, father to the new king.

So advantageous to the duke of Northumberland did this new version of the 'devise' seem to later historians, and even some commentators at the time, that it has been assumed that he was behind the whole idea to exclude Mary. And very possibly he was. After all, he was in a position to do it, given his influence over Edward, and the outcome was so much to his benefit that his involvement seems almost unarguable. Furthermore, the determination with which he pursued the idea, and forced others to accept it, shows his commitment to following it through. But was he alone in this?

It is quite clear that the change to the text that made Lady Jane heir was not part of Edward's original working. If it was, then the rest of the document, with its insistence on male heirs, would have made little sense. This reinforces the view that there were two, if not more, versions of the 'devise' on the same page. It is very hard to extricate Northumberland, or his supporters, from the second, which nominated Jane, but it is much less certain that he was responsible for the first.

For a start, he would have made rather a better job of it. The original text surely owes more to the excitable imagination of a teenage boy making his wish list, than to the thoughtful considerations of an experienced politician who would actually have to see through whatever was proposed. It shows a complete lack of awareness of the practical issues that would have to be overcome if England was to have no adult ruler, and also a surprisingly thoughtless, though perhaps simply immature, attitude towards the position and status of his own family.

There was also another aspect to the document that makes it almost certain that it came from Edward: it was treason. It could have resulted in execution for anyone who had a hand in writing it, except for one: Edward himself. The 1547 Treason Act, passed by Edward's own government, had made this absolutely clear: anyone who 'by open Preaching, express Words or Sayings, to depose or deprive the King, His Heirs or Successors, Kings of this Realm, from his or their Royal Estate or Titles…'[1] was guilty of treason. For Northumberland, his 'special friends', schoolteacher – all of whom have come under suspicion – even to have suggested that Edward write this document would have been extremely dangerous. And Northumberland, at least, was always cautious.

It is hard to imagine a situation in which Edward would have been encouraged by another person to write the original version of the document, especially if it involved such a radical step as defying an act of Parliament. Much more likely is that Edward, for whatever reason, decided to do it himself. Perhaps he had just studied his father's will in one of his lessons – there are enough similarities to indicate that he may have used it as a guide – and thought he might have a go with his own. We know that Edward produced papers for the Privy Council on important matters of state, so he was perfectly capable of doing this without help.

There is one interesting aspect, however, which is less often discussed, and that is the omission of Elizabeth. The reasons that Edward and/or Northumberland might have for excluding Mary are fairly straightforward; less clear is why Elizabeth – a Protestant - should also have been bypassed. Given that she appears nowhere, in either draft, we must assume that this decision was Edward's. The obvious reason is that to exclude Mary, and hand the succession to Elizabeth, would have created complications. Both had been declared illegitimate and so, if that was going to be the excuse, then Elizabeth had to go too. Also, to include Elizabeth would have been a statement against Catholicism which would have caused fury abroad and possible trouble at home.

And yet, if the aim was to ensure a Protestant succession, then Elizabeth, surely, would have been a safer bet than Jane, and it would have kept the succession within the Tudor family. Simply nominating the strongly-Protestant Jane would still not appease the Catholics and might, as it did, lead to rebellion. Admittedly, it would be a hard job to persuade Parliament why it should legitimise Elizabeth, and not Mary, and this is possibly why she was excluded, too. Another possibility, however, is that Northumberland would have known that he stood a better chance of dominating Jane, who might already have been his daughter-in-law, than the much less amenable Elizabeth.

In Jane's subsequent proclamation, which gave the public reasons for her succession, the key issue was that of legitimacy – Mary's official bastardy was highlighted, and compared with Jane's (the phrase 'lawfully begotten' is repeated over and over when describing Jane's status – particularly ironic given well-supported doubts over the legality of her parents' own marriage) - and the issue of religion only mentioned as the possibility that Mary might marry a Catholic. Clearly, religion was too sensitive an issue to use as a reason to exclude Mary, and thus if legitimacy was to be the *official* explanation then Elizabeth had to go, too.

In short, there are three possible interpretations of the 'devise': an attempt to secure a male heir (the first version), an attempt to exclude Mary from the succession (the first and final versions), and an attempt to nominate Jane as the next monarch (the final version). Whereas the first version is almost certainly Edward's, alone, the change to the wording that put forward Jane as the next queen is more easily attributable to outside help. And, of course, at that stage such involvement need not be considered treason since the mystery helper could claim to be acting on the will of the king.

The relationship between Northumberland and Edward is a fascinating one, and is, of course, key to an understanding of who was behind the 'devise'. Unfortunately, we have few clues as to the dynamics. Hoak, for example, has described Edward as Northumberland's 'crowned puppet'.[2] This is an extreme view and based mainly, it would appear, on reports from the Imperial ambassador, including the observation that at a diplomatic reception, the king kept glancing at Northumberland for guidance, and left the event at a nod from the older man.[3] This is conclusive of nothing, other than that Edward relied on guidance from those more experienced – he was, after all, a 14-year old boy at one of his first public engagements.

Certainly, Northumberland was in a position to influence Edward. He had surrounded him with his own supporters, and limited access from those he disapproved of. But Edward had schoolfriends, such as Barnaby Fitzpatrick, who could give different opinions, and his schoolmaster, Cheke, was by no means a mouthpiece for the duke. We also know that he was secretly fed extra reading materials on social and political topics by William Thomas, one of the council clerks. Some of the pieces he wrote in his schoolbooks, such as plans for the economy, show a more liberal attitude than Northumberland was noted for, and suggest he was quite capable of independent thought.

Furthermore, Northumberland was well aware that however powerful he might consider himself, his position always depended on the favour of the king. For Edward, however young he might be now, was still king, and in just a few years – assuming he lived - he would be able to make his own policies, and choose his own ministers, and he would be likely to remember those who had supported, or crossed, him in his youth. The care Northumberland took to surround Edward with his own men is not evidence of a lack of respect, but of an understanding of where real power actually lay. We don't know his exact feelings towards Edward as a person, but we can be sure that he was very mindful of his title.

So, is it likely that he approached Edward with a scheme for altering the succession to his own advantage, which left out Mary, and then forced, or manipulated, him into going along with it? Possible, yes; but likely, no. And subsequent events suggest that if he did, then he had done a remarkably good job, for Edward was to use all the power and influence at his disposal to push the scheme through. And besides, Edward's death was by no means a certainty, and if he had survived, and reached his majority, Northumberland's life, if he had proposed treason, would always be hanging by a thread.

We must be careful about how much to trust what Northumberland said or wrote – he was undoubtedly a cunning and unscrupulous politician – but on the scaffold he was to admit to his part in attempting to deprive Mary of her throne, though he tempered this by claiming that he was 'procured and induced thereunto by other',[4] who he refused to name. Suspicion has fallen on Sir John Gates, who had been closest to the king's person and who was in a position to persuade Edward, and there had been mutual recriminations, according to one observer, on the way to the scaffold,[5] but it may be possible that he was referring to Edward himself, whose name he loyally chose not to mention.

*

Everything would be so much clearer if we only knew *when* the 'devise' was written. To try and decide the answer to this question, we need to separate the different versions within it. There is no date attached to it – another clue that it was never intended to be an official 'will', but just a schoolboy exercise – and so again we will have to use deduction. It matters because it would help to pin down just who was responsible for it. Historians have generally concluded that it must have been written some time in 1553, between the bouts of illness that plagued Edward's last six months, probably in April or May. Clearly, he was well enough to pen it himself, and so cannot have been bed-bound, and as he must have had a reason for writing it, it would have been at a stage when he, and Northumberland, had cause to consider his imminent mortality.

Yet there are clues that it could have been written earlier, and possibly much earlier. For a start, there is no evidence in the text that Edward thinks he is going to die soon. The amendments to the opening sentence suggest that he considered it perfectly possible that he might have female issue. Yet, in 1553 he wasn't even married, nor were there any plans on the horizon, so he must have been expecting to live for some years at least. He then looks forward to a situation in the future when there might be male heirs, rather than to the present when a living successor might be needed very soon. if the document had been written in 1553, after he had suffered severe bouts of smallpox and measles – both potentially fatal diseases – and been diagnosed with tuberculosis – an illness that could result in death at any moment – it might be thought that he would view the succession with more immediate concern.

Edward may not have been quite the genius described by Roger Ascham, but he was exceptionally well-educated, and clearly intelligent. He may have been only a teenager in 1553, but he had been studying, and writing, documents on topics as varied as dress codes for different classes of society, new plans for the Order of the Garter, proposals for the economy, and the organization of the Privy Council, for several years, and it is hard to accept that as late as 1553, faced by the possibility of his forthcoming demise, he could have written something quite so impractical.

If so, when *was* the first version written? It could, of course, have been at almost any time, but something must have sparked off his train of thought, and it must have come from him, rather than from outside, because before the winter of 1552, there were no signs that he was going to die at all. Perhaps, as suggested earlier, it came after a study of his father's will, or perhaps there were more specific instances.

One of these may have been the tragic deaths of his schoolfriend, Henry, the former duke of Suffolk, and his younger brother Charles, from sweating sickness in July 1551. Like all victims, their deaths were rapid and came out of the blue, revealing just how fragile life could be in Tudor England. Although Edward made no comment in his diary, the death of one of his few close companions, in such a sudden way, cannot have failed to make an impression on the young boy, and possibly set those around him thinking, too.

And then there was the main purpose of the 'devise', which was to exclude Mary. If we are to accept that the reason for disinheriting her was frustration at her lack of cooperation over religion, then the most likely triggers are Christmas 1550, or March 1551, following the stormy meetings between the two when Mary refused outright to stop hearing Mass. If the combination of this motive, which continued to rankle, and the death of his schoolfriends, is considered, then sometime in the second half of 1551 is a reasonable assumption for dating the first version of the 'devise'. If this is the case, then it significantly reduces the likelihood of Northumberland being involved.

Exactly when the amendment nominating Jane was made is perhaps a little easier to decide, though admittedly not much. The activity that we know about, concerning changes to the expected succession, can be dated as early as 7 May 1553, when Northumberland had a cryptic conversation with the French ambassadors asking what they would do if they were in his shoes. That same month, on the 21st, the marriage of his son, Guilford, to Jane took place, which may have been connected to the amendment, and then came the report from the doctors on the 28th that Edward's condition was terminal, so it is likely that it was around this time that the 'plot' was hatched. On 11 June, Edward Montagu, chief justice of the common pleas, was summoned to court to convert the 'devise' into a legal document. Certainly, the 'devise' was not something that Northumberland wanted to leave lying around, and it is likely he would have tried to get approval for it from the Privy Council relatively quickly, though, naturally, he would have needed some time to prepare the ground.

Exactly how Northumberland discovered the original 'devise' is unknown. Perhaps Edward referred to it in a conversation, or perhaps the royal tutor, John Cheke, whose role in the affair is more than slightly suspicious, brought it up. Once the duke was aware of it, he could feel a little more secure since he had a degree of royal authority behind him, which gave a defence against charges of treason, and thus getting Edward to amend it would be easier.

We know that, at the start of June, Edward ordered the 'devise' to be copied out in fair hand for presentation to the lawyers. This is the missing link, since the copy has not survived. So sensitive was it that, fifty years later, James I ordered it to be destroyed. Somehow, the original 'devise' did survive, perhaps because it was seen as just a piece of Edward's schoolwork and of no great significance. How similar it was to the improved version we cannot tell. It is certainly very different in tone from the final letters patent, which contain reasons for the changes to the succession. It has been said that Edward signed the copy in six places, and this has been assumed to mean after each of the six paragraphs, though it seems hardly credible that Northumberland would have allowed it to see the light of day in anything approaching its original, confused, state. It was then left to the unfortunate lawyers to try and make legalistic sense of it, and convert it into letters patent.

*

Much has been made of the dastardly plot by the duke of Northumberland to alter the line of the English succession to his own selfish advantage, and Mary, and those who came after her, were more than ready to emphasise this aspect, both to blacken his reputation and to cement their own rights to the throne – a point of view that historians up to the end of the twentieth century were more than happy to accept. But was the line of succession so cut and dried? And how much did Northumberland and/or Edward really alter it?

Certainly, the precedents over the previous century were not good. Henry VI, in 1422, had had right enough to the throne through his father, and, indeed, during the long era of the Plantagenets, the succession had followed more or less smoothly - the murders of Edward II and Richard II notwithstanding - but after that, matters became more haphazard. In the hundred years before 1553 there had been eight changes of monarch, five of which had been violent, and one (Edward's own) highly contrived. To suggest that succession to the English throne was a seamless, automatic and unchallenged affair flies in the face of the evidence.

Indeed, there were even doubts over Edward's legitimacy. All those who, secretly for the most part, denied Henry's right to ignore the pope's refusal to sanction his divorce from Katherine of Aragon, would have seen Mary as the rightful heir. Furthermore, there had to be doubts over the manner, if not the legality, in which Henry had been allowed to organize his succession. In 1536, Parliament, whose independence of action at that time has to be questioned, granted him the unprecedented right to nominate his successors by letters patent. In other words, he now had the right to choose whoever he wished, without further check. This was unheard of, and was, arguably, an infringement of common law.

On a moral, though not a legal, basis, one has to wonder whether the decisions made by the parliaments of Henry VIII actually deserved the sanctity with which they were imbued. Parliament was made up of individuals, and these could be easily frightened off by a sovereign who was annoyed at their behaviour. To suggest that Commons or Lords could have freely opposed Henry VIII, without retribution, takes little account of the atmosphere of the time.

Henry had further challenged common law by including Mary and Elizabeth in the succession, despite their illegitimacy which made their right to succeed highly questionable. In fact, by June 1553 it might well be said that there was no indisputable legal succession to alter. Edward, arguably, had every right to clarify the situation by making his own decision. And this was possibly what he and Northumberland were trying to do in the letters patent that followed on from the 'devise'. Edward was simply behaving as his father had done. He and Northumberland fully intended to get approval from Parliament, and they immediately proceeded to issue writs for an October sitting, but Edward ruined the plan by dying in the meantime. In short, the duke of Northumberland may well have been guilty of tampering with the succession, but to suggest that there was something uniquely wicked about his actions is disingenuous.

However, it is this, more than anything else which has determined historical judgement of him, and given rise to his reputation as the 'bad' duke. Over ensuing centuries there was a radical shift in the power structure of the country, with Parliament effectively superseding the Crown, and the narrative of English history changed. Now, statesmen were judged according to their respect for, and relationship with Parliament, and Northumberland was deemed to have offended against parliamentary statute. The fact that Parliament itself had so cravenly delegated its own authority back to the king in the Third Succession Act is usually overlooked.

It is also worth considering *to what extent* the 'devise' altered the succession that Henry VIII had laid down. With the obvious exception of the exclusion of Mary and Elizabeth, it is similar in many important aspects. Both wills effectively put Jane next in line (after the princesses, in Henry's case). This is noteworthy because in terms of strict seniority, Jane's mother, Frances, should have come next. No explanation was given by either monarch for excluding her, and Frances appears to have accepted the situation. Henry's, and Edward's, motives are unclear, though both may have supposed she was too old to produce a male heir. The mysterious insertion in paragraph 1 of the 'devise', apparently stipulating that any male heirs of Frances had to appear before Edward's death, may have been put there to acknowledge her right, but effectively make it impossible for her to exercise it. But Northumberland had another very good reason for excluding her, for although the change of words that gave the crown to Jane could equally, and with perhaps more justification, have been applied to her, this would have given Henry, duke of Suffolk, her husband, the right to style himself king of England, and even allowed him to make decisions in that capacity. Henry was an important ally of Northumberland, but he was very much in his shadow, and there were serious doubts over his competence. He would be much less easy to control, and it is doubtful that Northumberland could have stomached having his protégé rule over him.

Another interesting similarity is the exclusion in both wills of two people who perhaps had even more right to the throne, namely the children of Henry's sister, Margaret. These were Mary, Queen of Scots, Margaret's grandchild by her first marriage; and Margaret Lennox, daughter of her second. The reason for them being ignored was political, for both were Scots. Henry had been enthusiastic enough about joining the two kingdoms through the marriage of Edward to Mary, but that would have kept England as the senior partner; subjecting his country to the rule of a foreigner was not something he was prepared to consider. After Henry's death, Mary's unsuitability became even more obvious once she was betrothed to the French dauphin, and the idea of having a Scottish queen, married to a French king, on the throne of England was, understandably, too much for Edward to bear.

This was also, presumably, the reason for not including Margaret Lennox's son, Henry, Lord Darnley, since he, too, was Scottish. The fact that he is nowhere mentioned is noteworthy since, if Edward really wanted a male succession, then here was the solution. Of course, it would mean that he would have to bypass the stronger claims of Henry's mother, but that did not seem a problem with choosing Jane over Frances. Darnley did not appear in Henry's will, either, and perhaps this is a clue that Edward was, essentially, just copying from his father's testament. At any rate, his omission seems to contradict the idea that Edward was *only* concerned with a male on the throne.

Thus, essentially, the only difference between the two wills was the removal of Mary and Elizabeth (and subsequently, in version two, the clear appointment of Jane), and a case could be made that Edward's 'devise' simply repeated the essence of Henry's will, while ironing out some of the legal anomalies. Far from altering the succession, Edward and Northumberland had simply brought it into line with common law, and made it a workable document, while Henry's will, being perfectly fine if Edward was to live and have children, looked like being made redundant by his imminent death.

All the above suggests that Edward and Northumberland had good legal justification for drawing up the letters patent which excluded Mary and Elizabeth and put Jane on the throne, but there was a problem: nobody believed it. And worse, it is quite clear from their subsequent actions that Northumberland, and possibly Edward, too, didn't believe it either. Despite all the, often convincing, legal arguments, it seems apparent that almost everyone in the kingdom, however much many of them might not have wanted it, expected Mary Tudor to be the next monarch if Edward should die childless. Despite historian Eric Ives's gallant attempts to portray subsequent events as Mary's plot against Jane, few at the time would have accepted this. In their view, Edward and Northumberland's actions were no less than a scheme to deprive Mary of her rightful inheritance.

And this was very forcefully promoted by Mary. Since her own claim to inherit the throne came from Henry VIII's will, the question of her bastardy was not one that she, or her supporters, or anyone with an iota of common sense during the subsequent reigns of the two sisters wished to dwell on. The focus on a plot, with the duke of Northumberland as instigator, nicely deflected from whether Edward had any right to change Henry's wishes, and whether Mary should be excluded through illegitimacy.

And it has continued to this day. Almost all the historical analysis of these events throughout the centuries has assumed that Edward and Northumberland plotted to change the succession, for whatever reasons, rather than whether they were, in fact, simply trying to determine the correct procedure to follow.

Two aspects have added to the appearance of a plot. Firstly, the supposed secrecy. Much of the complaint for this comes from the fact that what was going on was kept from the ambassadors, or at least Scheyfve, and from Mary herself, and of course the obscure manner in which the 'devise' was concocted. But this was only natural, both to avoid the possibility of Charles V intervening from abroad, and Mary stirring up problems from within the country. In fact, among those in important positions there was remarkably little secrecy. Although it was not revealed how the 'devise' originated – and why should it have been – the letters patent, and supporting documents, were witnessed and signed by 21 members of the Privy Council, most of the leading lawyers, most of the nobles in the country, the guards at the Tower, and the mayor and aldermen of the City of London, even before Edward's death had been announced.

The other issue was Edward's age. If he had been three years older, then there would almost certainly have been no talk of a plot. He would simply be doing what his father, and several kings before, had done – deciding on the succession himself. But because he was a minor, it was assumed that he had no right, nor the ability, to make changes, even though these changes were fully endorsed by the very council that was ruling in his name. It has been argued – and Mary always played this card, even when Edward was still alive – that he was a helpless youth completely dominated by the duke, and this may, to some extent, have been true. But if he had been an adult, ruling in his own name, even if still advised by Northumberland, it is doubtful that the accusation of a plot would have stuck quite so firmly.

One can also question how much actions carried out by a king and council could ever be termed a plot. They had the judiciary, albeit reluctantly, on their side, and only lacked the consent of Parliament, which they fully intended to obtain. It was only Edward's death, and the decision to put the scheme into effect before Parliament had approved the change, that gave it the semblance of a plot.

So clouded in mystery are the details surrounding the production of the 'devise' that it will probably never be decided where the truth really lies. But what was certain was that the succession laid down by Henry VIII was to be altered, and that Mary, seen by most as the rightful heir, was to be denied her inheritance. Time would tell whether she would accept the situation, or whether she would fight to claim her throne. Meanwhile, most of the country, in ignorance of what was going on behind the scenes, awaited the death of the king, and the accession of England's first queen.

4

Preparing the Ground

Since we don't know for sure when the two versions of the 'devise' were actually written, we cannot say precisely where they fitted into the course of the conspiracy. We don't know whether the second version marked the start of the idea to remove Mary from the succession, or whether it later became part of it. No-one was too keen to admit to their precise role in events, either then or subsequently. Given that Elizabeth, too, was excluded under the plan, then it would not have been safe to explain matters even during her reign, unless it was to defend oneself, as Cecil later did, or to heap further odium on the head of Northumberland. Thus, no-one involved in the inner workings of the plan could have felt safe to disclose details during their lifetime, and to have written anything, however private, could have been a potentially suicidal act.

The only vaguely knowledgeable sources of information we have come from foreigners, and they can only partially be relied upon. The ambassadors of the Empire, Venice and Spain wrote reports on the situation as it unfolded, but their access was usually only second-hand, and their interpretation was, naturally enough, coloured by what they thought their masters wanted to hear. Scheyfve, the Imperial ambassador, for example, was a competent and hard-working diplomat, and his full and frequent reports have come to represent the best guide to the course of events, but he was a strong supporter of Mary, and tended to overplay the role of France, and even, possibly, Northumberland, both of which he was encouraging his master, Charles V, to take robust action against. Commendone, the Papal envoy, also wrote an account, which seems to have been the basis of several later 'histories' by Italian writers, but his sources of information are unknown and it is unlikely he knew as much as he pretended about the behaviour of Jane on her accession. The best reports from the Venetian ambassador came after the crisis had passed, while the French envoys, Boisdauphin and Noailles, were irritatingly guarded, understandably enough if they were, as many suspected, involved in the conspiracy themselves.

From mid-June, the Privy Council went into secret session, and didn't emerge again until Mary was on the throne, so there are no clues from its records. Edward had long-since ceased to write his diary, Parliament was not sitting, and while onlookers such as Machyn and the writer of the *Greyfriars Chronicle* continued to observe what was going on in London, and give mention to the many rumours swirling about its markets and streets, there are few other sources of information to rely upon. Even those historians writing during the reign of Elizabeth, and later, James I – Holinshed, Knox, Stow, etc. – had to be careful what they wrote, and their access to information cannot have been much greater than that enjoyed by historians today.

To get to the truth of the matter, it helps to have a suspicious mindset; to automatically question every piece of information, and to tear oneself away from the accepted version of events that has prevailed to this day. Revisionist historians have attempted to do just this. Ives, for example, has presented the whole affair as a plot by Mary against the rightful queen, Jane, and while this is perhaps an extreme position, others – Beer, Hoak, Loades – have started to show Northumberland in a more positive light, and as a statesman and effective ruler, rather than simply as a selfish adventurer.

The problem for the historian is that one has to believe something, otherwise there is nothing to write about, but in an affair as murky and controversial as this there are always difficulties in knowing what to credit. Ives's psychological approach, in which he examines the personal motivation behind actions is certainly a promising one, though only applicable if human behaviour runs along consistent lines, which, of course, it seldom does. What will emerge, inevitably, is an interpretation rather than a definitive answer, with the historian choosing the evidence that seems most credible, or, as often in the case of academic history, which best supports the theory he or she wishes to put forward.

On 11 April 1553, Edward, whose condition seemed to be slowly improving, moved with his court from Westminster to Greenwich. There was nothing overtly alarming about this; it was a move which happened at around this time every year. But possibly, being further away from the city, it might also have been hoped that the location would be better for his health. However, by the end of the month, Scheyfve was reporting that matters had taken a turn for the worse, and that the king was spitting 'greenish yellow and black [matter], sometimes pink, like the colour of blood'.[1] Then, at the end of April, he had happier news to impart; the betrothal of Northumberland's son, Guilford, to Lady Jane Grey.

At the time, this created little surprise, and there seemed no particular reason why it should. Both fathers were dukes, and thus on the same social level; both men had been friendly for some time, and were mutually close on the Privy Council; both held similar religious and political views; and the engaged couple were of similar ages and therefore ripe for marriage. Northumberland could be pleased in that it connected his family, albeit distantly, to royalty, and to have won such a match for a fourth son was a significant achievement, while Suffolk now had a firmer link to the most powerful of the king's subjects. On the surface, it was a dynastic connection that was entirely logical and appropriate.

However, when news of Edward's 'devise' emerged, two months later, it came to have a very different complexion. For this document meant that Jane would now become queen, Guilford would doubtless be styled king, and Northumberland (and Suffolk) would be fathers of royalty. Those who are convinced of Northumberland's long-term cunning – Scheyfve, for example, who even as early as April was hinting at a plot to get Jane on the throne[2] - see this marriage as a response to the 'devise' (or, alternatively, the 'devise' as a response to the marriage). Having named Jane as future queen, the duke was now linking himself and his family to her, presumably so he could influence her better and maintain his hold on power.

The argument is persuasive because it is logical, plausible, and things nearly did work out exactly this way. If it is correct, it suggests that Northumberland may have known already about the 'devise', and the amendment in version two, and implies that Edward was resigned to his fate as early as April. Though, if this is the case, questions arise as to why he and Northumberland waited two months before getting it approved by the council, and why they did not call Parliament sooner to ratify it.

The couple were married a month later in a sumptuous ceremony lasting two days, 'with great magnificence and feasting',[3] according to Scheyfve, who may not have been invited, and who was therefore able to report, with a certain degree of satisfaction, perhaps, that many of the guests had subsequently gone down with food poisoning. Certainly, the French ambassador, and even L'Aubespine, a mysterious special envoy from Henri II, were present, which can have done little to improve his mood. It was, in fact, a triple wedding – Jane's younger sister, Katherine, was simultaneously married to the son of the earl of Pembroke, while Northumberland's daughter, Katherine, married the son of the earl of Huntingdon.

Although Pembroke was not a guaranteed supporter of Northumberland on the Privy Council, he was one who could be brought on board, and whose influence would be a bonus. Huntingdon was more obviously loyal, and so these unions could be seen as a way of strengthening the Northumberland–Suffolk axis. The fact that the ceremonies were joint was presumably intended to emphasise this point, though it doesn't mean that Northumberland actually instigated the matches himself; the parents of each couple had very good reasons for concluding their individual contracts. What the weddings don't automatically prove is that they were, at this early stage, all part of a plan by Northumberland to steal the throne from Mary.

Scheyfve, for the time being, was content just to hint his suspicions about the possible intent behind the marriages. What he was more worried about, during the month of May, was the worsening state of Edward's health, and some suspicious behaviour on the part of France. Keeping an eye on his master's principal enemy was at the top of his duties, and the unexplained, and rapid, visit of L'Aubespine had been highly concerning. If Edward were to die then the Catholic, pro-Habsburg, Mary would succeed, which was the natural and, from his point of view, highly satisfactory, outcome. So why, at this critical moment, was the French king sending over special envoys to have conversations with Northumberland that he wasn't party to?

The ambassador, naturally enough, had a network of informants around court, one of which seems to have been a remarkably well-placed member of the king's medical team. Consequently, he was fed up-to-date reports of Edward's deteriorating condition, and these did not make for good reading.

As early as 5 May, he reported that more doctors had been summoned to Edward's bedside and that the king was not thought likely to survive. It was forbidden to talk of his illness and some people had been pilloried, and had had their ears cut off, for doing just this. The doctors had noted not just a suppurating tumour on the lung, which they assumed, along with the continuous cough, to be a sign of tuberculosis, but also ulcers, a swollen belly, and a fever that he seemed unable to shake off. By the end of the month, he was able to add that the king's head and feet were beginning to swell, and that the poor lad had had his head shaved and hot plasters applied.

Yet it was not until mid-June that Scheyfve first mentioned the theory that Northumberland might be responsible for his condition, and referred to rumours that the duke might actually be poisoning him.[4] Later, when Northumberland's plans had become clear, these accusations grew more widespread, and were mentioned by several of the chroniclers, though he was never to be formally accused of such a thing. It would seem unlikely that Northumberland had much to gain from hastening the king's death. Admittedly, if the 'devise' had already been amended then he might want the king to die as soon as possible, before Mary got wind of it, but the fact that nothing was done to formalise the changes to the succession before 22 June, means that it was vital the king remain alive until at least this date, and even until approval could be granted by Parliament.

In fact, Northumberland, more a man of caution than a reckless adventurer, had very little reason to desire Edward's death at any stage, for he already had pretty much everything he wanted. His political position was secure, and he was making great progress both with the Reformation and improving the finances of the realm. He had spent much time and energy building up a positive relationship with Edward, whose youth had given him a golden opportunity to raise a king into the same way of thinking as his own. The country was unusually peaceful, so why should he want to risk all this for a highly uncertain future? Perhaps he did think that Jane and his own son would be easier to control, but that he should have taken the chance of deliberately upsetting the realm, and possibly opening the door to Mary, seems almost unthinkable for such an obviously intelligent and subtle politician.

Yet, ironically, Edward probably was to die from poisoning, and Northumberland was, to some extent, responsible. This was not down to any malice on his part, but more to his frantic efforts to keep the king alive. One of the benefits of royalty was access to the very best medical care of the age; the downside was that, with the public gaze focused upon them, this medical care had to be seen to be doing something. Tuberculosis was then an incurable disease, and resistant to most treatments, as the doctors well knew. While often fatal it can, however, remain largely dormant, often for years. In short, given the medical knowledge at the time, it would have been far better to have done nothing, and let the disease take its course, perhaps even allowing Edward to live for several years more.

But this was not a practical possibility. The extraordinary symptoms that Edward began to display, mostly atypical of tuberculosis, can best be explained by considering the likely cures employed. We don't know exactly what the doctors prescribed, but when one considers that mercury and arsenic were ever-popular remedies, then things start to become clearer. 'God deliver you from the physicians'[5] was what Sir William Petre wished Cecil when he was ill that May, and the same could have been wished on poor Edward, though it was not to be. When Northumberland sacked the doctors and replaced them with his own in early May, that just increased the pressure to try new treatments, which resulted in further abuse of the king's body. His appointment of a 'wise woman' added more uncertainty, besides provoking suspicions of his motives, though it was more likely just a sign of his desperation.

By this time, Scheyfve had wind of a plot, though not necessarily the right one. Aware of Northumberland's feelings towards Mary, he assumed, correctly enough, that the duke would take action to prevent her from succeeding to the throne. The sudden arrival of a special envoy from Henri II further aroused his suspicions, again rightly, for L'Aubespine's mission, though never precisely clarified, was seemingly designed to offer French help in the event of Edward's death. This help, which Northumberland appears to have declined, could have ranged from diplomatic, to even military, aid in the event of Charles V intervening to support Mary.

Which is interesting, because if Mary was to succeed naturally, which was the generally-supposed outcome, then Henri should have no reason to think that Charles might need to intervene. Did he already have knowledge of a plot, and was offering help? Of course, Henri had every reason not to want Mary to succeed, for that would have put England more firmly under the influence of the Habsburgs, and tipped the balance against him in the war he was currently waging with the Empire.

Henri II, studio of François Clouet

But Northumberland was right to turn him down, although he could have done with French help later, for this wasn't the only consideration of the French king. Naturally enough, Henri didn't want Mary to succeed, but he wouldn't have been particularly keen on Jane, either, if he even knew at this stage of Northumberland's designs. He was Catholic, and approved of the English Reformation only inasmuch as it kept England safely away from Charles. Also, as a monarch himself, he took a dim view on principle of hereditary rulers being overthrown. But, more importantly, he had his own candidate for the next ruler of England, one who, arguably, had a stronger claim to the throne, and who, fortuitously, happened to be currently betrothed to his own son: Mary, Queen of Scots.

Scheyfve was certainly aware of this ambition, though he didn't yet suspect Northumberland of backing it. Nor was he yet properly aware of the situation regarding Jane. He saw the main danger as coming from the Princess Elizabeth, and in May was warning his master of the possibility of Northumberland's son, Robert, marrying her, or even Northumberland divorcing his wife and marrying her himself.[6] Scheyfve was a close confidant of Mary, and would not have hidden his suspicions from her, therefore she must have been aware, at least from late April, of rumours that she was going to be disinherited.

On 7 May, the new French ambassador, Antoine de Noailles, had a meeting with Northumberland which threw more confusion than light on what was going on. He and Boisdauphin had originally scheduled an appointment with Edward for the 4th to formally mark the changeover of envoys, though this had been refused by the council due to the king's poor health, but a ceremony of sorts, without Edward, took place three days later. Afterwards, Northumberland chatted to them, and the question of the succession was raised. The duke turned to Noailles and reportedly enquired 'What would you do in my place?'.[7] The ambassador seems to have been nonplussed by this, but it may have been seen by the French court as an invitation, for Henri promptly dispatched L'Aubespine on his secret mission.

Northumberland's comment is interesting on two levels. Firstly, it implies that he was thinking of doing *something*, when, strictly speaking, there was no need for him to do anything. If Edward died, then Mary would succeed, as laid down by statute. Clearly, at this relatively early stage, he was considering intervening in this process. Secondly, he was evidently trying to involve France. Interestingly, the same day, his ambassador in France, Wotton, was instructed to deliver to Henri a formal offer of mediation by England in the war between France and the Empire.[8] This, by itself, is curious because surely the last thing that Northumberland should have wanted was peace in Europe and for Charles V to be given breathing space to concentrate on events in England. He also should have been aware that Henri was very much the aggressor in this struggle and would have been highly unlikely to take up the offer, as, indeed, he didn't. Was this initiative perhaps just a gesture of friendship from Northumberland to Henri, in return for French help against Charles if he should need it later? This might explain part of the purpose of L'Aubespine's journey – to find out just what it was that Northumberland actually wanted.

Nothing is known for sure about this mission, which was hurried and seemingly inconclusive. While the discussions were private, and nothing appears to have been written down, L'Aubespine himself hardly kept a low profile – even attending the triple wedding – and Scheyfve inevitably read the worst into it and saw it, probably correctly, as an offer of French help against Mary. He also noted, as did Noailles, that defences in London and Windsor were being hurriedly reinforced, and that privy councillors, many of whom were lords lieutenant and therefore responsible for law and order in their counties, were being sent to all parts of the realm, and especially to coastal areas, presumably to forestall any invasion, and to keep the country peaceful in the event of Edward's death.

Yet surprisingly, in view of the efforts of his doctors, the king's condition underwent a small improvement during May, and on the 18th he was able to have a brief audience to say farewell to the departing Boisdauphin. Petre, secretary to the council, reported to Cecil that the king was much better, and Sir Philip Hoby, English ambassador to the Low Countries, assured the regent that the king was 'but a little sick of a cough'.[9] Scheyfve, however, who had been unable to get an audience, didn't accept these rumours of recovery and raised the stakes in his efforts to persuade Charles to intervene by reiterating talk of poisoning, and noting that 'Northumberland is hated and loathed as a tyrant, whilst the said lady [Mary] is loved throughout the land.'[10]

Throughout May, while Edward's health fluctuated, outwardly business continued as usual. On the 20th, an event took place that was to have major implications for the country's future, though its significance was little realized at the time. An expedition of three ships, led by Richard Chancellor and Sir Hugh Willoughby, sailed from Greenwich to investigate the possibility of a north-east passage to China. As the ships left, members of the council, several of whom had invested in the expedition, flocked to the windows and towers of the palace to see it off. Edward, unfortunately, was too sick to witness it, though he doubtless heard the enthusiastic firing of the ships' guns as they slowly made their way downstream. He had signed letters of greeting to whichever rulers they might meet along the way.

Despite the care that had gone into setting up the voyage, and the long and fearsome list of rules that governed behaviour on board, Willoughby was to prove a lacklustre commander. They had only reached Harwich when they found that part of the food had gone rotten, and the hogsheads of wine were leaking. Progress was dilatory, with frequents stops and delays, and he was not helped by the weather, so it was late in the year by the time the three ships reached the northernmost tip of Norway. Here, a terrible storm caused the fleet to be scattered, and Chancellor's vessel became separated. Willoughby with the remaining two, was driven by storms into an uninhabited region and decided to winter there. Despite sending groups of men in three different directions on four-day treks to try and make contact, they found no trace of other humans. At some stage, in early 1554, the crew of both ships perished, either from cold or hunger, or both, Willoughby's log being found some years later.

Chancellor, however, had better fortune. Finding harbour in northern Russia, he made it overland to the splendid court of Ivan IV in Moscow, where he was well-received. He was able to return with trading privileges which led to the founding of the Muscovy Company. This was the precursor of the other great trading companies which were later to provide the stimulus for the development of the British Empire.

Although largely a privately-financed expedition, this venture should not be overlooked. The same year, Thomas Wyndham attempted to open up a trading route to Benin, now Nigeria, and two years before he had journeyed to Guinea on the coast of West Africa. Such activity, tentative as it initially was, owed much to current conditions in Europe. The Habsburg-Valois war was disrupting trade, and the Channel was full of unrestrained piracy. Northumberland had indicated with his return of Boulogne to the French that he was not interested in pursuing an active foreign policy in Europe, and so attention turned further afield. These expeditions were the first English trading ventures beyond Europe, and they marked an important, though perhaps unintended, shift in foreign policy, that was to come to fruition under Elizabeth.

Meanwhile, at home there were more immediate matters to attend to. On 28 May, Northumberland met with the king's doctors who informed him that they had run out of ideas, that Edward's illness was terminal, and that he would be unlikely to last two months. He now had to make up his mind what to do. L'Aubespine met with the Privy Council on the same day, and whatever was said may have given the duke and his supporters the confidence to proceed.

Few clues have emerged about what was happening behind the scenes over the next two weeks, but we can guess that the finishing touches were being put to Edward's 'devise'. On 2 June, Sir John Cheke, Edward's 'scholemaster', was sworn in as a secretary, and therefore member, of the Privy Council. This seemed a strange, and largely unnecessary, move, since there were already two secretaries, although there were suggestions that the others – Cecil and Petre - might be considering resigning, especially Cecil, who (according to his later version of events) wasn't totally on board with the plot.

Cheke was a highly-regarded academic and, as provost of King's College Cambridge and tutor to the king since 1544, and a member of Parliament, was a distinguished member of the establishment, even more so since Edward had recently ennobled him. It is unlikely, however, that any of these qualities were what singled him out for the job. Far more important was his absolute commitment to the cause of religious reform, and thus his presumed distaste for any change that the accession of Mary might bring about.

There is also the lingering suspicion that his proximity to Edward must have made him aware of what was going on, and that possibly he was being brought into the council so that he could share responsibility: effectively to shut him up. The fact that the oath that all privy councillors were required to swear included the admonition to 'keep secret all matters committed and revealed unto you' may back up this assertion. What this suggests about his exact role in the affair is unclear – it is not inconceivable that at some stage it was he who had originally set Edward the task of composing the 'devise'. Strype, in his biography of Cheke, describes him as 'always at his [Edward's] elbow, both in his closet and in his chapel, and wherever else he went, to inform and teach him',[11] thus suggesting it is more than likely he knew about the plot.

Added to this is the strangely vindictive way that he was later pursued by Mary, once she had become queen. He had, admittedly, written the council letter in July that denied her claim to the throne, but after an initial period of arrest he was formally pardoned and allowed to travel abroad. However, as late as 1556, he was kidnapped while still in the Low Countries, and brought back to further imprisonment. This might have been due to his unrepentant Protestantism, but it could suggest that the queen held a particular distaste for him due to his special involvement in the conspiracy against her.

The next task for Northumberland and Edward was to persuade the lawyers to convert the 'devise' into a legally watertight document, and this does not appear to have been straightforward. The lawyers, more than anyone, were aware of the implications of being associated with such a thing, and it is clear that they were unhappy. Our only evidence for their attitude comes from an account by Sir Edward Montagu, chief justice of the common pleas (and thus the second highest lawyer in the land), written early in the reign of Mary, at a time when he had been stripped of his office, heavily fined, and imprisoned in the Tower. The account was shown by Montagu's great-grandson to historian, Thomas Fuller, sometime during the seventeenth century.

According to Montagu, he was summoned by command of the Privy Council (and he took care to name the signatories of the instruction) to attend the court at 1 pm on 12 June, along with three other senior lawyers. They all duly arrived, and were brought before the king, who was accompanied by Northampton, Gates, and a couple of other councillors. Edward launched into an explanation of his worries that Mary might marry a foreigner and that his changes to the religion of the country might be altered. He then ordered the lawyers to draw up in legal form a 'bill of articles', presumably referring to the fair copy of the 'devise'.[12]

Straight away, the four lawyers saw problems with the form of the 'devise', and the fact that it went against the Act of Succession, and they began to object. Edward, however, would have none of it, and forcefully instructed them to draw up the document anyway, and to be quick about it.

The next day, the lawyers met among themselves and engaged in an apparently semantic argument as to whether simply drawing up such a will was treason, or whether only putting it into effect after Edward's death would incur the charge. Of course, to them the argument was anything but semantic; if the former were true it would possibly be them heading for the scaffold. This anguish amongst the lawyers is a reminder of just how high the stakes were. It might be thought that lawyers will do anything for a fee, but risking their heads was clearly a step too far.

But they were under pressure. That same day, Petre summoned Montagu to Ely Place and demanded that he hurry up. Montagu flatly refused to comply, and he and the others went straight to Westminster, where councillors were in session, and reminded them all of the dangers of what they were proposing. At that moment, according to the account, Northumberland, who had been in an adjoining room, burst into the chamber 'in a great rage and fury, trembling for anger' and called Montagu a traitor and threatened to 'fight in his shirt with any man in that quarrel'.[13] Thoroughly intimidated, the lawyers returned home, though for now they did nothing further in terms of drawing up the will.

On the afternoon of the 15th, they were again ordered to attend court. Those councillors who were present in the ante-room glared at them crossly before they were taken to see the king. Edward was equally displeased, and demanded to know why they had refused his command. Montagu repeated that the succession could only be altered by Parliament, and that until this was done, any such documents would have no legal force. Edward replied that he had every intention of calling Parliament, and demanded that in the meantime the document be drawn up. Montagu was somewhat relieved to hear this and, concerned by the mutterings of some of the councillors standing behind that they would be traitors if they didn't do the king's bidding, the lawyers grudgingly acquiesced.

Nevertheless, aware of future danger, Montagu requested that the instruction be given under the safeguard of the great seal, and that they should be granted a general pardon, to which the king agreed. Yet, despite this, one of the lawyers – Justice Hales - still refused to comply and, as Montagu darkly noted, how Northumberland 'handled him he can tell best himself'. The lawyers then departed in some degree of dread to draw up the final articles.

This vignette is fascinating in what it reveals, or doesn't reveal, about the inspiration behind the plot. It shows Edward as confident, and committed, enough to browbeat distinguished lawyers on his own, with Northumberland being brought in to give back-up when required. If the latter was simply acting on orders of the king, he certainly seemed enthusiastic enough about doing it. It also showed the rest of the Privy Council – or at least those of them present – as being in agreement with the situation, though Montagu did note that they were 'all afraid of him'.

Whether the purpose of Montagu's account was to set the record straight, or to exonerate himself, or both, is unclear. It is doubtful that he was in fear for his life – he had already been punished by other means – but he may have been hoping for some sympathy, and even redress, from Mary, and certainly his description of Northumberland's role would have been just what she wanted to hear. His opinions on the extent to which Northumberland held the council in thrall may, or may not, have been accurate, but at least we can believe that *someone*, be it Edward, or Northumberland, or the council as a whole, must have put considerable pressure on the lawyers to be party to what they evidently viewed as a clear act of treason.

Not that Montagu was the only one with reservations. Archbishop Cranmer, too, appeared reluctant, and he later refused to sign the subsequent Engagement which committed signatories to carry out Edward's wishes for the succession, and only agreed to the letters patent after persuasion from the king. But there is something slightly untrustworthy about his claimed behaviour. He was the one who had declared Mary and Elizabeth illegitimate in the eyes of God, and he was the one who had most to lose if Mary came to the throne and turned back the course of 'his' Reformation. In fact, he had every reason to fear for his life if Mary succeeded, and it seems that his protestations were a case of hedging his bets. There is a suggestion that it was not the exclusion of Mary that he objected to, but Elizabeth, and given her Protestant leanings this would make more sense. He had asked to speak to the king in private, to explain his concerns, but this had been refused – probably the councillors were worried he might be able to talk Edward round.

There also exists an extraordinary letter, written long after these events, in October 1573, from Roger Alford, previously assistant to William Cecil, to his master 'reminding' him of his behaviour during those days.[14] Cecil had requested this letter, either because his loyalty was currently in doubt, or as an insurance against any future investigation. The purpose was clearly to exonerate him from having any part in the conspiracy, even though his signature is clearly affixed to the letters patent. According to this letter, Cecil had opposed the whole idea, and had had as little to do with it as possible, siding with the arguments of the lawyers, and only signing once they had already done so, under pressure from the king. Interestingly, Cecil did not seek to blame Northumberland personally, but attributed the 'devise' to Edward and a few in the council.

Alford then painted a picture of Cecil's unusually frequent, though unexplained, nighttime visits to London, where he went about armed, in apparent fear of arrest, and where he began moving belongings to a safe house, including money and blank passports to help with an escape, and even passing on his lands to his son. Alford further denied any involvement by Cecil in Jane's brief reign, and painted his master as one of the first to welcome Mary.

One can either accept this letter at face value, and see it as illustrative of the febrile atmosphere at the time, and as clear evidence of an underhand conspiracy by a few in authority, or see it simply as a means of Cecil extricating himself from any accusations of being part of a plan to deprive his current mistress, Elizabeth, of the throne. There is something slightly comical about Cecil's reported fears, especially given his close friendship with Northumberland, and the idea that he knew little or nothing about what was going on is hard to swallow.

William Cecil, attributed to Marcus Gheeraerts the Younger

The final document, drawn up by the lawyers on 21 June, has been known variously as Edward's will, his letters patent or, as he seems to have preferred, a 'declaration and limitation concerning the succession of the crown'.[15] In it, he makes the case for changing the succession, namely that Mary and Elizabeth, as bastards, and as half-sisters, had no right to inherit the crown from him. Whether these were Edward's real reasons is, of course, unknown, but they did, at least, establish some sort of a legally-defensible motive.

However, the document then goes on to slightly tarnish this reason by emphasising the dangers of the princesses marrying foreigners who might interfere with religion and the peace of the realm. Denying the throne on this basis was certainly not legal, and simply removed some of the force of the previous argument, and anyway the princesses were forbidden under Henry VIII's will to marry without Privy Council permission.

Likewise, the subsequent sentences extolling the characters of the daughters of Lady Frances were hardly relevant. The rest of the will still stressed the principle of male succession, as any future son of Frances would be first in line, but it did at least nominate Jane in second place, if Frances should have no son in Edward's lifetime.

But perhaps this document, and subsequent proclamations justifying the exclusion of Mary, is more revealing than it seems. After all, unlike the 'devise', it does actually give *reasons* for what Edward was intending. Those mentioned – particularly those concerning fears over a marriage to a foreigner - have conventionally been regarded as mere 'window-dressing', as excuses to cover Northumberland's grab for power. Yet they are the same reasons that would be given by Wyatt as a justification for his rebellion later that year, and the same ones that were to justify opposition throughout Mary's reign, and almost certainly the reason for Henry insisting on Privy Council approval for her marriage. Northumberland may have been shrewdly tapping into existing fears, but those fears were genuine.

By 15 June, Edward and Northumberland had what they wanted in terms of legal backing for ensuring the exclusion of Mary from the throne, apart from confirmation by Parliament, but they clearly did not yet feel secure. At some stage, presumably during the following week, they drew up a document normally referred to as the 'Engagement',[16] which they insisted that members of the Privy Council and senior lawyers sign. All it basically said was that the signatories promised to uphold Edward's will, but since their signatures on the will committed them to uphold it anyway, it seems, in a practical sense, to have been rather pointless. In fact, it was an extraordinary, almost laughable, attempt to ensure loyalty, and is more reminiscent of a group of boy scouts sitting round a campfire making vows with their own blood rather than an instruction at the highest level of government. It reeked of conspiracy, had no legal force, and was testament only to the lack of trust among the leading players, and an indication that some of them, at least, were well aware they were doing wrong.

On 14 June, the duchess of Suffolk, Jane's mother, had been summoned to an audience with Edward.[17] Given that this was in the midst of the attempts to legalise the 'devise' it seems probable that the purpose of the meeting was to inform her of the preferment of her daughter, Jane. There is some doubt over this because popular tradition has it that Jane was in ignorance of the conspiracy when her accession was announced after Edward's death, though this seems somewhat implausible. With Edward's demise apparently imminent, it appears obvious that Jane should be prepared for her future role, and anyway her father was already in the loop, and he was unlikely to keep it secret.

What the duchess made of this news we can only imagine. She had always enjoyed good relations with Mary, and must have been anxious at the implications of this change. How she felt about being upstaged by her own daughter, when she appeared to have the better claim, is also unknown. Later, she was to play her subservient role with apparent grace, and as she had always been ambitious for Jane she was perhaps content with this outcome which, in any case, would elevate still further the status of her family.

Meanwhile, the ambassadors had got further wind of something going on. Scheyfve noted on the 15th that top lawyers were being summoned to draw up Edward's will, though he seemed unaware as yet of what it contained.[18] Noailles, the following day, observed nobles and guards being summoned to the Tower, and was alarmed by this unusual activity.[19] Also, on the 16th, the council had its last recorded meeting. Thereafter, all its sessions would be secret, with no records of attendance, or matters discussed. The following day, Noailles met with councillors and observed that they seemed calmer and happier. They claimed to be optimistic about the king's health, but Noailles was not taken in. With commendable intuition, or possibly fore-knowledge, he ascribed their relaxed and united appearance to some difficult decision that had just been taken.[20]

The ambassadors were not the only ones whose suspicions were aroused, however. On the 19th, Scheyfve transmitted a message from Mary, who was 'in sore perplexity', to Charles V asking for advice on what to do in the present crisis.[21] She was, at present, in her house at Newhall in Essex, within easy reach of London, and she was clearly being kept up to date on matters regarding Edward's health, both through the Imperial ambassador and his agents, and her own network of informants, and also, more surprisingly, by Northumberland. She may not have known exactly what was going on behind closed doors at Westminster, but the fact that she made this request shows that she had her suspicions.

And she would have had every right to worry, even if she didn't yet know the full details. If she was to be denied the throne, what would then happen to her? Northumberland could not just leave her to go into secluded retirement; that would be far too dangerous. She would be a magnet for any opposition to the new regime, and her previous form suggested that meekly acceding to such a situation was not in her character. Nor could he allow her to flee abroad, where she might get support from Charles and launch an invasion. That left few alternative options, and none of them particularly agreeable.

But it is more likely that these were minor considerations. Mary is often portrayed as weak and vacillating, and, indeed, trying to bring her to a decision could be a tortuous process. However, once she had made up her mind and determined on a course of action, she was relentless and unbending. Compromise did not come easily to her, as demonstrated by the lengthy and uncomfortable stand-off with her father over acknowledging him as head of the English Church, and in her dealings with Edward over the saying of Mass. When she considered that she had right on her side she was immovable, and courageous. Her request to Charles should be seen less as the plea of a helpless victim asking for rescue, than as an active request for help in getting what was rightfully hers.

Surprisingly, perhaps, relations between Mary and the council throughout 1553 had shown outward signs of improvement. Since the confrontations of 1551, both sides had decided to observe a mutual stand-off. It can hardly be supposed that Mary actually went two years without hearing Mass, so we can deduce that there was a tacit agreement that so long as she did it in private, and did not make waves, the council would leave her alone. In March 1553, perhaps as a reward for her compliance, she was permitted her triumphal entry into London, her status and arms as royal princess were restored to her, and in May she was given large areas of land in Norfolk and the east of England.

Some, even at the time, were suspicious of this apparent *volte-face* and, ever distrustful of Northumberland, assumed that it was an attempt to lull her into a false sense of security. While possible, this seems unlikely. The council had been trying to get Mary to come to London for some months, and the lands that she was awarded were mainly exchanges to keep her further away from the coast from where she might flee, or welcome an Imperial army. The restoration of her title is more problematic, but perhaps the simplest explanation is that there was no good reason not to. In March, Edward was not in imminent danger of death, so there was little thought of the possibility of Mary succeeding, and it is unlikely that at that stage any plot was being seriously considered. Northumberland now felt confident enough to try and ingratiate himself with Mary – she still had the potential to be the focus of opposition – and this could simply be seen as a way of righting a wrong. Northumberland may well have been a devious politician, but the idea that he deliberately raised her status, showed her to the people, and extended the area where she might find loyal supporters – all of which would make things more difficult if he ever did try to disinherit her - just to make her less suspicious is perhaps a little too subtle.

Scheyfve's report on the 19th made no mention of the will or Engagement, so clearly the council, now meeting in closed session, had managed to keep this a secret from him.[22] What he was intrigued about was the rumour that some councillors were suggesting an arrangement by which Mary would agree to maintain the religious changes, not restore Church lands, and keep the present council in power. Others, more alarmingly, were apparently in favour of excluding Mary completely. The chances of Mary accepting the first option appeared slim, and it was far from what he or the emperor would want, but it was certainly preferable to the alternative.

His report did, at least, have the effect of stirring the emperor into action. On the 23rd, Charles, incapacitated by gout, and weary of the demands of administering his vast empire – a matter he took too seriously for the care of his own health – wrote separately to Edward, Mary, Northumberland, and the Privy Council announcing the sending of a team of three special ambassadors, headed by one of his most capable diplomats, Simon Renard, ostensibly (and untruthfully) because he had been starved of news about the king's health.[23] The true purpose of their mission would be revealed in person – not even Scheyfve was initially informed.

The confidential instructions to this team made clearer the purpose of the visit.[24] Charles was, somewhat belatedly, responding to the L'Aubespine mission of the previous month, and he wanted his envoys to ensure that Edward (and the council) were aware that Charles' feelings for him were greater and more sincere than those of the French. More importantly, however, the team were to try and ensure the safety of Mary, and assist her in succeeding to the throne. Charles appeared aware of a possible attempt by the council to disinherit her, though not the details, but his main interest was, quite clearly, to prevent France from taking advantage of the situation to gain a foothold in England.

The instructions went on to echo the information provided by Scheyfve. He advised the ambassadors to make it quite clear that Charles understood the concern that Mary might marry a foreigner, and to encourage the belief that he would be happy for her to choose an Englishman, though he recommended they try to set English suitors against each other so that in time a 'better solution' might be arrived at. Likewise with religion, Mary must be encouraged to promise to make no changes, at least until an opportunity emerged 'to guide affairs in the right direction', and she must also promise not to punish the current government for any offences that may have been committed.

Charles ideally wanted the ambassadors to visit Mary first, to get her opinions on these issues. They were then to relay these to the emperor before proceeding further. Charles clearly did not regard his cousin as a weak and helpless woman who he could easily bend to his will, and was happy to leave the initiative to her, though he still intended then to try and micro-manage the situation. He ended his instructions by reiterating the principal objects of the mission as 'to preserve our cousin's person from danger, assist her to obtain possession of the Crown, calm the fears the English may entertain of us, defeat French machinations, and further a good understanding between our dominions and the realm of England'.

The instructions show Charles' pragmatic attitude towards the situation, but not such a great understanding of his cousin. Mary was highly unlikely to accept these compromises. Nor is it clear whether he had fully understood the nature of the plot. If Edward, Northumberland, and the Privy Council were genuinely concerned by the prospect of Mary overturning religion, purging the government and marrying a foreigner, then his advice sounds wise. It would enable Mary to succeed without a constitutional, religious, or international crisis. If, however, the plot was all about the ambition of Northumberland, and the other issues merely excuses, then he had missed the point: there was nothing in these orders about how to neutralise the duke.

Meanwhile, everything hung on Edward's health. On the 24th, Scheyfve reported that his condition was so bad he would surely die the next day. His nails and hair were dropping out, he had difficulty breathing, and he was covered in sores.[25] A special prayer for his recovery had been posted up throughout the city, causing astonishment among those many passers-by who were still unaware of the gravity of his illness. Yet, three days later he announced that there had been a change, and that Edward was better, and on the 30th the special ambassadors appear to have been told that the king was able to 'eat, drink, and enjoy repose'.[26]

To confirm this, Edward actually appeared at a window of his palace at Greenwich to show himself to the people, but his appearance was so wasted that this did little to convince anyone of his chances of recovery. On Sunday 2 July, he was due to appear again, and a crowd assembled, only to be told that it would be done the following day, though this, too, was cancelled as the weather was 'too chill'.[27]

Mary, meanwhile, had not sat idly by. Aware of the king's fading chances of survival, at the end of June she moved to Hunsdon, another of her properties, closer still to London. On 3 July, she was apparently summoned to Greenwich to be with her dying brother, but was alerted on the way that it could be a trap. She hurriedly returned. Aware now of the imminent danger, she decided to move further away, and settled on Norfolk, which was closer to the sea and where she had a concentration of supporters. She secretly left Hunsdon with just a couple of attendants at dead of night on the 4th, claiming sickness in her household.

By this time, Scheyfve had firm details of Edward's will, and was aware that Northumberland intended to install Jane as the next queen. He reported on the 4th that the councillors had begun arming and readying their retainers, as well as stockpiling weapons and ammunition, and fitting out warships for some unexplained purpose.[28]

Around 9 o'clock in the evening of 6 July, Edward finally gave up the long struggle. With the words 'I am faint. Lord have mercy upon me, and take my spirit',[29] he died in the arms of one of his favourite companions, Sir Henry Sidney. As with his father, courtiers and the council intended to keep his death secret until steps could be taken to secure the succession, but the Imperial ambassadors, who arrived the next morning, were able to report the same day on the king's demise.[30] The stage was now set for the conspiracy to unfold.

5

The Rebellion Against Mary

From the moment of Edward's death, the plot against Mary began to unravel. While alive, his existence had lent some sort of authority to the scheme, but now dead, all that was left was some papers of dubious legality, and the commitment of only a handful of councillors to seeing matters through. Most of the country, when eventually it learned of the king's death, would automatically hail the new queen, Mary.

It could be argued that the unravelling had begun even before Edward's death, for the success of the venture had never been solely in the hands of the plotters. Much depended on what Mary would do, and the fact that she had moved from Hunsdon even before the 6th showed that whatever her intentions – fight or flight – she was not going to come quietly.

Those who have *not* seen Northumberland as a treacherous and ruthless adventurer – Jordan and Beer, for example – have preferred to portray him as a loyal servant, bamboozled by the king into following his scheme, and then having to face the consequences alone. This works up to a point, and only up to the death of the king, for now Northumberland was free to do what he wanted. Nor was there much of a dilemma. On one side there was the will of a king too young to legally make one, together with letters patent still not bearing the royal seal; and on the other a parliamentary statute, and the will of a king authorized by Parliament. Legally, there was no contest: the council *had* to proclaim Mary.

We do not know what went on in the council meetings at Greenwich and in the Tower over the next few days, but it would be naïve to assume that the question of whether to actually proceed with the plot was not discussed. It is almost a truism of this period that Northumberland was completely in control of the council, and that the others meekly followed his wishes, but this is hard to justify given what little evidence we have. The idea that the plot was his, and that he forced it on his reluctant colleagues, was one all too readily espoused, subsequently, by councillors eager to absolve themselves of responsibility, and one which later monarchs, and historians, have adopted as being simpler and less messy than the alternative.

Northumberland was undoubtedly a dominant individual, prone to bursts of rage – his threat to fight anyone who disagreed with him when forcing Montagu to approve the 'devise', is one example, as is his earlier ban from the council for striking Stephen Gardiner, bishop of Winchester, during a meeting (though anyone who knew Gardiner would have found such behaviour readily excusable) – but he was hardly a dictator, despite attempts by the Imperial ambassadors, among others, to portray him as such.

For a start, he had none of the security apparatus needed to establish a dictatorship. He had no army, no police, his personal 'manred' – his retainers - was no greater than that of most of the other nobles in the land, and the limit of his intelligence-gathering technology was the ears and eyes of watchers in his pay whose level of efficiency could be gauged by the fact that it took three days for those watching Mary (if there even were such people) to realise she had gone missing. True, he had a majority of supporters on the council, but many of these had their independent power base, and were beholden to him only for their seat on that organization. Certainly, he had ruthlessly disposed of opposition in the form of Somerset, and this may have scared the others, but he had nearly been a victim himself of the initial attempt against the protector. Northumberland's real power had always come from his relationship with the king, and now he no longer had that.

In fact, the number of those on the council who he could genuinely rely on was small. The earl of Suffolk, for all that he was worth, was possibly the most loyal, as were the earls of Northampton and Huntingdon (at least for now) and Sir John Gates. Pembroke and the Marquess of Winchester could be persuaded more easily than most, and possibly Cheke, but few others were automatic loyalists. Even Cecil, hitherto a close ally, wanted nothing to do with this scheme. The reaction of the others seems to have ranged from grudging acceptance of the plan to disguised hostility, though if we are to go by the snivelling letter later dispatched to Mary after her victory it would appear that all had been against it from the start, and they had only gone along with it because Northumberland had forced them.

But there must have been something more than this. As could be seen from the coups against Somerset, the council was a centre of intrigue, and councillors were not shy of taking extreme measures against leaders of whom they disapproved, even if they were the king's own uncles. Northumberland had always been at pains to position himself *within* the council, and to show himself as one of them, and not, like Somerset, an aloof outsider. This meant that decisions taken were not unilateral, but discussed at the table. How much Northumberland listened to, or acted upon, contrary opinion we do not know, but whatever was decided could be seen to have come from Whitehall rather than Durham Place. Which all suggests that what came next was the responsibility of the council as a whole, and not just Northumberland.

So, if it wasn't just fear, why did the other councillors go along with him (or, because we honestly don't know the truth of things, persuade *him* to go along with *them*)? The best legal advice in the land had already informed them that there was no lawful basis to what they were proposing, and that their actions amounted to high treason. How much easier it would have been just to call the whole thing off, put the blame on the dead king, and declare for Mary. The sooner they did this, the less chance there would be of any retaliation against them, and besides, they had not yet declared Jane, and they could always argue – with justification - that they had been forced by Edward to sign the incriminating documents. And yet they didn't. Something must have persuaded them that it was in their interests to go ahead with the plot.

Some of them may have felt a moral duty to follow Edward's plan, and fulfil the promises made in the Engagement. There is some mileage in this. They would all have known Edward well, would have seen him grow towards adulthood, would have worked with him on his special council, and helped him formulate his policies. Many would have genuinely liked him. His tragic and premature death would have undoubtedly had an impact – the death of a monarch is always a profoundly significant event, both on a national and a personal level –

and it is not beyond the bounds of possibility that, cynical and worldly-wise as they were, they would have felt an emotional obligation to fulfil his dying wishes.

Most of the councillors were Protestant, and therefore feared a loss of office, and possibly persecution, if Mary succeeded, and all had been involved, to greater or lesser extent, in building the new religion, and would therefore be reluctant to see their work destroyed. They would also have genuinely shared the fear of Mary marrying a foreign prince, despite their theoretical ability to prevent it. They had enjoyed the previous six years of power, and had worked hard to put right the problems left by Henry and Somerset, and the accession of Jane promised more of the same. Mary, on the other hand, would be no pushover and, if they kept their jobs at all, they might have to put up with major decisions being made outside the council chamber. Furthermore, and perhaps most significant of all, there was always the possibility that Mary might try to restore monastic lands to the Church, much of which was currently in their possession. That would entail a major loss of income.

For now, the present government seemed to hold all the cards. If it came to a fight, they had a significant number of their own retainers, and the navy was apparently loyal. They also had the Tower, into which they had been stockpiling weapons, and they had the royal mints, as well as the capital, under their control. They had their own people in all areas of local administration throughout the country, and they had the moral authority of being the recognized government. They also had good legal arguments why Mary should not become queen, and if the question boiled down to which religion the country wanted, they should have a major advantage there, too. As for Mary, she seemed to have nothing in her favour, and besides, she was under virtual house arrest – they presumed – and could be easily taken at any time. So why not go through with it?

It should be noted that, initially, none of those councillors present attempted to leave and join Mary. We do not know how heated the discussions were around the table, but there was no outward show of dissent over the next ten days. All appear to have acquiesced, with differing degrees of enthusiasm perhaps, in the scheme, and all must be held accountable. Only later, when support for Mary grew, did cracks start to appear.

As to how many councillors were present in the Tower, accounts vary. We know the names of the main players, for example those who signed the letters emanating from Jane, and those who were present in Pembroke's house on the final day, and it appears that there were probably about twenty-five, out of the full membership of thirty-three. Whether this implies that the remainder were absent because they disapproved of the scheme, or simply because they were in the country on their estates, we cannot say, but we can be sure that the majority of the council were initially prepared to go along with the plot.

Later, once Mary had come to the throne, we start to get a different picture. Cecil, in a letter sent to ingratiate himself with the new sovereign, asserted that he had never been in favour of the scheme, despite the appearance of his signature on several of the incriminating documents.[1] He had tried to have Windsor Castle handed over to Mary, and hinted at helping the rising against Jane in Lincolnshire where his lands lay. He had refused to write any of the letters aimed against Mary, and had also made efforts to flee the Tower. He named a number of councillors who could vouch for his claims, and his statements, however much we should take them with a large pinch of salt, might indicate an atmosphere of uncertainty and possible dissension within the government rather than unity.

*

Those who have chosen to depict Northumberland as the sinister and Machiavellian schemer have been hard-pressed to explain the awesome level of incompetence that he, and the council, now proceeded to demonstrate. From a position of such strength that even Charles V was reduced to abandoning any attempt at intervention, hardly even considering the prospect of saving his cousin's life, Northumberland managed to throw it all away, and within a fortnight was proclaiming Mary queen himself.

Given his previous record of skilful and ruthless political manoeuvring – most notably in the two coups against Somerset – one can only conclude from what happened next that either he was never wholly committed to the scheme in the first place, and that he had only been carrying out Edward's wishes, or that he suffered a virtual breakdown, for his actions seem more akin to those of the proverbial rabbit caught in the headlights than to a cunning and ambitious plotter.

That Mary had been allowed to leave Hunsdon at all while Edward was *in extremis* seems extraordinary. The entire success of the scheme had to rely on neutralizing her, and that, at the very least, meant controlling her whereabouts. The Imperial ambassador was able to report her departure from Hunsdon on the day she left,[2] yet Robert Dudley was not dispatched to Hunsdon to arrest her until the 7th - three days after she had gone. Northumberland appears to have had no effective intelligence of her movements – a basic, and fatal, error.

It has been argued that he could not just turn up and arrest the princess without good cause, at least not while Edward was still alive, but this is nonsense. This was the very time when she *should* have been apprehended – with whatever excuse – since it could be done under the royal seal. Some accounts say that she was summoned to court on 3 July, which may have been an attempt to do just this, but no escort was sent and, warned of the danger while *en route*, she was able to turn back and leave Hunsdon the next night. It also appears as if he didn't even have her under observation. She seems to have had her own informants at court, but Northumberland had no-one in her household, or effective watchers in the area, to keep an eye on her.

There are various theories that explain this fatal lapse: that Northumberland had cut a deal with Mary for her to renounce the throne in exchange for land grants[3] (extremely unlikely, for a number of reasons, not least her character); that he thought he had lulled her into a false sense of security with the land grants (slightly more plausible);[4] and that he was 'very ready to despise the plans of a mere woman' (probable).[5] Soranzo, the Venetian ambassador, with the benefit of hindsight, averred that Mary was well aware of what was happening and was simply stringing Northumberland along.[6] Whatever the cause, Northumberland, and others, had clearly taken their eyes off the ball, and handed the initiative to her.

Over the next three days, the plotters did little or nothing of any significance to ensure the success of their enterprise. They did at least secure the Tower, various councillors arriving hotfoot from Greenwich at 2.00am on the 7th, to install Edward Clinton – lord high admiral - as the new constable. To outsiders, they maintained the fiction that Edward was still alive, even though as early as the 7th, the Imperial ambassadors and Noailles were aware of his death, and, according to the latter, so were many of the inhabitants of London.[7] Both sets of envoys asked for audiences with the king, to be told that he was currently indisposed, but that the council would pass on a message.

The visits to the court by the envoys did nothing to decrease the alarm of either. Each was convinced that the other was planning something that would alter the balance of power in Europe. Noailles did not believe that the Imperial ambassadors had arrived simply to renew the old treaty of friendship with England, as they claimed, and Scheyfve and Renard were convinced that the French were offering armed help to counter any possible moves by Charles. Each looked at every tiny move by the council, as well as the comings and goings of the other, to try and work out exactly what was going on.

They need not have worried, for it appears that very little was going on at all. Northumberland politely refused offers of French help, claiming that he had the situation in hand,[8] while the Imperial side had given up completely on Mary. In a despatch to Charles on the 7th, Renard was full of gloom. He guessed that Mary had decided to fight for the crown, a resolution he considered 'strange, full of difficulties and danger'. He advised Charles not to send troops since that would only push England into the French camp, and declared that Mary's ambition was 'so difficult as to be well-nigh impossible'. Possession of power was the key factor, 'especially among barbarians like the English', and Mary, particularly due to her religion, did not have it.[9]

Charles, usually so astute in his understanding of English affairs, got this one completely wrong. Not that he can really be blamed; almost everyone else did too. He was hardly helped by the information from his ambassador, assuring him one moment that everyone loved Mary and all were dying to see the end of Northumberland, and the next saying there was no hope for her. In the event he made one intervention, which may have been critical; he instructed Scheyfve to negotiate with the council on behalf of Mary, to suggest that she would not force a return to Catholicism, and would not necessarily marry outside the realm.[10]

Mary, at this critical moment, was on the road to Framlingham, via short stops at Sawston in Cambridgeshire, and Kenninghall in Norfolk. It is not clear whether she was aware of the fact that she had been abandoned to her fate, and whether this had an effect on her subsequent behaviour, but at some stage she had made up her mind, and by the time she reached Norfolk her journey, which had begun as a flight from danger, had turned into a strategic withdrawal.

East Anglia

Her decision to head for East Anglia was the result of an irony. By the terms of her father's will she had been bequeathed lands, though the nature and position of these had not been specified. In May 1553, the council had decided that those which had belonged to the duke of Norfolk, which had reverted to the Crown after his attainder and imprisonment, would be suitable, and these she duly took over. Of course, the duke of Norfolk was a Catholic, as inevitably were many of those in the area beholden to him. Mary had not just been awarded high-value land, she had been presented, presumably accidentally, with a natural-fitting power base.

There is an interesting sub-plot to the story of these lands, as many of them were transfers rather than outright gifts. Mary's lands had previously been centered on Essex, many of them close to the coast. After her suspected escape attempt in 1551, the council had come to the conclusion that they were too close to the sea for comfort, and decided to swap them for ones further inland. It has been noted that these new ones were of considerably greater value than those she was giving up, and that, surprisingly, they were awarded at a time when the council was doing its best to save money by getting the most value from Crown lands.

There could be a perfectly simple explanation for this: Mary was simply being encouraged not to make a fuss at the transfer by ensuring that she came off better from the deal – a price worth paying. However, there have been suggestions that they may have been part of an agreement by which Mary would accept these improved holdings in return for not pursuing her claim to the throne. Elizabeth was also given new lands at the same time.[11] While conspiracy theories are always intriguing, this one does not hold much water. The idea that the sisters – neither especially noted for being amenable to pressure – would willingly give up their inheritance, and betray the sacred mission of their father, for a few parcels of land, is hard to swallow: the fact that Northumberland chose never to mention it is even more so.

Much has been made of Mary's indecisiveness, particularly on her agonizing over her decision to flee the country in 1551, but nothing over the next two weeks suggests anything other than determination, clear-headed resolve, and courage. While the council in London dithered, she acted, and looking back at events, it is clear to see that as early as the 7th, if not earlier, she had taken charge of her fate. For on that date, she had begun to write letters proclaiming herself queen, so that her supporters would be aware of her position and would hopefully flock to her.[12] Since she couldn't have sent such letters before Edward's death, for that would have been treason, the date indicates the superiority of her own intelligence system, and possibly even how much better prepared she was.

In truth, Mary did not do a lot more during the crisis *than* write letters, but in the event she did not have to. All she had to do was sit tight, wait for supporters to arrive, and watch while Northumberland and the council obligingly imploded.

The only other remotely positive thing the council seem to have done during those early, crucial days, was gradually add to the list of those in the know about the conspiracy. On the 7th, the lord mayor and aldermen of London, and the city guard, were summoned to Greenwich to swear an oath of loyalty to the new queen, Jane. This may have come as quite a surprise to them, especially as Edward's death was still a secret, and it served little purpose other than to enable further rumours, and suspicions, to seep out as to what might be going on. It also committed the council still further to their chosen course of action. With events shrouded, ineffectually, in secrecy, and with rumours abounding, the only logical conclusion that could be drawn by the public at large was that something unnatural and underhand was unfolding.

On the 8th, the council sent letters to lords lieutenant and justices of the peace warning of Mary's departure from Hunsdon, and asking them to suppress any risings, and to be vigilant, especially around the coasts, both to forestall any possible invasion and to prevent her fleeing abroad.[13] The letter affirmed that Edward was still alive, even though he had already been dead for two days. Apart from hinting at some sort of conversations between Mary's household and the Imperial ambassador, there was no evidence of exactly why she posed such a danger to the country, and why leaving her house without expressly asking the council for permission should have been a matter of such national importance. Considering that she was still, publicly at least, the heir to the throne, it must have caused some surprise among the lords lieutenant to hear that she was plotting to have foreigners invade what was likely to be very shortly her own kingdom.

Edward's death was kept a secret for three days. There was nothing unusual about this, the same had happened after Henry VIII had died, but then the intervening time had been spent in setting in motion the necessities for a seamless transition to a minority rule. Now, the Privy Council simply tried to keep it a secret, without making any practical provision for what to do when they had to announce it. Apart from the capture of Mary, the other 'must-do' task, which they also singularly failed to do, was to introduce Jane.

Of course, this was bound to be difficult given the nature of the plot. Nothing could be done until Edward had died, but during the period of secrecy there were opportunities to smooth the transition. At the very least, propaganda questioning the legitimacy of Mary could have been disseminated via handbills through London from the moment the letters patent were signed two weeks *before* Edward's death. This could have been ramped up after the 6th – the previously-discussed letters to the lords lieutenant could have suggested an alternative to the 'traitorous' Mary. But nothing was done. Thus, when on the 10th, Jane was proclaimed queen in the streets of London, without any prior warning, the news was greeted, unsurprisingly, with bemusement.

And, to some extent, it still is. Apart from those who have studied the period, few are even aware that she has a claim to be the first queen of England. She appears in few chronologies of kings and queens – the list of British monarchs on the souvenir ruler sold in the Tower of London does not include her, even though she spent her entire reign within its confines – and she is still rarely acknowledged as a legitimate queen, which is ironic since her own claim to legitimacy was arguably greater than Mary's. She is little more than a supporting player in this story, despite the high rank she temporarily held, significant mainly because she *wasn't* Mary.

Although forgotten by most, she has been remembered with a high degree of devotion by a few. It is remarkable how much has been written about such an historically insignificant figure as Lady Jane Grey, and about one for whom there is so little real information. Countless histories, novels, poems, plays and films have been produced throughout the centuries about a figure who ruled for only thirteen days – nine if you count from the date of her proclamation – without ever being crowned, legally approved, or having made a significant executive decision. For these reasons she has become more of a symbol than a flesh and blood figure; more a myth and a cipher than a real person.

Presumed portrait of Lady Jane Grey, unknown artist

So insignificant was she, that, apparently, it was not until the evening of 9 July that the council bothered to inform her that she was now queen of England, and in fact had been for the previous three days!

Because of the amount of myth-making it is not always easy to see through it to detect the facts beneath. Some stories have been told and retold so many times that they have gained the status of truth. A good example is the scene in which Jane, having been summoned on the evening of the 9th to Syon House to meet with the duke of Northumberland and a few other councillors, is informed that she is now queen.[14] According to the story, which seems to have originated with Commendone, it is the first that she has heard either of Edward's death, or of her elevation, and she is shocked and protests that she shouldn't be queen.[14] It is a terrific set piece; the young and inexperienced girl, tearfully protesting her reluctance, and then being bullied into submission by a gang of elderly and important men, including her own father. But how true is it, and how do we know?

While there is nothing particularly surprising, or unbelievable, about her upset – Edward was her cousin, after all, and on top of that to suddenly be told you are now queen would be enough to cause disquiet in most people – can we really believe that this was the first she had heard of it? Was Northumberland worried that she might reveal the secret if he warned her beforehand (and did her parents give nothing away?), or did he have so little consideration for her that he thought she needed no notice, or training, for the role? Or was her 'surprise' invented to blacken his reputation and add to the image of her as an innocent victim?[15]

At least, on the 9th, Londoners did get some clues as to what was afoot. Those attending the Sunday sermon at Paul's Cross, an open-air pulpit in the grounds of the cathedral, would have heard the bishop of London, Nicholas Ridley, preach a fiery sermon in which he described both Elizabeth and Mary as bastards. Whether this was on his own initiative, or on the orders of the council, it seems to have backfired as it was not well received by the congregation who were 'sore annoyed with his words, so uncharitably spoken by him in so open an audience'.[16] The *Greyfriars Chronicle* also refers to a sermon the previous week in which a Dr. Hoskins failed to offer the customary prayer for the princesses. Neither preacher appears to have mentioned Jane, however.

So, when Jane was finally escorted to the Tower on the afternoon of the 10th, as ritual demanded, few were fully aware of what was going on. Again, the council seems to have missed an opportunity, either through negligence, or concern over how Londoners might react. Far from bringing her in through the streets of the capital, where she could be seen and welcomed by the people, she was surreptitiously sneaked in by river, presumably with the intention that the people should *not* see her. Nothing so much demonstrates the lack of confidence of the plotters, and the irregularity of what they were doing, than Jane's back-door entrance into her kingdom. Much was made of the fact that no-one shouted 'God save the Queen', or showed any enthusiasm for her, but this was hardly surprising given that she had yet to be publicly proclaimed, and few of those watching – and there can't have been many of them - can have had much, if any, idea of who she was and what she was doing there.

Later, in the evening, heralds were sent to the principal spots in London - Tower Hill, Cheapside, St Paul's - to proclaim Jane to the population. Again, there was almost no public reaction. This is less surprising when one examines the document they were obliged to read. Far from being a succinct, and no-nonsense, affirmation of Jane as the next monarch, the proclamation was an over-long and mind-numbingly tortuous justification of why she and not Mary or Elizabeth should be queen.[17] Even if we assume that the citizens were given a cut-down version, in the unlikely event that those present were still listening, or even still there, by the end, the only impression they were likely to have come away with was that something very fishy was going on. That they were unenthusiastic at the news was, therefore, unsurprising; that they were not openly rebellious was remarkable.

History relates that only one person openly opposed the announcement. Young Gilbert Potter, an apprentice vintner, was heard to protest that Mary should be the rightful queen. He was denounced, apparently by his own master, and for his pains was forced to stand in the pillory with his ears nailed to a post, while an officer of the law informed passers-by of his crime. Before being taken down, his ears were then sliced off. His fate aroused some disquiet, and the appearance of a seditious pamphlet entitled 'Poor Pratte',[18] which circulated the London streets defending his action. It is said that he was later rewarded with lands by Mary. Some sort of immediate revenge may have been exacted as, that same afternoon, his master, attempting to pass through London Bridge in a wherry, was drowned when his boat overturned in the rapids.

So, what do we know of the person who was, temporarily, to beat Mary to the race to be England's first reigning queen? Very little, in truth. For starters, we don't know when she was born, where she was born, or even what she looked like. We have only a handful of anecdotes about her early life (which was pretty much her whole life) from which to draw conclusions. Typically, as a minor and distant royal, and as a female, she was not considered worthy of much mention until such time as she became queen, and for some time after that no-one was much inclined to write about her, either. Since then, the very lack of detail has been a frustration to historians, and a godsend to romantic novelists whose imaginations have known no limits in filling in the missing gaps.

It is believed that she was 17 when she died in 1554, which would probably put her birth in 1537. Her family seat was Bradgate in Leicestershire, so she may have been born there, or possibly in London, or indeed in any of the other properties that her father, then marquis of Dorset, owned. She was a cousin to the future king, Edward, and had two younger sisters, Katherine and Mary, both of whom were to play significant roles during subsequent reigns.

Apart from the fortune of her birth into a noble household, and all the material comforts that that promised (although membership of this particular household was, of course, to result in her early demise), she was also able to benefit from the extraordinary changes that were happening around her. For this was the period in which Renaissance values had a significant impact on her upbringing. For all his faults – and he had more than his fair share of these – her father, Henry, was a passionate believer in the value of education. How sincerely he believed in female education we don't know, but since he had no sons, he was content to lavish his enthusiasm on Jane and her sisters.

His wealth and status, and his evangelical beliefs, meant that Henry could use his connections to secure the very best tutors for his daughters. These included a young Cambridge graduate, John Aylmer, as her main teacher, but she was also encouraged to correspond with Protestant luminaries, such as Bullinger and Ulm, who her father patronized. These went into encomiums of admiration for Jane's academic abilities, though whether this was more down to the fact that they depended financially on Henry, or whether she really deserved such praise is uncertain. It is said that she was proficient in Latin and Greek, and probably French, and maybe even Hebrew, and Roger Ascham, tutor to the king and Princess Elizabeth, and whom we have already seen present a gushing comment on Edward's academic abilities, wrote about 'that most excellent maiden, Jane Grey... whose mind is more cultivated in the teaching of Plato and the eloquence of Demosthenes than distinguished by mere fortune'.[19]

One vignette, often repeated by biographers, is the time that Ascham paid a surprise visit to Bradgate and discovered Jane sitting inside reading

Plato while her parents were out hunting. Jane apparently assured him that this was what she preferred to do, leading writers to assume that she was naturally bookish. At this same meeting she apparently explained how much she was grateful for the gentleness of her teacher, Aylmer, compared to the rough handling by her parents who 'sharply taunted' and 'cruelly threatened' her with 'pinches, nips, and bobs and other ways that I will not name for the honour I bear them'.[20] Since Ascham included this passage in his book 'The Scholemaster', in a section extolling the virtues of good teachers, there may have been an element of exaggeration, but it was enough to tar the reputation of her parents.

At any rate, Jane was exceptionally well educated and, by all accounts, intelligent as well, but there was another motive for her parents putting so much expense and energy into her upbringing. For Jane was a marketable commodity, and the better educated she was, the more valuable. Once Henry VIII's will had been published, she became more valuable still, for she was now in the line of succession, and this brought her to the notice of that notorious schemer, Thomas Seymour, brother of the new protector, the duke of Somerset, who offered to make Jane his ward.

Placing a 10-year-old in the vicinity of this well-known rogue was hardly an example of exercising a duty of care towards his daughter, but Henry had good reasons for doing so. Firstly, Thomas was prepared to pay the not inconsiderable sum of £2000 for taking on the wardship; and next, he suggested that he might be able to get her betrothed to none other than his own nephew, the young king. Thomas's motives, naturally enough, were not altruistic. He wanted to spite his brother by scotching Somerset's intention to marry Jane to his son, and he wanted to get Henry's support in his attempts to achieve a more prominent role in the government of the kingdom, and even, as it later transpired, to overthrow his brother.

Yet the deal turned out well for Jane. Thomas had secretly married Henry VIII's widow, Katherine Parr, and it was into her household that Jane was to move. Katherine was an intelligent woman, well-connected with reformist, humanist, society, and her court was lively, intellectual and stimulating. The 18 months Jane spent there were probably the happiest and most rewarding of her life. However, it came to an end when

Katherine died in childbirth, and Thomas sent her back to her parents. Although she was to return for a second spell, Thomas's arrest, and subsequent execution, meant that her wardship, and faint hopes of marrying the king, faded.

By 1553, Jane had achieved a small reputation for her intelligence and her devotion to the new religion, and it may have been this, as well as her position in the line of succession, that determined Northumberland to choose her as a bride for his son, and for he and Edward to decide on her as a successor. It is noteworthy that no-one, not even those with a motive for doing so, had a bad word to say about Jane as a person; criticism was purely on the grounds of her right to be queen.

However, one thing her education had not prepared her for was how to rule a country. Edward, and his father before him, had received the very best teaching in how to be a prince, and in the arts of government. He had even been given a degree of experience during his minority, and would, arguably, have been the best-equipped, and most comprehensively-trained king so far. Jane had been prepared for life as a lady of the court; to be witty, knowledgeable, pleasant company, and skilled in how to run a household, but no more than this. Now she was expected to take on a far different role.

Not that this bothered Northumberland particularly. All he wanted of Jane was that she should be tactful, malleable, obedient, and a figurehead for a regime dominated by himself and Guilford. Of course, it was not just Jane who was uncertain of how a queen should rule; no-one in England had any experience, either. Interestingly, the ambassadors of France, Venice and the Empire barely mentioned her, and, if acknowledging the new regime at all – and Charles did his utmost not to - referred to 'King' Guilford, for it was automatically assumed that he would be the actual ruler, and therefore the one to do business with.

But Jane had other ideas. From her first day in office, she flatly refused to make him king. Defying the protestations of Northumberland, his wife, her parents, and Guilford himself, she would offer him only the dukedom of Clarence. And there was not much that they could do about it because she was now queen. This story is interesting for it reveals her as not just a meek and obedient puppet, but as someone with her own mind. We do not know why she did this. As there was no precedent in

England, there was no special reason why Guilford should have been given the royal title (though Mary was subsequently to have her husband, Philip, titled, though not crowned, king). It may have been that she did not consider him suitable for the role (we know almost nothing about him), or that she wanted to distance herself from Northumberland, or that she simply wanted to rule herself.

Those who have wanted to paint Jane as more in control of the situation, and not as a helpless victim, have highlighted this as an example of her capacity for independent action, but it seems out of character. If she was so able to assert herself now, why had she not, the day before, refused the throne, given her proclaimed reluctance? It has been suggested that she was persuaded to take the crown in the belief that she was carrying out Edward's wishes, and this may have been the case. The truth is that we know nothing for sure. It is even possible that we can turn accepted wisdom on its head, and see her as someone of ambition, who had bought into Northumberland and Edward's vision of an evangelical crusade that she was now heir to, and that her 'reluctance' – the existence of which relies mainly on her later (lost, and disputed) exculpatory letter to Mary - was simply a way of subsequently appealing for mercy.

All we know is that she persisted in her refusal, and put up with the fury of Northumberland's wife, who tried to persuade Guilford not to sleep with her. Nor does she appear to have made any further complaint about her new role. Her refusal, however, may have had consequences. Some councillors, especially those who were not fully on board with the plot, may have been prepared to put up with a female ruler on the understanding that her husband would be the one they would deal with; now that they seemed destined to serve a woman, this may have weakened their resolve. Admittedly, Mary, too, was unmarried, but at least, according to Henry VIII's will, they would be in charge of approving a husband for her.

However, by this time such matters were becoming increasingly irrelevant, for on that same day – the 10th – a letter arrived from Mary which would have a significant impact on subsequent events. It was carried by an elderly retainer, Thomas Hungate, and, as luck would have it, arrived at the worst possible moment, while the council was in session.

It was opened, and read before all those present, and it produced consternation.

We do not know whether it was written by Mary herself, or by one of her advisers, but as she signed it she must take the overall credit. It is a veritable masterpiece, and may well have been the single most important factor in ensuring her victory. The tone was respectful, confident, and restrained. She began by restating her right to the throne, emphasizing that 'there is no true subject that is, can, or would pretend to be ignorant thereof' before expressing surprise that the council had not yet contacted her. She trusted that when they had debated the issue more fully, their 'loyalty and service' would reach the same conclusion. She showed herself aware of efforts to disinherit her, but assured them that she would fully pardon them. She ended with a sting in the tail with the hope that she would not have to use those 'true subjects and friends' who God might send to her cause.[21]

To the waverers among the council members, of whom there were doubtless several, it offered a way out; to those more obdurate it issued a warning that Mary would be prepared to fight for her crown. Any hope that she would peacefully accept the situation was now over. Northumberland promptly sent Hungate to the Tower – a clear case of shooting the messenger – in what appears initially a cruel and pointless act, but which, on reflection, was perfectly understandable. He, better than any, realised the importance and impact of the letter. Although he still seemed to have the cards stacked firmly in his favour, from now on he acted even more like a dead man walking.

Not that Mary had much more reason to feel confident, and at the time of writing the letter was little more than a bluff. She was still on the run, had few if any of the loyal friends she was hoping to attract, and had been written off by the Imperial ambassadors who declined even to send anyone to hear what she was intending to do. Robert Dudley was, presumably, still in pursuit, though it is far from clear where he had got to, and the six ships that Northumberland had been fitting out over the previous month were lurking around the coast to cut off any chance of escape. However, flight does not appear to have been in her mind, and at Kenninghall she was within her own lands, and as safe as it was possible to be for the moment.

Still, Northumberland was able to rally the council to pen an immediate reply, reiterating the right of Jane to be queen; reminding Mary that she was illegitimate, as confirmed by Parliament; ordering her not to 'vex and molest any of our sovereign lady queen Jane's subjects'; and advising her to 'show yourself quiet and obedient (as you ought)'. It ended 'Your ladyship's friends showing yourself an obedient subject', and was signed by 23 councillors (including Cecil).[22] Nowhere, however, did it promise pardon, as Mary's own letter had done.

The same day, the council sent out another circular to lords lieutenant in the counties announcing, for the first time – four days after Edward's death – the accession of Jane. The instructions ordered officials to 'defend her just title, and to assist her in the possession of her kingdom, and to disturb, repel and resist the feigned and untrue claim of the Lady Mary, bastard-daughter to her [Jane's] great-uncle King Henry VIIIth'.[23] The text was drafted by Northumberland in person, as Cecil refused to write it, but signed by Jane, who seems to have been getting into the swing of her new role. The gloves were off; Mary was effectively an outlaw in her own realm.

These letters were all very well, but they were at least a day behind Mary's. To a population, and local officialdom, unprepared for what was going on, but, presumably, under the assumption that Mary was the rightful successor, and who were now being canvassed for support by both sides, the letters from Mary would have caused less surprise than those coming from the government. Admittedly, the council had already sent letters on the 8th, warning county officials to be on the lookout for Mary, but these had given no inkling of a change of regime. Now, suddenly, these officials were presented with the *fait accompli* of a new queen, apparently pulled from a hat. It would have been surprising if many did not see greater reassurance in Mary's demands for support.

Belatedly, the council now realized that something needed to be done about Mary, and urgently. But this was easier said than done. There was no standing army to call upon. The *gendarmes* that Northumberland had mobilized in the wake of his coup against Somerset had been stood down. There were the retainers that individual councillors could call upon, but most of these would have been going about their usual business in their own areas some distance from London. In the end, the council had to send messengers and a proclamation out into the streets of the capital to recruit men on the spot, with the promise of inflated rates of pay. Fortunately for him, Northumberland had, at least, taken the precaution of ensuring that arms and armour had been stockpiled in the Tower, so he was not short of weapons.

Aware now of Mary's opposition, the council suddenly seemed to see danger in the presence of the three Imperial ambassadors. If Mary was going to fight, then obviously she was going to need help, and this was most likely to come from Charles V. The ambassadors had allegedly come to enquire about Edward's health, but this, in itself, was suspicious, and why were they still here? It now seemed clear that their purpose was to help Mary, and maybe even spy out the land for an Imperial army to come to her assistance. Two councillors – Lord Cobham and Sir John Mason – were dispatched to get rid of them.

The council was correct in believing that Charles favoured his cousin to be the next queen, but wrong in fearing that he was going to do anything about it. In further instructions to the ambassadors on the 11th, he made it quite clear that he had his hands full with France and could not spare the men. Any action to secure the right result would have to be diplomatic, or by encouraging support for Mary within England. He urged his envoys to impress upon the council that he did not want to force a foreign husband upon Mary, or get her to change the country's religion.[24]

As the envoys had been trying to get an audience with the council ever since they had arrived, they were happy enough to receive the visit of Cobham and Mason on the 12th, even though these two had come to tell them to pack their bags. Nevertheless, they duly went through the spiel recommended by the emperor, and were gratified to note that the two councillors were so 'astonished and confused' that they were speechless and sat looking at each other not knowing what to say'.[25] The meeting ended with the promise that the message would be reported back to the full council, and that the ambassadors meanwhile could remain in the country.

The ambassadors had also gone through their set routine of complaining that France was trying to get involved so that it could install Henri's future daughter-in-law, the young Mary Queen of Scots, on the

English throne. Some historians have assumed that it was this that caused such consternation among the two councillors, but this is unlikely. Scheyfve had been trotting out this line for years – bad-mouthing France was an essential part of his brief - and it would certainly not have been the first time Mason and Cobham had heard it. The knowledge that Mary, with Charles's blessing, might be prepared to compromise on religion and marriage was, however, a genuine game-changer.

Since we have no evidence of what the council was discussing in private session, this meeting is all the more revealing. At some stage, councillors must have convinced themselves that Charles would attempt to force Mary's succession. Evidently, the French had been encouraging this belief for some time, and L'Aubespine's mission had presumably been to offer French help for this eventuality. But this offer had been declined, and besides equipping six ships, and sending some councillors to look at coastal defences, precious little had been done to forestall an Imperial invasion. Probably this was due to complacency, and the belief that Mary would just accept the situation, but her resistance had raised suspicions that the emperor might be behind it. The councillors' reaction to this new information that Mary would be prepared to leave things more or less as they were seems to have been one of intense relief, and it very possibly acted as a turning point in the affair.

What is even more interesting is what these two did with the information: they relayed it back to the council. This is noteworthy because Mason and Cobham had been instructed to tell the ambassadors to leave, and the easiest course of action would have been simply to fulfil this task. Instead, they urged them to stay. If they had been committed to Jane, then the very last thing they would have wanted was for the ambassadors to tell their colleagues of Charles's attitude, since that would serve to sway opinion and probably divide the council. It suggests that as early as the 12th, these two, and probably others, were already looking for a way to ditch Jane, and Northumberland.

The latter had further problems of his own, particularly a dilemma over who should lead the expedition to tackle Mary. Originally, it seems that Suffolk was nominated as commander, an unusual choice since he had virtually no military experience and was notoriously incompetent. The only thing in his favour was that he was loyal, and with his daughter back in London he would be less likely to go over to Mary. It seems that it was Jane who put her foot down and vetoed this suggestion, either because she was well aware of his failings, or because she wanted some sort of moral support from her father in her dealings with the council. Instead, the council nominated Northumberland.

This was an unfortunate, though possibly unavoidable decision. Northumberland undoubtedly had military experience, though not significantly more than others on the expedition – Huntingdon, Grey and Clinton, for example – and he had the necessary charisma, but he was also sorely needed in London. Dealing with Mary did not, at that stage, seem to require a high degree of military skill or knowledge – she appeared to have few supporters and no artillery – so he would not have been needed on that account. Furthermore, he acted as though he mistrusted other members of the council, and that if he was away from the capital he would be leaving himself, and his plan, wide open.

Stow relates the arguments put forward in favour of Northumberland – his experience, the fact that he had already won a victory in Norfolk and was therefore feared by the people there, and that he had good motivational and organisational skills.[26] All of these may have been true, but they counted for little in comparison with the need for him to hold the council together in London. It seems perfectly feasible, however, that certain in the council were pushing him into leadership simply to get him out of the way.

That he accepted the commission is perhaps another sign that he had lost his nerve, and his control over the situation. For a man who was used to bending the council to his will, he now seemed to be sheltering behind its decisions, and not wanting to be seen to be acting without its permission. It was madness for him to leave London at this moment, and he must have known it. Either the council, or Jane, must have insisted that he lead the expedition, or else he simply didn't trust another commander not to defect to Mary.

Meanwhile, Mary had moved from Kenninghall to Framlingham, a well-defended castle deep in the Suffolk countryside. Already, things were looking up for she had been joined by a number of nobles, among them the earls of Sussex, Bath and Oxford, Sir Edward Hastings and Lord Wentworth, together with their retainers, and many others from the local area which contained several of her estates. Although neither properly trained nor armed, the sheer numbers gave confidence to her, and dismay to those in the capital. The ambassadors reported that she had 15,000 men, which seems an exaggeration, or possibly a misprint, but it is quite possible that she had a tenth of that number. On the 12th, she felt sure enough of her position to demand that Norwich, the second largest city in the kingdom, proclaim her queen. With a short delay to get confirmation of Edward's death it obliged the following day.

On the 13th, Henry Dudley, Northumberland's son, was sent to France with a message for Henri II. It has never been clear what this contained, for by the time it was delivered it was too late. The Imperial ambassadors, who cannot have known, claimed that it was a request for French military aid in return for Calais being returned to France. This seems highly unlikely. At the time, Northumberland had superior forces to Mary and could have expected to win on his own. To have done it at the cost of Calais would have been so deeply unpopular that it would certainly have ensured the speedy end of his own ambitions. It is possible that he was asking for French help to *protect* Calais in the event of Charles exploiting the uncertain situation in England, and the constable of France did send a letter to the governor of Calais suggesting exactly this (to which he got an unsurprisingly undiplomatic reply). Otherwise, the rumour can be seen as just another attempt to blacken his reputation.

Northumberland's expedition left London on the 14th. The night before, he had a farewell dinner with fellow councillors, after which he made a speech calling on them to remain faithful to Jane, who, he reminded them, they had all put in this situation. So passionate was he in his calls for loyalty that it is perfectly clear he expected none. The scene has been built dramatically by later writers to be vaguely reminiscent of the Last Supper, except that this time there would be many to betray him. The earl of Arundel made a special point of assuring the duke of his loyalty, thus casting himself unequivocally in the role of Judas.

The behaviour of Henry Fitzalan, earl of Arundel, was suspicious throughout. One of Henry's original executors, he had been dismissed from the council in 1551 for his connections with Somerset's alleged plot against Northumberland, and had spent time in the Tower. Then, despite his known Catholicism, he had been mysteriously brought back onto the council to sign Edward's will. It is not clear why he should have agreed to this, nor why Northumberland should have recalled him, unless to add greater weight to his plans, and send out a message that religion was not the reason for excluding Mary. Quite possibly, Arundel had planted himself in the council for the purpose of later helping Mary, and he may even have been her secret informant. Certainly, his later career, in which he was involved in several of the plots against Elizabeth, including, ironically, promoting the claims of Jane's sister, Katherine, as a successor, reveals him as having a naturally treacherous character.

Henry Fitzalan, 12th earl of Arundel, unknown artist

Northumberland had good reason to see treachery, for that same day, and doubtless taking advantage of his absence, Cobham and Mason had arranged a meeting between certain, picked, councillors and the Imperial ambassadors at Baynard's Castle in the city, home to the earl of Pembroke. The earls of Shrewsbury, Pembroke, Bedford and Arundel, together with Petre, met to hear the envoys repeat Charles V's intentions regarding Mary, and also accusations that the French were trying to take advantage to install Mary Queen of Scots as the next monarch. The impact of this meeting would shortly become clear.

Despite the lack of time, and having other things on his mind, Northumberland had managed to put together a sizeable army to deal with Mary. Estimates vary, but it seems that on the morning of the 14th he may have taken with him as many as 1000 cavalry and 3000 footsoldiers. Many of these were trained, and some had experience – many of the Gentlemen Pensioners, roughly half of whom were in the force, had fought in Henry's war in France - and so would be more than a match for the local peasants who formed the bulk of Mary's supporters. Crucially, he also had the major advantage of nearly all the heavy artillery in the kingdom, which would be particularly useful in the event of a siege, and which had been so effective in dealing with the Norfolk peasants during Kett's rebellion in 1549. As he rode out of London, in a somewhat sombre mood, Northumberland noted the lack of enthusiasm from passers-by on the streets and remarked to Grey, 'the people press to see us, but not one says God speed us'.[27]

Unknown to him, fate had already turned against him. The previous night there had been a storm, and five of the ships that he had sent to patrol the coast to prevent Mary's escape had been driven into Orwell Haven. The sixth, the *Greyhound*, had sought shelter in Lowestoft. There is some confusion as to the exact sequence, and timing, of events – the most revealing testimony comes from the master and certain members of the crew of the *Greyhound*, but this is coloured by the fact that they gave their depositions during Mary's reign, and as part of litigation against the ship's captain, Gilbert Grice.[28] From what can be gathered, Grice, a personal appointee of Northumberland, was persuaded to go ashore, whereupon he was promptly arrested and delivered to Mary at Framlingham. The crew claimed that they were now solidly behind Mary, though they promptly began to ransack the captain's chest and share out the proceeds, so politics may not have been their only motivation.

The remainder of the fleet lay in Orwell Haven, where, coincidentally, Francis Jerningham, one of Mary's supporters, was at that moment in the area trying to recruit men for her cause. He met the captains, who had come ashore, and tried to persuade them to swap sides. He appears to have succeeded for they then rowed back to the ships and called on the sailors to join them, which they did, enthusiastically. Apparently, they were behind on pay, and were on the point of mutiny – a detail which Northumberland, as former lord admiral, should have taken care of. As well as the extra men - and the ships' crews may have included trained marines - there was the more significant matter of the guns and cannon on board. The duke now seemed to have lost his crucial advantage in artillery.

It is taken as fact that this was another of the turning points that defeated Northumberland, but its effect was probably more moral than practical. There is no evidence that the cannon ever were removed from the ships, and the logistical difficulties of unloading and transporting heavy ordnance, even if they did have the necessary equipment handy, would have involved time and effort, and it is unlikely they could have made it to Framlingham before Northumberland. Letters ordering the removal of the guns were only sent by the alternative privy council that Mary had established at Framlingham on the 16th,[29] so it is unlikely they could even have been taken off the ships before the 18th. Symbolically, however, it was a blow. He had taken the trouble to ensure that the captains were loyal to him, and their apparent betrayal must have hit hard.

It is not clear when Northumberland was made aware of the loss of his navy. Dates are confused, and the turning of the *Greyhound* was separate from the other ships, but we can suppose that by the 15th, the navy had effectively gone over to Mary. The news probably reached him while he was at Cambridge, and then a possible course of action would have been to not wait for his own ordnance to catch up – most of the cannon left London a day after him, and were far slower – but to race to Framlingham before Mary's guns had a chance to arrive.

But the councillors in London soon knew, and it further weakened their resolve – 'each man', in the words of a chronicler, 'then began to pluck in his horns'.[30] They were aware by now that lords in the counties of Oxfordshire, Buckinghamshire and Middlesex, far from Framlingham, had come out in favour of Mary, proclaiming her queen and sending men to help her. This double blow served to convince them that Jane's accession would not be easy, and that there was a strong risk of civil war. It also brought home the fact that they might very likely lose, and that their heads would shortly be on the block. In front of them, enticingly, was the letter from Mary offering them pardon if they admitted their errors and acknowledged her as queen, and the assurance from the ambassadors that Mary would not make changes to religion or the government.

Besides signing letters to her officials in the country, and appointing an ambassador to the imperial court – Richard Shelley, whom Charles refused to meet - it is not clear how Jane passed her time in the nine days that she was queen of England. At one stage she asked to see the crown jewels, and was able to select some for her personal use – embarrassingly, since Mary later did an inventory and claimed that some had gone missing – but other than that she appears to have left no impression. Guilford, on the other hand is reputed to have taken on airs, and sat at the head of the council table as if he really were king.[31] Perhaps the two were given belated coaching in the necessary skills needed to be monarch, but it is more probable that they were both simply helpless observers of the chaotic, and increasingly dispiriting, events that were unfolding around them.

One curious anomaly, which is little remarked upon, is Jane's actual status as monarch. She had been proclaimed queen, but at 17 she was still a minor. The 'devise' had placed great emphasis on male heirs being unable to rule until they had reached 18, but no such stipulation was put on Jane, and, of course, there was no legal precedent regarding a queen. In practice, this was irrelevant, since Northumberland intended to make the decisions himself, and he generally acted as though he was in charge, but in theory perhaps Frances ought to have been established as 'governess', and perhaps even Guilford, who was 18, had more right to consider himself king.

Meanwhile, Northumberland, the man of action and instigator of the crisis, dithered. He reached Cambridge on the 15th, a good 40 miles from Framlingham, and then stayed three days, apparently doing nothing. Part of the reason was to await the arrival of the artillery, which he clearly saw as the key to the success of his expedition, but this delay simply gave Mary more time to gather her forces. He believed himself still short of men and ordnance, and wrote to the council for reinforcements, which he did not receive. His son, Robert, had apparently given up his pursuit of Mary, and was currently spending his time trying to raise men in the surrounding region, managing, at least, to secure the important port of King's Lynn for Jane.

After being joined by Lord Clinton with a sizeable force, probably at Newmarket, Northumberland made his way to Bury St Edmunds, some 20 miles closer to Framlingham, but remained there only a day, before retreating back to Cambridge in the evening of the 19th. By this time, his scouts could confirm that Mary had as many as 10,000 men, far more than he could boast, and these were being trained, and were well entrenched before the castle. His artillery was still lagging behind him, his men were beginning to get restless and starting to desert, and support from the council was drying up. It is said that, while at Bury, he had received orders from the council to return to Cambridge, but it is equally likely that he had just lost his nerve. The next day, after news came from London that the council had declared for Mary, he went to the marketplace and, with tears rolling down his face, threw his cap in the air and proclaimed her the new queen.

On the surface, Northumberland's behaviour throughout the campaign, if not through the whole crisis, seems lacklustre and uncommitted. Much has been made of his skill as a military commander, but, in truth, the only time he had actually *led* an army was against the peasants of Norfolk in 1549, and even then he was under the orders of the protector. Now, he was leader of the council, and carrying out a plot which he knew was unpopular, and illegal, and he seems to have got cold feet. Partly, he felt unconfident without artillery, and they were dragging him back, but also he didn't want to do anything without the instructions and endorsement of the council, which he evidently hoped to hide behind if things were to go wrong.

But the council was no longer behind him. Stow reports that as early as the 15th, Cheyne and the earl of Pembroke asked to leave the Tower to 'consult' in London, but were not allowed.[32] Although letters continued to go out to local authorities denouncing Mary's rebellion, and Ridley was instructed to give another sermon at Paul's Cross extolling Jane and vilifying Mary, it was clear that there were divisions. Suffolk, Northumberland's closest political ally, was clearly incapable of holding the council together, and Jane on the 16th felt obliged to have the gates of the Tower locked, to keep those inside in, and the keys handed to her.

That same evening the marquis of Winchester was reported to have slipped out of the Tower, and a party was sent out to find him and bring him back.

On the morning of the 19th, several of the councillors succeeded in leaving the Tower and, on the pretext of a meeting with the French ambassador, headed towards the earl of Pembroke's house. On the way, Shrewsbury and Mason met the lord mayor out riding, and asked him to round up secretly some of his aldermen and sheriffs and come within the hour to Baynard's Castle. Arundel, despite his previous protestations of loyalty to Northumberland, was a key figure in persuading those present to change allegiance and support Mary. The others needed little persuasion and, having made the decision, they proceeded to Cheapside, pushing with difficulty through the crowd, which had obviously heard rumours of what was afoot, to proclaim her, amid scenes of great rejoicing.

Arundel and Paget, the latter recently restored to the council, were dispatched to ride hell for leather to Framlingham, with a cringing letter from them all, to convince Mary of their loyalty – 'we, your most humble, faithful, and obedient subjects having always (God we take to witness) remained your highness true and humble subjects in our hearts…'.[33] Back in the Tower, Suffolk had learned of his colleagues' betrayal, and stood down the guard. He came into the room where Jane was eating dinner and tore down the canopy of state from above her. She is said to have expressed relief, and stated that she was happier with this news than that of her elevation less than a fortnight before. He then left the Tower, and abandoned his daughter to her fate. The rebellion was over. Mary had her inheritance at last.

6

Mary the Queen

In hindsight, after all the troubles of her youth and early middle-age, Mary's accession seems easy, and almost inevitable. Subsequently she, and later her sister, would effectively airbrush out the brief reign of Jane so that the succession of Henry VIII's eldest daughter would seem to follow naturally on from the tragically short rule of his son, to such an extent that for most people today Jane is a barely-remembered figure, with few being able to place her accurately on a timeline. The Tudor dynasty continued on its relentless path with barely a hiccup, and Mary is always known, with dubious accuracy, as the first reigning queen of England.

Yet, on the death of Edward, her closest supporters, among whom were her cousin Charles V and his ambassadors, wrote off her chances, telling her she had no hope, and advising her to lie low and wait for rescue – a modest enough option that Charles was unwilling in practice even to consider, believing it too risky. So how had she turned the situation around and overcome the odds?

The first reason is that the odds were probably in her favour all along; they simply needed unlocking. It became perfectly clear from the earliest days of Jane's rule that the majority of the population still believed that Mary was the rightful heir, and saw Jane as little more than an imposter foisted upon them. Many would have been aware of Henry VIII's will, confirmed by Parliament, putting her second in line to Edward, and few would have understood, or been convinced by, the arguments for her illegitimacy.

Mary was also genuinely popular. The country had rejoiced at her birth, followed her progress through childhood, and taken her to their hearts. Before the troubles began, Henry VIII had been an extraordinarily popular monarch, and his young family had been as attractive and iconic as royal families today. For years, it was taken for granted that she would be the next ruler, and she attracted considerable attention. Many sympathized with her over her parents' divorce, and her subsequent, harsh, treatment by her father, and they admired her courage and loyalty to her mother.

She also seems to have been personally likeable. It is always easy to forget this, given the errors and excesses later in her reign that earned her the soubriquet 'Bloody Mary', but much of this reputation was fostered by the Protestant writers under Elizabeth who created an image that has since been credulously followed. Reports of her character before this paint someone who was devout, generous, and loyal.

If we can look through the bias of the Catholic writers who came to her at Framlingham during those difficult days in July, it really does seem that many of those who arrived to help were inspired as much by love of her, rather than simply her constitutional right, and that she managed to engender an atmosphere among her followers which would have made them willing to lay down their lives for her. One anecdote tells that when her troops were lined up for inspection, there were so many that her horse shied and she had to review them on foot. It is said that she then spent three hours walking along the lines chatting to her men.[1]

Such devotion led to outrage over the inexplicable decision to deny her the throne. We have a few accounts of ordinary individuals – Gilbert Potter, for example – who were astonished and who openly protested, and those who flocked to her – not just retainers and bondsmen who were obliged to follow their lords, but also common people who went of their own volition - were clearly moved by a desire to put matters right. Several towns quickly declared for her – Norwich and Coventry, among others – while those which didn't were motivated as much by political calculation as by a genuine belief in whose claim was the most just.

Although London went for Jane - to the astonishment of the Imperial ambassadors who had been reporting for months the popularity of Mary and who now saw before them an apparent acceptance of the new regime – its loyalty was only skin deep. The capital was more tightly under the influence of the government, and the mayor and aldermen had sworn an oath to accept Jane. The rigid guild system meant that many others were obliged to follow, especially the apprentices who could, on occasion, form riotous mobs. Potter, for example, was denounced by his own master. Furthermore, the government had been posting proclamations against loose tongues, and public punishments in the pillory, and even the occasional hanging, were sufficient to cow the city into submission. London did not cheer the accession of Jane, and the atmosphere could best be described as one of sullen resentment. In contrast, the news of Mary's triumph was greeted with days of genuine celebration.

There is some debate over the extent to which religion played a part in events. On the surface, there seems to have been a very obvious, binary, choice. Mary was excluded by Edward because of her Catholic views, and therefore it might be expected that adherents of the new religion would flock to Jane, and the old to Mary. But this wasn't necessarily the case. Admittedly, those who came to her at Framlingham were mainly Catholic - the earl of Sussex was one notable exception, though his support may have been due more to Mary's forces having taken his son hostage - but the towns and cities elsewhere, most notably London, were not, and yet they needed little encouragement to proclaim her when the moment was right. Although the majority of Catholics saw Mary as their champion, many evangelicals did so too, and not for religious reasons.

Partly, this ambivalence was due to time: there was very little of it. Just ten days to work out what the issue was really about, and first impressions therefore counted higher. Mary, sensibly, did not use religion in her call to arms; she kept things simple and concentrated on the main issue: her right to the throne. Even the council, which did mention the fear of her bringing back the old religion, kept this as a secondary factor, and chose to concentrate on her legitimacy. Given more time, and if things had become bogged down in conflict, there may have been something akin to a war of religion in England, but this was clearly not the moment for it.

There is a fascinating personal account of what it was like to live through the uncertainty of this period, written by Richard Troughton, a bailiff from Rutland, who spent the days of Jane's reign wandering around the Stamford area allegedly trying to persuade people to support Mary, and declaring Northumberland 'the vilest traitor and villain that ever was'.[2] He had heard news of her proclamation in Bury and had decided that she was the legitimate choice. Most of those he met appeared to agree with him, though some were reluctant at first to commit themselves. Most significant was the reaction of Sir John Harington, a local landowner, who demonstrated his opinion by fetching a book of statutes and laying his finger on the page containing the Act of Succession. Throughout his account, religion is not mentioned. Troughton refused to join the forces that were being mustered to help Northumberland, and scratched his name off the list, taking a risk by doing this, and by telling the soldiers that they could go and drink 'horse piss'.[3] The account was written during the reign of Mary as a petition to the Privy Council against charges of having supported Jane, so it should therefore be viewed with some caution, but the fact that he did not ingratiate himself further by claiming to be a Catholic gives it slightly more credibility.

As well as this general belief in her right to rule, it must be acknowledged that Mary played her cards faultlessly. Not that, to be honest, she did an awful lot. Her justified suspicion of the council's invitation to visit the dying king caused her to escape in good time, and from then on it could be said that she held the initiative. It may have been impossible for her to leave the country, so her decision to stay and fight may have been forced upon her. However, once the decision was made she acted with resolve. The letters to her followers asking for support pre-dated those of the council denouncing her – some historians even believe that they were written in advance, ready for just such a situation - and so gave her an advantage, and her letter to the council was superbly worded, and well-timed. Nor should her courage and determination be doubted, and her move inland to Framlingham was a clear indication to all of her intention to stay and fight.

In a sense, the episode could be seen as a personal duel between herself and Northumberland; a game played for very high stakes. Both were aware of their likely fate if they were to lose, and it became a case of who would blink first. Mary was buoyed by her conviction that God was on her side, and that she was the rightful queen. Unfortunately for Northumberland, it seems that he may have believed it too.

As always, luck played a role. The timing of Edward's death – before he had a chance to secure parliamentary approval of Jane's succession -

was unfortunate. As was the storm which blew the ships into harbour and gave Mary the moral advantage of the guns. It cannot be said the whole scheme was doomed to failure, however, since if Mary had been put out of the way, either legally through Parliament, or in some more drastic manner, the population would have had little choice but to have accepted Jane. Yet there was a fundamental lack of belief in what the council was trying to achieve, particularly within itself. Throughout the whole affair, councillors behaved as though they were committing a crime, and this meant that when they were challenged their lack of self-confidence caused them to act irresolutely.

Northumberland's expedition was half-hearted. He didn't want to go, and he shouldn't have gone. He was the only one who could have held the council together, and he wasn't there to stiffen its resolve when opposition grew. In retrospect, there possibly needn't have been an expedition at all. The council could have waited in London, given time for Jane's regime to bed in, and then challenged Mary to move against it, which would have put her, strategically, in a more vulnerable position. But the council was not to know that Charles had no intention of helping, and was not confident of the level of support within the country. Once at the head of his troops, the fearless warrior, Northumberland, was dilatory, unwilling, and at the end simply surrendered without coming in sight of his target. By this stage, the feeling among those at the time, and later historians, was that right had triumphed, justice had prevailed, and that history had resumed its chartered course.

And this could be seen in the celebrations that greeted the council's capitulation. Three days of rejoicing, bonfires in the streets, church bells ringing, and councillors, who only hours before had been defending Queen Jane, throwing their caps in the air – Pembroke's, apparently, full of money - and leading the festivities. And then the race to Mary, to prostrate themselves on the ground before her, dagger pointed towards their breast, craving pardon for the wrong they had committed. And, in the majority of cases, receiving the forgiveness they desired. Though not for all.

Surrounded at Cambridge, the duke of Northumberland read the instruction from the council requiring his troops to put down their arms and freely disperse. Pointing to it, he argued that this must include him as well. Bemused, his captors freed him. When the earl of Arundel arrived the next morning, he found the duke booted and spurred and promptly re-arrested him. Although it appeared that Northumberland was on the point of a quick getaway, it seems extraordinary that he had not taken advantage of the hours of darkness. Perhaps the idea had not occurred to him, or perhaps he was still in the throes of the confusion and self-doubt which had so often afflicted him, and which seems to have been his constant companion in the days following Edward's death. He was escorted back to London, and into the Tower, advised by Arundel to remove his cap on approaching the city to avoid being recognized, and possibly lynched, by the angry crowds.

The stage was now set for Mary's triumphal entry into London. This was something she was very good at, for she was always aware of the power of her personal appearance and the almost god-like reverence in which the monarchy was held. So, no restrained and almost furtive coming to the Tower, as had been the case with Jane; this was to be a show of power and celebration. To build expectation, and allow time for the spectacle to be prepared, she did not enter the city until 3 August, a full fortnight after her victory. In the meantime, she moved slowly, via stays in Ipswich and Colchester, receiving greetings and adulation along the way.

Accompanied by her half-sister, Elizabeth, who may or may not have shared in the general happiness, she was met at the gates by the lord mayor and aldermen, who presented her with a sceptre of office. To the sounds of trumpets, and the deafening boom of cannon firing from the Tower, and the 'marvellous rejoicing'[4] of the tens of thousands of people lining the freshly-gravelled streets, she rode in procession through the city. According to one account there were reckoned to be up to 3,000 horsemen accompanying her.[5] The buildings had been bedecked in flags and tapestries, and here and there were signs bearing the motto *Vox populi, vox dei*, a sign that Mary was there by popular as well as divine right.

The French ambassador, Noailles, had already ridden 15 miles out of London in order to pay his respects to the new queen.[6] He was well aware that he was close to being *persona non grata* for his supposed links to Northumberland's coup, and he was anxious to rehabilitate himself. He came with the good wishes of Henri II, and, somewhat brazenly, offered his support to establish her authority. One wonders how much patience Mary had left with the streams of well-wishers who only a fortnight before had been part of the plot to deny her the crown, but he claimed that he was well received, and that he had kissed her hand, though Renard made a point of reporting that he was later absent from the procession.[7] The two envoys were at each other's throats, and with neither of their reports being wholly truthful it is often hard to work out the real story.

Once inside the Tower, the place where monarchs traditionally went to prepare for their coronation, she had other duties to perform. Within its walls were some who she viewed with favour; those who had fallen foul either of her father, or of Edward, and who she now declared free. These included the duke of Norfolk, premier peer in the realm, and a staunch Catholic; Stephen Gardiner, former bishop of Winchester, who had refused to accept the new Prayer Book; and Edward Courtenay, a young noble, with whom there had been a suggestion of an earlier romance. Also within the walls was the former queen, Jane. She was not to be freed, and history does not relate whether the two then met.

We have a pen portrait of Mary, admittedly written a year later, by the Venetian ambassador, Giacomo Soranzo.[8] He described her as 'of low stature, with a red and white complexion, and very thin; her eyes are white and large, and her hair reddish; her face is round, with a nose rather low and wide; and were not her age on the decline she might be called handsome rather than the contrary'. He went on to declare that she was not strong and that she suffered from headaches and heart palpitations, for which she was regularly blooded. His impressions of her were largely positive, however, and he mentioned that she would work regularly until after midnight, that she was merciful and generous, that she was intelligent and spoke Latin French and Spanish, and understood Italian.

He confirmed her devoutly religious character, but the impression he gives is far from that of an ascetic. On the contrary, she loved to play on the lute and spinet, in both of which she was proficient, and adored rich and sumptuous clothing. She also had a great liking for jewels and, in the opinion of the ambassador would doubtless have bought many more if she had had enough money. One guesses that, whatever their political or religious concerns, the ladies and gentlemen of the court would have breathed a sigh of relief at her accession;[9] out again could come the finery and ostentatious costume that had had to be shut away during the more austere reign of Edward.

And so, with the cheers of the people fading into the distance, Mary now turned to her most urgent task; that of taking control of the country and establishing her regime. Despite the adulation that had greeted her up to this point, she was by no means secure, and the events of the previous month had made it clear that the Tudor dynasty was there only so long as it enjoyed the support of the people. She could count on no help from within her family – only Elizabeth was still around (and Anne of Cleves, though she had withdrawn from public life, and had no interest in re-involving herself), and she was unlikely to be supportive. Other than that, she was surrounded by a coterie of powerful, ambitious men, vying to gain influence over her.

History has not been kind to Mary, at least not the History written by the English. In the broad sweep of time, her reign has traditionally been portrayed as an anomaly, a stunted thing, a mistake, and ultimately pointless. The wider story is one of the steady and inevitable progress of English (then British) nationalism, and its bed-fellow, Protestantism. A ruler who sought to turn the clock back to the old, outdated Catholicism, and, moreover, hand the kingdom to a foreigner, simply does not fit in with this narrative. And thus historians, though less so recent ones, have either tried to play down her achievements, or to characterize her reign as an unfortunate blip.

This, of course, was not the perception among people at the time. Mary was all too real to them, as was her programme of counter-reform. And, barring the misfortune, albeit largely predictable, of being unable to produce an heir, this programme could have been expected to take the country forward in a different direction entirely. In that case, it would have been the reign of Edward that was pointless. History is lived looking forwards, but interpreted looking backwards. To be understood, however, it has to be viewed from both directions.

Besides, Mary's reign was only an anomaly from a narrowly English perspective. In a European context it fitted in, both temporally and ideologically, with that revival of a dynamic, militant Catholicism that was the Counter-Reformation. And in much of Europe, that movement was successful, even up to the present day, and there it provides the mainstream narrative. The fact that it failed in England was not, as 'Whig' historians like to imply, inevitable or divinely-ordered, but simply due to Mary's barrenness and early death. This does not justify writing off her reign as unimportant.

Each of the Tudor reigns was characterised by a definite purpose, one that provides a key to understanding all their twists and turns. Both Henrys were concerned - obsessed almost - in establishing and guaranteeing the survival of their dynasty, while Edward's project was the introduction of the new religion. Elizabeth was concerned also with this, and with furthering the defence and international standing of the realm. Yet Mary, too, had a project. So easy did her victory over Northumberland appear that she could only conclude that God had given it her. And if He had, then He must have had a reason for putting her on the throne. That reason was obviously to lead her people away from the confusion and sin into which they had been unwittingly drawn, and back to the true faith. Her reign may have seemed an anomaly, but it was not without purpose.

Several problems presented themselves immediately: how to establish her legitimacy; who to select as her Privy Council; what to do with those who had joined the rebellion against her; how to rid herself, and the country, of the new religion; how to prevent France from trying to unseat her; how to cope with the perennial problem of royal expenditure; and - one which had not hitherto concerned her, but which her advisors were already falling over themselves to bring to her attention - who she should marry.

These problems were not exceptional; in fact, several were routine. But what was exceptional was Mary herself. Not only was she a lone woman among men, and no-one, least of all her, had much idea of how to deal with this, but she was completely inexperienced in political affairs. She had not expected to become queen, and had therefore received no training. For years she had been absent from court, and had had to rely on rumour for any idea of what was going on there. She had an agenda, of a sort, but almost no idea of how to go about achieving it. Her reign was going to be one long voyage of discovery.

The most pressing issue was the question of who she should choose to conduct the everyday task of governing. Once her Privy Council was formed, then it could help her with the other matters. She had no shortage of men to choose from. Almost all the previous council had already come to beg forgiveness and pledge themselves to serve her. These may have, technically, been traitors, but they were also men of experience in government, and Mary was aware that, if the transition was to run smoothly, she would have to make use of at least some of them. She also felt a debt of gratitude towards men of her own household, and those who had flocked to her at a time when things were still in the balance, and she couldn't bear not to reward them and have them around her. She had already formed a council of her own at Framlingham, and many from this body - men with no previous experience, such as Rochester, Englefield and Jerningham - also found their way onto her Privy Council.

While many of the principal councillors under Northumberland lost their jobs, some significant figures survived, notably the marquis of Winchester as high treasurer, and eleven others, including the earls of Bedford and Pembroke, and Petre, Mason and Cheyne. Paget and Arundel who had been on the board under Somerset, and who had come lately to Jane's council, were also retained. Five others, among them the duke of Norfolk and Gardiner, had served under Henry. All these men had been active members of previous governments, and so, despite the flurry of new entrants, Mary at least had a core of experience and competence at her disposal.

This may have resulted in a significantly larger council than usual - over 50, which caused Paget to drily remark that England 'was now governed by such a crowd that it was much more like a republic'[10] - though in practice this was not a major problem since many councillors did not attend meetings, and gradually a more manageable inner circle developed, as it had under Edward. Records of council meetings show that on only a few occasions were there as many as 25 councillors present – the same number as attend a modern British cabinet - and usually only half that number. What was potentially more of a problem was that, within this group, many councillors did not see eye to eye, and very quickly factions developed. The leading lights of these were quickly identified as Paget and Gardiner, previously allies and friends in the later days of King Henry – indeed, Paget owed his career and advancement to Gardiner – but now bitter rivals. Both men were devious, self-serving and hungry for power, but both were astute and able politicians and could be useful if handled properly.

They were also different in personality and outlook. Stephen Gardiner was more of an ideologue. As bishop of Winchester under Henry his favoured position seemed to be the reformed Catholicism of the king's later years. He was happy enough with the royal supremacy, and with the break with Rome, and so was hardly a die-hard conservative. Indeed, he had been able to accept some of the aspects of the new religion, but had baulked over the issue of the Prayer Book, and this had ensured his sacking, and his sojourn in the Tower. Once freed, he had a clear agenda to bring the country back to the old religion, and his new promotion to the position of lord chancellor gave him the opportunity. He was an ill-tempered and abrasive character – 'an outward monster' with 'a vengeful wit',[11] in the words of John Ponet, a not entirely disinterested observer

Stephen Gardiner, unknown artist

who had replaced Gardiner as bishop of Winchester under Edward and then been replaced by him under Mary - and was not a popular figure to lead her government.

William Paget was a more complex character. Dubbed a 'master of practices', he was the third of those shadowy, self-made, men who realized the opportunity for wielding power in the position of royal secretary under Henry. He followed in the footsteps of Wolsey and Cromwell, though was smart enough to avoid the fate of either. He was uncommitted on religious issues, which gave him the freedom to align himself wherever he chose, and he is generally regarded as being the brains behind Somerset's seizure of power. Closely linked to the protector, he fell foul of Northumberland, and spent time in the Tower on somewhat dubious charges of corruption. Restored to the council at the

William Paget, attributed to Jan Vermeyen

end of Jane's brief reign, he was, typically, the first to reach Mary and proclaim his allegiance to her. His expertise was in foreign policy, though his agile and tireless mind could be turned, equally successfully, to all aspects of government.

It has often been taken as read that the divisions in the council during Mary's reign were a bad thing, but this need not have been the case. A truly useful advisory body would have a variety of opinions, giving all sides to the question, and her council certainly contained these. But if this dynamic was to work, it required a decisive ruler to listen to both sides, accept the differences as positive, and come to a conclusion. This was Mary's weakness. Resolute enough once she had made up her mind, she was a ditherer in the making of it, and this made her appear weak and added to the impression that she was not really in control. Renard, the new Imperial ambassador, described her as 'easily-influenced, inexpert in worldly matters and a novice all round',[12] and this seems, at least at the start, to have been pretty much the case.

One area where Mary, being a woman, was at a major disadvantage, compared with her father and previous monarchs, was in her more distant relationship with that shadowy fixture of Tudor government: the Privy Chamber. This was formed of those trusted friends who, at least under Henry, had been allowed intimate contact with the royal person, to the extent of seeing and helping him rise and dress in the morning, and then surrounding him throughout the day, both at work and leisure. These men held official positions and grand titles – great chamberlain, comptroller of the household, master of the king's horse, etc. - and some of these carried automatic entry into the Privy Council – the grand master of the household was also lord president of the council, the device by which Northumberland had gained control of both the council and the Privy Chamber. As such, the chamber held a semi-official, and vital, advisory role for the monarch, and its access to information, and to the king's person, as well as its special loyalty, made it a significant arm of government.

Its significance, however, cannot be explained by the notional positions and titles of its incumbents, but by that very intimacy that it allowed. The position of monarch was, *ipso facto*, a lonely one. The Privy Council was largely made up of politicians who were loyal only so far as the king was able to control them, but the chamber contained his personal *friends*, those who he could trust, and as such it was an important link with the council, and a means of controlling it.

During the minority of Edward, the chamber had occupied an even more significant role. The king's vice chamberlain, Sir John Gates, had acted as the unofficial conduit between the king and Northumberland, and the organization had formed something of a protective shield – some might argue, prison wall - around the royal person, preventing access from those it distrusted, and ensuring that the duke always enjoyed the royal favour.

Mary, however, could not benefit from the same advantages that the chamber had bestowed on her predecessors. Obviously, those most intimate to her were women, and they, however loyal and helpful (and some, such as Susan Clarentius, were both) simply did not have the same degree of access to information and political influence. The official Privy Chamber still existed – men such as Rochester and Jerningham, both Framlingham loyalists, were part of it - but at one remove from the monarch, denying her much of the support that closer intimacy would have encouraged.

One effect that this distance between her and her government had in the early days was to cause her to pay less heed to the council and to seek advice elsewhere, among her Framlingham faithful and, arguably worse, the Imperial ambassador. Simon Renard appears almost immediately to have become one of her most important and trusted confidants, and one councillor, the ever-watchful Paget, recognizing this, understood that here was a possible route to gaining Mary's favour. This carried the soon-to-be-realized risk of England falling further than it might have wished into the Habsburg orbit. Not that it is always easy to gauge the extent of this. Renard was tireless in his efforts to keep his master, the Emperor Charles, informed of the situation in England, and as his voluminous and detailed despatches survive, it is easy, as a historian, to fall into the trap of putting too much emphasis on his role, which, naturally enough, he took pains to emphasise.

Renard's reports are admirably detailed, but they cannot all be taken at face value. Apart from the issues of their accuracy, there is also the matter of their intent. Renard, like those, equally assiduous, Imperial ambassadors before him, wrote both what he thought the emperor wanted to hear, and what he thought the emperor *should* want to hear. Much of the latter was also concerned with stressing the importance and skill of Renard, himself. In the case of the early part of Mary's reign, one can easily come away with the impression that he was her closest advisor, and that it was he, rather than the council, on whom she relied. Nevertheless, the course of events indicates that he must have played this role with skill, and with considerable success, since Mary was to become heavily influenced both by him and his master.

Perhaps she could have done worse. Charles was a hugely-experienced ruler of an extensive and unwieldy empire that stretched over much of Europe, and even as far as South and Central America. He had had to deal with different languages, cultures, religions and political systems, and somehow, generally hanging on by his fingertips, he had steered a course that had kept his dominion largely intact. His treatment of Mary had revealed his intuition and empathy, being closely-involved but always respectful. He had an acute understanding of English affairs, often superior even to that of his own ambassadors, and he shared Mary's desire to bring back the old religion. Yet, despite all this, he had an agenda, and it wasn't an English one.

While Mary dithered, and councillors and ambassadors jockeyed for her favour, the country held its breath. No-one knew what to expect. Would there be a blood-letting of all those who had opposed her? Would there be a rapid change of religion? Who would she marry? What would life under England's 'first' queen be like?

The first crisis point, surprisingly, concerned Edward. In all the excitement of the previous weeks, no-one had yet seen fit to bury him. His body still lay at Greenwich, apparently forgotten. Putting him in the ground was easy enough, but the problem arose over what sort of service he should have. He, of course, had been deeply committed to the new religion, and so it was expected that he should be laid to rest according to its rites. But the new queen did not share his views. Could she allow his soul to remain filled with sin, or should she insist on him receiving the proper sacrament which would ensure his admission to heaven? Her decision on this point might send important clues as to her intentions for everyone's religious future.

The ambassadors were aware of the problem, and of Mary's wish to have a Catholic service. They wrote to Charles, urging him to dissuade her, and also to Mary herself, emphasizing how sensitive a matter this was – 'so important and thorny'[13] - and pointing out that Charles had already informed the council that she would not tamper with the country's religion. If she were to insist, this would get her reign off to a bad start, and she must remember that there were still supporters of Northumberland at large. Edward's soul was damned in any case, so what difference would it make?

But Mary was adamant, and it took more persuasion to finally reach an agreement by which the council organized the funeral, in which Edward would be buried according to the Protestant rites, while Mary heard a Mass for his soul in the Tower chapel. It was a compromise, but not much of one. Mary's absence from the funeral defied protocol, and appeared a clear snub, and it sent an obvious signal that no matter how undecided she seemed to be over matters of state, there were some things on which she was not prepared to give ground.

On 8 August, over a month after his death, Edward was finally laid to rest in the burial place of kings in Westminster Abbey. He was at least afforded the dignity of a state funeral, and Thomas Cranmer, still archbishop of Canterbury, performed the service. The crowds who lined the streets were genuinely moved. He had been a young man of real promise, who had shown every indication of becoming a great king. The absence of Mary was a worrying sign.

The next pressing item on the new queen's agenda was what to do with those who had plotted to deprive her of her inheritance. Charles, ever-aware of the need to allay fears, instructed his ambassadors to advise Mary to punish only those most responsible, and those who might give trouble later, but to show mercy to most. However vague this advice, they declined to pass it on, allegedly because they were confident in 'her great goodness and natural clemency', but actually because they were busy promoting a general bloodbath that would include Jane and Guilford, and the Princess Elizabeth for good measure.[14] Mary, however, had no intention of proceeding this far, recognising that Jane was just a cipher, and that, while she agreed with Renard's opinion of Elizabeth that she was 'clever and sly', it would be enough just to send her away.

But over one person, at least, there was to be no disagreement. Northumberland could never be allowed to escape, and so, on 18 August, he was led from the Tower to Westminster Hall to be tried for high treason. Along with him, came his close ally, William Parr, earl of Northampton, and his son John, earl of Warwick. This was a public, and much-publicised, trial and no expense had been spared to give it the solemnity and distinction it deserved. A great stage had been erected, with tapestries and hangings, under which sat the duke of Norfolk, who had spent the years of Edward's reign imprisoned in the Tower, and several of the Privy Council who, the previous month, had been seated with Northumberland around the table plotting Mary's own fate. This should have given him some inkling of the likely result.

Not that he could have been in much doubt, anyway. He wouldn't have forgotten the last major trial in the same location, when he had helped arraign Somerset on a similar charge. He would also have been well versed in the format of Tudor treason trials, in which lawyers were not present, at least not for the defence, and in which the purpose was pretty much limited to publicly announcing the sentence. We don't have a record of the precise charge; high treason was the only recorded accusation, almost as if this didn't require further explanation.

Northumberland began with an interesting line of defence which, if lawyers had been present, might have engaged the judges for rather longer than the minutes it otherwise took them to reach their, pre-ordained, verdict. First, he questioned whether someone acting under the royal seal, and the instruction of the monarch, as he had been careful always to do, both when plotting to disinherit Mary, and when taking up arms against her, could be considered guilty of high treason. Secondly, he wondered whether those who had shared in his alleged treason had any right to be sitting in judgement over him.

Norfolk had evidently been expecting these questions, for his reply was brusque and uncompromising. The royal seal, he argued, was not that of a usurper, but of the rightful queen, so Northumberland's actions could not have been lawful. As for the right of those sitting on the bench to try him, anybody who was not under an act of attainder had the right to be a judge if the monarch permitted it.

While the second answer was stretching things a bit, the first was more justifiable. Although Northumberland, ever-mindful of his father's fate, had taken care to ensure that he was always protected by royal authority, even to the extent of fatally delaying his march against Mary by waiting for council instructions, this was no use to him now. The very justification for Mary being the current queen was that she was the rightful successor to Edward, and so her reign must have begun immediately after the late king's death. Therefore, Jane's warrant held no validity. This argument was now official, and in Privy Council records the period of Jane's rule was referred to merely as 'the late time of the rebellion'.[15]

But there is some confusion over which seal Northumberland was referring to. In the records of the trial, the exact definition of the accusation is not explained. If Northumberland was being tried for taking up arms against Mary, then the seal referred to must be that of Jane, and therefore invalid. If, however, the crime was that of trying to alter the succession, then Northumberland was acting under the seal of Edward, in which case his defence was more robust. Either Norfolk misunderstood the distinction, or (more likely) he deliberately ignored it. Either way, Northumberland decided not to pursue the point.

Aware now that he had failed to dent the confidence of the judges, and it is unlikely that he ever really expected to, Northumberland immediately switched to 'Plan B'; to admit everything and fall on Mary's mercy – an unlikely option, but just about the only one remaining to him. To have argued further would only have annoyed her, and since she seemed to be sparing others in the council, there was just the slimmest chance that he might escape as well.

Not from the judges, though. Once the admission of guilt had been made, their job was done, and, as per the script, they promptly sentenced him to be hanged. Following the normal ritual, he was allowed to make requests, asking Norfolk to intercede with Mary for a pardon; for the nobleman's death of beheading; for mercy for his sons; for a priest to be made available to clear his conscience (doubtless a lengthy process); and, more interestingly, for four councillors to be sent to him so he could inform them of 'such matters as shall be expedient for her and the common weal'.[16]

Then it was the turn of his co-accused. William Parr blustered that he had been away from court, hunting, while the plot against Mary was unfolding. Unfortunately for him, he was well known to be a close confidant of Northumberland, and his signature was there on letters from the council during the rebellion. Warwick's line of defence was his tender years, but this, likewise, cut no ice. Both were sentenced to the same fate, and were returned to the Tower, the dreaded axe turned backwards to signify to the waiting crowds the anticipated result. The next day, Sir John Gates, Andrew Dudley - Northumberland's brother - and Sir Thomas Palmer were also condemned. Only the latter showed any sign of resistance, taking on the judges by claiming, untruthfully, that he had not taken up arms against her.

Among all the others who could potentially have been executed, Palmer seemed a curious choice. He held no high office, and was no more prominent in the rebellion than others who were to escape death. One possible explanation is his involvement in the fate of Somerset. It was his, concocted, evidence which had been crucial in establishing the former protector's plot against Northumberland, a version of events that several of those still on the council had been happy to go along with. Now, those councillors wanted that issue closed, and their involvement forgotten. Palmer's death would achieve both those ends.

This was not, however, the end of the story. The verdicts were a formality that had to be gone through to establish guilt, and to justify Mary's position. Whether the sentences would actually be carried out was the prerogative of the queen.

So now it was the turn of the ladies, those whom Charles warned his ambassadors about, who were only out to better themselves.[17] The duchesses were first, using their personal contacts with Mary to argue and achieve pardon for the earl of Warwick and the other two Dudleys (Andrew and John), and then, more dubiously, the duke of Suffolk, who somehow, despite having been one of Northumberland's main backers, and who in the words of one contemporary chronicler, 'no man judgeth he can live',[18] escaped even a trial. William Parr was also released. So it was that the original seven were whittled down to just three, which rather belies her reputation as 'bloody' Mary; Henry would doubtless have kept the headsman much busier.

On 21 August, a large crowd assembled at Tower Hill, at the very spot where, 18 months before, many of them had come to see the duke of Somerset suffer the same fate. However, they were to be disappointed. An announcement was made that there was to be no execution that day; Northumberland had just announced that he wished to hear Mass.

This was, to say the least, a bombshell. Northumberland was one of the main instigators of the Reformation in England, a movement that had seen enormous changes, not only in beliefs, but also society. Now he was announcing that it was all a sham, that he had been 'seduced these 16 years past by the false and erroneous preaching of the new preachers',[19] and that he was really a Catholic after all. Nor was he alone. His fellow conspirators – Andrew Dudley, Gates and Palmer – also announced that they were ready to join him. The four of them then made their way to the chapel of St Peter ad Vincula in the Tower in order to take the sacrament. This was, of course, a terrific propaganda triumph for Mary, and she was to make the most of it, ensuring that this 'conversion' was witnessed by a hastily-assembled group of city merchants and other notables, and known to all.

The word 'enigmatic' is a lazy one when applied to people, since in reality all humans are by their very nature changeable and unpredictable, but Northumberland has certainly made it difficult for historians to understand him. There are various theories as to what was behind this remarkable *volte face*. Quite possibly, his Anglicanism was only ever skin deep. We can be fairly sure that he was not particularly devout, and that the religious changes were done more for political reasons, such as enriching the country from Church lands, and getting more power for himself by removing it from the bishops. He had previously shown that he knew little about religion and could not take part in religious debates.[20] He had 'relapsed' already into Catholicism in 1550 during the coup against Somerset when it looked as though his life was in danger, so it is likely he saw religion as simply a means to an end.

His principal motivation at this present time seems to have been to try to save his life. He may have used his conversations with those councillors who visited him in the Tower – Gardiner and Arundel – to persuade them to intercede with Mary, and his conversion could well be seen as a similar tactic. There are suggestions that he had been told his life would be spared if he did this,[21] and that would explain the even more surprising fact of the others joining him in his conversion. Cooper, in his chronicle, asserted that this was, indeed, the case, and that Gates and Palmer, having then realized that this was not going to work, died as Protestants.[22] At any rate, it evidently failed, as the same evening he was informed by the lieutenant of the Tower that he would die the next day. He spent some of his remaining hours writing a grovelling note to Arundel begging for Mary to spare him – 'a living dog is better than a dead lion'[23] – which suggests that simple human weakness was the likeliest explanation.

How he must have rued his whole involvement in the plot. It had failed completely, Mary was on the throne, the religious experiment seemed doomed to fail, and he was headed for the scaffold. If his motive had been ambition, then he could not even console himself with the thought that he had given it a proper go. If he had simply been concerned with his own safety, then he must have been doubly regretful. Mary, it seemed, was not such a vengeful woman after all. If he had accepted her accession in the first place, he would, almost certainly, have lost his pre-eminent position, but possibly the worst fate that would have awaited him would be a comfortable retirement on one of his many estates.

Jane was one of those who was disgusted at this turnaround. She blamed Northumberland for her present predicament, which she was all too aware could soon result in her own death. He had assured her that her becoming queen would guarantee the continuation of the evangelical Reformation, and now he was cynically betraying it to try and save his own life – something she would never consider doing. 'Like as his life was wicked and full of dissimulation', she is reported as saying, 'so was his end thereafter'.[24]

The next morning, he seemed to have recovered his composure, and as he, Gates and Palmer made their way to the scaffold they were almost cheerful. He and Gates had a brief, and somewhat untimely, discussion on who was at fault for their current predicament – each blaming the other, but then offering forgiveness - but once on the scaffold Northumberland, while alleging that he had been pushed into the conspiracy, declined to name names.

He then launched into his final speech, one which, in the printed form in which it was widely distributed, was so self-condemnatory, and so much what Mary wanted to hear, that there have to be suspicions about its authenticity. We have no details of how these things were managed – whether those condemned wrote their last speeches beforehand, or, far less likely, there was a scribe at the execution taking down every word – so we cannot judge on their accuracy, but it seems perfectly feasible that the final version was heavily massaged.

It was another age, and attitudes to dying and the promise of the hereafter, were, presumably, very different, but it is hard to feel anything other than admiration for the brave and stoical way that so many of these victims met their end. Although beheading was probably the quickest and least painful way of meeting one's death - 'though somewhat sharp',[25] as the priest had helpfully informed them shortly before - nevertheless it was hardly a moment to look forward to. The coolness of these three men, as they went through the prescribed rituals, with death only moments away, is humbling. Palmer, the third to die, is reported to have thrown his cap into the crowd, and wished them all good morning, adding that he fully expected to have a good morning, and a good evening as well, almost as if he were performing a stand-up routine.[26]

Some of the descriptions of Northumberland's behaviour on the scaffold indicate, from his long-winded speech, and the time he took fussing around with his clothes, that he was expecting any moment to hear news of a reprieve. If so, he was to be disappointed. He, like the others, was dispatched with a single stroke. He couldn't really have expected to be pardoned, nor could Mary have spared him. That would have confirmed all the judgements about the weakness of women and their unsuitability to rule. As it was, she was as merciful as she reasonably could be, and few were likely to mourn the deaths of these three.

Northumberland had not done his reputation any favours, either, what with his last-minute conversion and his begging letter to Arundel. One of the most powerful and telling narratives of English history is the triumph of Protestantism, which allegedly dragged the country out of the superstitions of the Middle Ages and into the modern world. Any figure who obstructed this 'inevitable' march must needs be evil or misguided, which partly explains the subsequent dire reputations of both Mary and

Northumberland. If the latter had gone to his grave still faithful to the new religion, he would doubtless have found a more comfortable space in Foxe's famous 'book of martyrs'. As it was, the 'bad' duke was the image that has survived.

Which is a shame, because he doesn't wholly deserve it. He had proved an efficient and effective ruler, stabilizing the currency, improving the economic situation, bringing about an extraordinary change in religion with very little opposition, and ensuring peace and stable relations with England's neighbours. On the debit side, he had been greedy for power, ruthless in his disposal of Somerset, and, above all, he had sought to alter the natural succession in his favour. This last has, until recently, always overshadowed any of the good that he did.

So much of the surviving historical sources about Northumberland portray the negative image, and so enduring is this interpretation, that it feels almost wilfully perverse to question it. But so many things about him are unclear. Was it really him who was behind the whole scheme to disinherit Mary, or was it Edward's idea and he was just the loyal servant – 'the faithful servant who shall become a perpetual ass',[27] in his own words - faithfully carrying out his master's orders? Certainly, he appeared an enthusiastic supporter of the plan, and it is fair to say that it would never have come to fruition without his backing.

Suspicions that he was aiming for the ultimate goal, and that his real intention was to make himself king were aired at the time, and have been repeated since. They are simply a smear, and it is doubtful that he ever seriously considered it. The idea that he could hold on to the throne, even if he somehow managed to take it in the first place, hardly merits consideration.

Those usurpers who had managed to seize the throne – Edward IV, Richard III, Henry VII (even Jane Grey), to name but a few – all had royal blood and some, however tenuous, link to the ruling family; Northumberland had none. He was a *nouveau-riche*, and the idea that the established nobility would ever have tolerated him occupying that position is unthinkable. And he would have known it. Besides, there was little motive. The situation he would have found himself in if the plot had been successful – a position of control over the government, and over the

Crown - was little different from the one he already occupied: a position arguably stronger than the monarch's anyway.

Strype's verdict was that he had simply 'grown too big for a subject',[28] and perhaps it was this that caused his downfall. Accustomed to the trappings of power, he could not bear to see these taken away, and his support for the plot was to a large extent a matter of maintaining his pre-eminent position. Ambition is a motive that most observers and historians have accused him of, and although by then he had probably reached as far as he wished to go, he doubtless had no immediate desire to step back and give it all up.

Yet there is a fascinating letter, written by him to Cecil early in January 1553, in which he paints a very different picture of himself.[29] It comes from a time when he was away from court for a long period with 'extreme sickness' and was clearly being badgered to return. The tone is world-weary and resigned. He talks of his 'long travail and troublesome life' during which, while others were out enjoying themselves, he 'went to bed with a careful heart and a weary body; and yet abroad no man scarcely had any good opinion of me'. 'What should I wish any longer this life, that seeth such frailty in it?'. We can either read this, as Tytler does, as 'an accomplished piece of hypocrisy', or perhaps see a window into a more complex and sympathetic soul. Less than six months later, however, he was plotting to change the succession to his undoubted advantage, and give himself yet more of the labour and unpopularity that he was so bemoaning. Perhaps, to misquote a proverb, having found himself on the tiger's back, it was just too difficult to get off.

But now he was gone, and Mary could look forward. The first few months had been spent mopping up the detritus from the revolt against her. The main plotters had been executed, the old council had been disbanded, and Edward had been buried. Some loose ends were still waiting to be tied up – the fate of Jane and her husband had yet to be decided – but new administrators had been appointed to a council of her own choosing, and it was now time to move on. For Mary had a job to do: to bring the country back to the old religion, and then move it forward along a righteous path. This was not going to be easy.

7

Establishing the New Regime

Paul's Cross stood in a patch of open ground within the precincts of the great cathedral. In front of the cross was a pulpit where it was the tradition for a sermon, or sermons, to be preached every Sunday. This had been the site of the rabble-rousing discourse by the firebrand bishop, Nicholas Ridley, on 9 July, in which he had called Mary a bastard, a theme he had repeated the following week. On this day, Sunday 13 August, there was a very different feel. Gilbert Bourne, archdeacon of St Paul's, not only offered up a prayer for the dead, forbidden under the New Prayer Book, but also launched into a speech decrying the punishment under the Edwardian regime of the highly-unpopular, and recently re-established, bishop of London, Edward Bonner.

At this, some in the crowd became restless and began shouting 'Pull him, pull him', meaning that Bourne should be removed, and complaining that Bonner had 'preached abomination'.[1] Tempers flared, and some began climbing the pulpit to physically remove the preacher. In the confusion, someone threw a dagger at Bourne, which struck the pulpit and rebounded back. The situation was saved, surprisingly perhaps, by two evangelical priests standing nearby - Bradford, who climbed into the pulpit and began calming the crowd, and Rogers, who somehow managed to hustle the preacher away to the safety of the nearby school.

Mary was understandably displeased when news of the incident was brought to her. She gave orders via the Privy Council to the London authorities to instruct householders to keep their 'children, apprentices and other servants in such order and awe',[2] and threatened that if they could not guarantee to keep the peace then they should hand over their powers to her. The next Sunday, on her instruction, the pulpit was surrounded by 200 guards armed with halberds, as well as several senior councillors and members of the City livery companies. This time, the sermon, delivered by a Dr. Watson, chaplain to Gardiner, went ahead without protest.

The incident was a salutary reminder that, no matter what her inclinations in terms of religion, she would have to move cautiously. This advice had already been recommended to her by Charles, and, for a time, she seemed to take it. Yet she was not inclined to do nothing. At the start of August, following her entry into London, she had released Gardiner and re-appointed him bishop of Winchester, and had then done the same for Bonner and Tunstal, allowing them to take over their former positions as bishops of London and Durham respectively. Other bishops who had been removed during Edward's reign were also re-installed in their sees.

Although these re-appointments were a telling sign for what was to come, they did not, initially, impinge upon the lives and beliefs of most of the people. Mary could argue that these men had been unfairly dismissed, simply because of their beliefs, and that they could now return to the places they had been rightfully put by Henry VIII, before the child king, heavily influenced by misguided councillors, had removed them. On this basis, she did not yet remove Archbishop Cranmer, an appointee of Henry's, even though she must have been dying to do so.

On 8 August, she tempered these changes with a well-timed and well-phrased proclamation on religion. In this, she expressed the hope that, over time, everyone would return to the religion which she held so dear, but that, until such time as Parliament might decide otherwise, everyone would be free to follow their own conscience in matters of faith. And to calm high spirits, there should be no calling of names like 'heretic' or 'papist', and unlicensed writing or preaching on matters of religion, which could inflame feelings, would be forbidden.

This pronouncement would doubtless have come as a considerable relief to many, though it was more subtle than it first appeared. It implied that the Edwardian laws against non-attendance at church would not, for the time being, be enforced; that Cranmer's prayer book would no longer be compulsory; that Catholics could begin to worship in their own way without fear of arrest; and that, through censorship, the government could control what religious messages were being put out. Under the guise of religious toleration, it actually began the English counter-reformation, and sugared the pill by announcing that when this happened, it would be done not by royal diktat, but legally, by Parliament.

In terms of her own personal beliefs, Mary wanted to put the clock back much further than many of her fellow Catholics. She wanted to return to the era before the break with Rome, when the Pope was still head of the English Church, and England was following an unreformed Catholic agenda. But this was easier said than done. Some changes, like abolishing the evangelical doctrines and services, and even restoring the primacy of the pope, could, at least in theory, be done by Parliament. They would lead to opposition, undoubtedly, but Mary always had the belief, not wholly unfounded, that the majority of the people would not object. Other issues, such as the re-establishment of the monasteries, would be nigh-on impossible.

To encourage the process, the pope, evidently keeping a keen eye on events in England, immediately appointed Cardinal Pole, an old friend of Mary's who had been exiled by Henry, as papal legate, with instructions to return to England and begin bringing that country back into the fold. Pole was keen to set off straight away, but alarm bells rang with Charles V, who, among other concerns, realized that Pole would be a divisive figure who would stir up opposition by pushing for immediate changes. He advised Mary against allowing him back so soon, and then used every means at his disposal to delay and impede his journey.

Apart from expelling some of the more radical foreign, Protestant, preachers, who had been equally a thorn in the side to Somerset and Northumberland, and whose loss was mourned by few, Mary showed that she was prepared to wait, at least until she could shelter behind the authority of Parliament. Then she could use its power to legally remove all the doctrinal changes made during the time of Edward. She had her bishops back, and now it was time to move against Cranmer.

Mary had a special, and very personal, loathing for Cranmer. Not only did she hold him responsible for the Reformation, and, by implication, the persecution she had been subjected to throughout Edward's reign, but he was also the man who had approved Henry's divorce from her mother, and who had declared her, repeatedly, a bastard. The fact that he had been reluctant to join in the plot to exclude her counted for nothing; he had ruined her life, and her mother's, and had brought the entire nation into sin. Since her accession, she had refused to meet him, and had ignored all the pleas he had sent through others. Revenge would be sweet.

On 13 September, the council sent Hugh Latimer, an evangelical preacher, to the Tower for 'seditious demeanour',[3] presumably for continuing to preach the new religion, and the following day it was Cranmer's turn to appear. After a long discussion, he was committed for treason and sedition. Mary and the council, due to a fortunate accident, were then able to add the charge of heresy, which gave even more justification for imprisoning him. This was due to a letter Cranmer had written in which he quashed widely-circulating, and damaging, rumours that he had said Mass. The letter had found its way to others who had had it published and widely distributed. Its denial of the Mass gave Mary the perfect opportunity to keep Cranmer behind bars. She did not yet, however, have a reason to deprive him of his title, which he was to keep, though no longer to use. Now she could begin the process of wearing him down, and getting a recantation of his faith.

Thomas Cranmer, unknown artist

Although privately denying her position as head of the Church, Mary was not shy about issuing instructions in her name for how religious changes should proceed. On 15 August, an order went out to London aldermen for the restitution of goods removed from churches during the Reformation. This began the public process of turning the clock back. Gradually, altars began to re-appear in place of the Protestant communion tables, and vestments and church plate, handed back by those who had hidden them either for safe-keeping, or who had purloined them and now feared discovery. Feast days were re-instated, and singing and the Mass were heard again at St Paul's and several other London churches, not, as the chronicler, Wriothesley, avowed, 'by commandment but of the people's devotion'.[4] Although the Venetian envoy, Soranzo, claimed that the majority disliked the return to Catholicism,[5] protest tended to be individual – the records of the Privy Council show isolated cases of priests giving inappropriate sermons, or people criticizing the changes, or, in one case, a man shaving a dog to look like a priest.[6]

Low-level persecution of Protestant priests was now stepped up. Those who had married were given the option to divorce their wives, or lose their benefices, a stark choice for those who were already poor. Not all acted with the initiative of one parish priest who resolved these problems by selling his wife to the local butcher.[7] In fact, such was the shortage of trained priests that many are reputed to have found employment elsewhere, presumably with 'housekeepers', rather than wives, attached.

Those who kept quiet and made the required changes had to deal with their consciences, but some could not. The reports of the Privy Council from this time are full of those who were arrested, pilloried or jailed for 'lewd' and 'seditious' words. One such was Thomas Montaigne, who had the twin misfortune of not only refusing to change his views, even after a personal confrontation with Bishop Gardiner, but having served with Northumberland's army against the queen.[8] He was committed to the Marshalsea prison, without trial, where he remained in isolation, denied food donated to the 'non-heretic' prisoners, refusing to recant, and refusing even to accept an offer of release from a representative of Wyatt during the latter's rebellion. Later, he was sent, via a short stay in the Tower, to Cambridge Castle, where he managed to talk the over-enthusiastic keeper out of hanging and burning him the next day. Altogether, he was three years in prison before fleeing to the continent. Perhaps the most surprising aspect of his tale is the number of times he was offered his release if he would only recant: the desire of the authorities seemed less to punish than to achieve the propaganda victory of redeeming lost souls.

Another case with a more tragic outcome concerned the justice of common pleas, James Hales, noted for having been almost the only judge who had refused to sign Edward's 'devise' on legal grounds. Again, following the letter, rather than the spirit, of the law, he had ruled in a court case against a Catholic who denied Mary's supremacy. Gardiner, furious, had him imprisoned, and subjected him to pressure to convert. Hales had refused and tried, unsuccessfully, to kill himself with a knife. By now severely unbalanced, he had agreed to conversion, was released, and achieved his aim by drowning himself in a stream so shallow that he had had to force his head down into the water.[9]

The sensitivity of the authorities towards religion could also be seen in the case of Edward Underhill. By his own admission a 'hot gospeller' – a devout Protestant – Underhill was a well-connected squire from Warwickshire, who was summoned before the council, even before Mary had arrived in London, for having written a ballad, the contents of which were undisclosed, but were obviously critical of 'papists'.[10] Despite having served in the army of Henry VIII as one of his bodyguard of Gentlemen Pensioners, he was snubbed by councillors, one of whom he had served alongside in France and whom he had tended to when sick, and another whose son he had saved from drowning. He was summarily sent to Newgate prison, and only released after a month when, having contracted an illness, it seemed he might die. Underhill was loyal enough towards the new sovereign to rise from his sickbed to see her pass through London to her coronation – so gaunt and emaciated that even close acquaintances failed to recognize him – and later to volunteer to defend her against the army of Thomas Wyatt. Furthermore, he had not joined the rest of the Gentlemen Pensioners who had formed part of Northumberland's army against her. It is unlikely Mary had any knowledge of his ordeal, but that someone of his standing could suffer such treatment is clear evidence of a much wider persecution.

While the campaign to restore Catholicism, a process which would gather momentum after successfully gaining the support of Parliament, was being ramped up, Mary had further unfinished business to attend to. Two people still posed a threat: Jane, and Mary's own half-sister, Elizabeth. Jane would be the easier to deal with since the people's lack of interest in her had already been demonstrated by their failure to come to her aid during her brief reign. Few felt any loyalty towards her – 'a queen of new and pretty invention'[11] as she was contemptuously referred – but her mere existence created an alternative if the people should become disenchanted. Although not directly naming her, Charles and Renard had been heavily implying that she should be executed, and the latter had even quoted a story from the classics to illustrate the point.[12]

However, Mary resisted. Whether out of a genuine merciful temperament, or the pleading of Jane's mother - her old friend, Frances - whose skill at persuasion had already been demonstrated by her ability to have her husband freed without so much as a trial, or the understanding that the beheading of a 17-year-old girl, who everyone knew was a mere puppet of Northumberland's, would not look good and would do nothing to enhance her reputation, we cannot be sure. Probably a bit of all of these. For the time being, Jane remained in the Tower, but was kept apart from the judicial circus involving Northumberland and his allies.

Nevertheless, something had to be done, and seen to be done, and in the event Mary chose the best and most effective option. Jane would be publicly tried, found guilty – an inevitable outcome – sentenced, and then, instead of an immediate pardon, remain in the Tower at the queen's pleasure, with the sentence of death hanging over her, in case she, or anyone else, should attempt anything in her name. In effect, she would be a hostage – far more useful than if she were executed – and it meant that whoever tried to rebel would have Jane's blood on *their* hands. Perhaps, at some later stage, she could even have been freed. The solution would have been perfect if Mary had not underestimated the reckless stupidity of Jane's father.

The trial of Jane and Guilford was set for 11 November, and went according to plan. Neither offered a defence to the charge, though Guilford might have wondered what on earth he had done to deserve his fate, and both behaved quietly, and bravely. Jane must have felt momentary disquiet at the passing of the sentence of death by burning, as was habitual for a woman, but she could be confident that this would be altered to beheading – some slim consolation. They were returned to the Tower, where they passed the next few months separately within its confines, albeit in some degree of comfort. The Tower, although a prison and a place inspiring terror, was also the site of the mint, the royal menagerie, and various government offices. Accommodation for prisoners was dependent on various factors, and could range from the dank dungeon of popular tales, to quite comfortable quarters, attended by personal servants. The two ex-royals were in the latter category, so were allowed a certain amount of freedom within the walls, and probably had as agreeable a time as was possible within the obvious limitations.

The other problem was more complicated: Elizabeth. She and Mary had always had an uneasy relationship, due mainly to the fact that she was the daughter of Anne Boleyn, the woman who had usurped Mary's mother and brought such suffering to the lives of both. As far as Mary was concerned, Elizabeth was damned by birth, and later by her choice of religion. As Mary had moved closer to the centre of power, so had her half-sister, and now she was within clutching distance of the throne. There was something unsettling in Elizabeth's character; the ability to dissimulate, to wait and not commit herself - from one point of view essential survival tactics, from another sly and untrustworthy behaviour.

She had dutifully celebrated Mary's accession, and played the part required of her at the triumphal entry into London, and would do likewise at the coronation. Like Mary, she had taken the opportunity to be seen, and to be seen as princess of England, bringing with her a large and impressive retinue. She had professed loyalty, and had written to congratulate the new queen, but this had not impressed everybody. In mid-August, Renard had warned Mary about Elizabeth's presence at court, describing her as 'clever and sly'.[13] Mary told him that she had the same opinion and would send her away. In truth, Mary had little hard evidence that her half-sister was plotting anything - Elizabeth had taken no part in Northumberland's conspiracy, which affected her as much as Mary - but if there was a threat to her rule, this was its most likely source, and subsequent events would suggest that she was more than partly justified in her fears.

By this time, rumours were swirling around the court over marriage prospects for the two spinsters. A young nobleman, Edward Courtenay, son of the deceased earl of Surrey, had spent the whole of Edward's reign cooped up in the Tower for crimes committed by his father. He was rumoured to be an old flame of Mary's, and on his release it was hoped by some that this past friendship would lead to something more permanent. As a handsome and dashing young man, he quickly became a popular figure. The only impediments, apart from the rather important fact that Mary was clearly no longer interested in him, was his tendency towards dissolute and immature behaviour, and his dubious commitment to Catholicism.

Given the queen's lack of interest, rumours then began to spread about the possibility of a match between Courtenay and Elizabeth. This could have created an evangelical dream team, and consequently a nightmare for Mary. The combination of the younger couple, capable of producing an heir, was a perfect alternative to the older queen, both for dynastic and religious reasons, and was an obvious focus for any opposition to her rule. Renard noted this possibility with apprehension, and worried that Elizabeth was 'greatly to be feared for she has a power of enchantment'.[14]

Some of Elizabeth's deviousness, or cleverness, could be seen at the beginning of September when she wrote to Mary informing her that she wished to convert to Catholicism, and asking the queen to send her the necessary trappings to enable her to hear Mass. This may have fooled Mary, but not Renard, who, suspecting trickery, kept a close eye on the situation. A fortnight later he reported that the princess had failed to attend Mass the previous week, and seemed to be backtracking on her resolution. Mary then accosted her, and while Elizabeth swore that her conversion was true, she was 'very timid and that she trembled when she spoke'.[15] This cut no ice with the ambassador, who interpreted the trembling as deceit, rather than submissiveness.

Renard's reports during these early weeks, and his conversations with Mary, were full of suspected plots and threats to her rule, and reading them presents a picture of a country teetering on the edge of revolt. It is hard to know how much this was due to the hysteria that he was often wont to show, and how much he was trying to make the situation sound worse to encourage Mary to take action against any possibility of trouble.

He also, of course, wanted to raise the temperature for the attention of Charles, both to justify his own worth, and to get the emperor to intervene more actively in English affairs, particularly in respect of a project very close to his heart: Mary's future husband.

Another, more immediate, concern, or opportunity, was the forthcoming session of Parliament, already called by Edward for October, which would provide the chance to get legal backing for her regime. This much she could feel confident about, but the other items on her agenda, namely the religious changes she had in mind, might be more of a problem. There was also the matter of her coronation, and the sooner that was done the more established she might feel, and the easier it would be to forget the reign of Jane. There was a problem, however. She was still officially illegitimate, and would remain so until she could convince Parliament to declare her otherwise, so should she delay her coronation until she was legally entitled to take the throne?

There were arguments on both sides. Renard reported that some people – Gardiner, for example - were urging her to wait, arguing that the coronation would be a farce if it was not legally watertight, though he, Renard, believed that if she met Parliament as queen she would carry more authority for the tasks that needed to be done.[16] Not for the last time, Mary took the side of the ambassador against the head of her own government, and her enthronement was scheduled for 1 October, four days before the proposed date for the opening of Parliament.

Putting on a show was something that Mary excelled at, and she didn't disappoint this time. No expense was spared, and for two weeks Londoners were engaged in preparations. The streets were freshly gravelled, pageants were prepared at all the major landmarks – the Chepe, Cornhill, Leadenhall, Fenchurch, St Paul's, and more – flags and hangings set up along the processional route, grandstands built for members of the City guilds, and the statues and conduits freshly painted. On 27 September, she moved from St James's Palace to Whitehall, and then by barge to the Tower, followed by a procession of boats carrying the aldermen of the city, decked with streamers, and with minstrels playing, and cannon firing a salute from the Tower.

At 2 o'clock on the afternoon of 30 September, she rode back through the city to Whitehall in a carriage covered with cloth of gold, followed in another by Elizabeth and Anne of Cleves – the two next senior ladies in the kingdom. Behind them came a mighty cavalcade of bishops, knights, lords, councillors, aldermen, and all the great and good. At each stop on her progress, the future queen was entertained by pageants, including one at Gracechurch in which a model angel set up high appeared to blow a trumpet, the sound coming from a well-hidden trumpeter 'to the marvelling of many ignorant persons'.[17] Conduits flowed with wine. Several of the pageants were performed by children, which Mary seemed particularly to enjoy.

The most spectacular was reserved for a daredevil – Peter, a Dutchman - who stood at the absolute top of the steeple of St Paul's, his feet upon the weathercock, and waved a flag as the queen came past, and then balanced on one leg on the vane while shaking the other, a feat for which he was deservedly, and handsomely, rewarded by the City authorities.

Superficially, the celebrations seemed a model of good organization and efficiency, yet actually they were anything but. English royal coronations were not supposed to be some randomly-devised ceremony, cobbled together at the whims of the new monarch; they were carefully-prescribed rituals, used for hundreds of years past, with rule-books (the *Liber Regalis*) governing all the details. The monarch's sojourn in the Tower, his procession through London, and the timings of his coronation were not accidental; they were laid down in protocol. Even down to exactly what he should wear, which symbols of office he should hold, and which words were to be used in the service. This was what the waiting crowds were used to, and what they expected to see and hear.

The problem was that Mary was a queen, and a queen regnant to boot. The rule books prescribed precisely the rituals for a king, and for a queen, but never before for a queen who was a king. Mary and her household literally had to make things up on the hoof. The indications are that several of the issues were not very well dealt with. The procession through London was traditionally marked with pageants, comparing the monarch with flattering instances from biblical or classical history, for example Mary as Judith, the slayer of Holofernes – an obvious reference to her victory over Northumberland. Contemporary reports indicate that those pageants prepared by the immigrant community far outshone those of native Londoners, an issue that may well have been down to confusion and embarrassment as to how to approach this unprecedented situation.

Most interesting of all, however, was the debate over what she wore. This should have been obvious enough, especially since several of the chroniclers and ambassadors claim to have been eye-witnesses. Curiously, most of these do not mention her dress at all – a surprising omission that either might be because it was exactly what they expected, and therefore hardly worthy of comment, or because they were discomfited by what they saw. An official court record has it that she was dressed in the traditional garb of queens – white cloth of gold, with a magnificent be-jewelled headdress (the latter detail remarked on by several of the eye-witnesses). But later historians, especially those writing at the time of Elizabeth, disagree, and claim that she was wearing a gown of blue velvet, the traditional colour of *kings*. The fact that this later evolved to a *purple* gown (the colour of emperors) shows the significance of such iconography, and the implication that, in the eyes of some, Mary had not quite got it right, and that she had begun her reign on the wrong foot. More fairly, it was an indication of how much she was treading new ground, and how potentially fragile her position could be due to her gender.[18]

For the coronation itself, there was some recent precedent for change in that the service had been altered for the young Edward, who had not been deemed strong enough to hold the heavy symbols of state, nor even to last the full length of the traditional service. Mary was crowned queen of England not by the archbishop of Canterbury, who was currently in the Tower, but by Stephen Gardiner, but the ceremonies, at least, were conducted according to the old rituals, with certain modifications having to be made for the fact that she was not a king – for example a special crown had been made for her, and she held two sceptres, one for a king and the other for a queen. She was anointed with holy oil that had been secretly sent from the Low Countries through the Imperial embassy, since she didn't trust the quality of the English oil (presumably because it had been subjected to six years of Protestantism). She had also been given special dispensation from the Vatican to allow the title of supreme head of the Church to be pronounced, an issue over which she had been plagued by worry. She emerged, officially, though not universally, acknowledged as England's first ruling queen.

Four days later, on 5 October, after hearing Mass in Westminster Abbey, she formally opened Parliament. As the writs had been sent out under Edward, she had had no time for much engineering of who should attend, and so it was to some extent a Northumberland-inspired collection of Commons with which she was faced. With the Lords, it was different as she had already made changes, both ecclesiastic and lay, and with the presence of her extended and, hopefully loyal, council, she could hope for less opposition. Otherwise, no-one really knew what to expect. Charles and the ambassadors advised her to proceed carefully, and not to bring in too many changes at once.

Although largely retrogressive, her programme for the November sitting was one of the most radical yet seen. She was basically intending to turn the clock back to at least 1533 – the date of her parent's divorce - deep into the reign of her father, in order not only to legally secure her own position, but also the status of the Church for which she had far-reaching plans. Even on the first day there was controversy, when two of the remaining Protestant bishops withdrew rather than take part in the religious service, though this can hardly have been a disappointment to her. Following this, both houses assembled to hear Gardiner read out the government's plans.

Religion obviously topped the list, and the lord chancellor made no secret of his intention to restore Catholicism to the country. Next came plans to improve the financial state of the realm. Rather strangely, Gardiner had been in charge of working on the government's financial proposals, while Paget, who was never terribly concerned with matters of faith, had dealt with the religious measures. Whether this was a deliberate plan by Mary, or others on the council, to steer the chancellor, who was even less patient than the queen, away from more extreme proposals, is not known. There may have been some sighs of relief from the Lords in particular, many of whom feared that the religious measures would include the confiscation of the monastic lands they had recently acquired from the Crown.

Overall, she seems to have been largely successful. Since records of speeches and discussions within Parliament were not then made, it is hard to gauge the strength of support or opposition, so we have to go by the decisions finally reached. On 28 October, a bill recognizing the legality of Henry's marriage to Katherine of Aragon, was passed, which therefore legitimized Mary. The bill did not affect Elizabeth's illegitimacy, so effectively she was killing two birds with one stone by weakening any chance her half-sister might have of unseating her.

In terms of her religious programme, the most significant measure was a bill revoking all of the nine religious acts passed during the time of Edward. No longer would priests be allowed to marry, Cranmer's new Prayer Book was removed, and the sacraments regained their place within the service. After five days of debate - an unusual length of time, which suggests some strong opposition - the bill was passed by an estimated 350 votes to 80 in the Commons.[19] This was an important start. Equally contentious, and requiring several days of debate, was a bill repealing all the treasons acts since 1352. This would ensure that no-one could be prosecuted for disputing the royal supremacy, and many members rightly saw it as a first step towards restoring papal rule over the English Church. This was as far as she dared go for the time being: it did, at least, re-open the question as to who was head of the Church. With these amendments under her belt, Mary now felt she had the authority to proceed.

But not everything had gone her way. Although Parliament was happy enough to pass a bill against those who tried to disrupt church services, aimed clearly against the more extreme Protestants, it threw out one which made attendance at church compulsory – interesting, since it had been happy enough to pass the Act of Uniformity insisting on just this for Anglican Church services some 18 months earlier. It also refused to pass an act re-establishing the full extent of the bishopric of Durham, which Northumberland had been in the process of dismantling. These setbacks, although relatively minor, were a warning that Parliament's acquiescence to her planned changes could not be taken for granted. Mary would still have to tread carefully.

For now, she could turn her attention to other, more mundane though no less important, issues. Among these was the economy, which was still in a fragile state, despite having been put on a firmer footing by Northumberland. Mary had the good sense to keep in place two men who had helped bring back financial stability under the previous regime, namely the marquis of Winchester as lord treasurer, and Gresham, the agent in Antwerp. On 4 September, she issued a proclamation stabilizing the value of certain gold and silver coins, and remitting that part of the subsidy, granted in March, that had not yet been collected. This may have been costly, but it earned her instant popularity throughout the country, and provoked a 'marvellous noise of rejoicing'[20] in Cheapside when the news was read out. In the same proclamation she vowed to pay off all Edward's debts, attributing them, unjustly, to Northumberland's failures – repeating the charge that he had previously laid at Somerset's door, and continuing a tradition that has since stood the test of time. This news slightly tempered the announcement three days earlier of a forced loan of £20,000 that she demanded from the citizens of London.

Another issue that Mary had to keep an eye on, and one which had implications for the security of her regime, and for the country, was England's international situation. The two major European powers – France and the Empire – continued at war with each other, which gave Mary some breathing space, but it could hardly be denied that her accession had the potential to alter the balance within the continent. Henry VIII had flitted between the two powers, but had essentially followed a non-aligned policy, made more secure by a treaty of friendship with Charles V that allowed him to make occasional forays against France and Scotland. Somerset had continued this course, but Northumberland had adopted a more restrained approach in which he tried for good relations with both, successfully batting away Charles's attempts to involve him in the conflict, and even offering, unsuccessfully, to mediate between the two warring parties to bring peace. During the crisis over the succession, he had appeared to move closer to France, but had refused their offers of active help. The accession of Mary, cousin to Charles V, now seemed to put England more firmly within the Habsburg orbit.

Renard had been quick off the mark in making himself invaluable to the new queen. Whereas, a few weeks before, the Imperial envoys had watched in frustration the comings and goings of French diplomats who seemed to have a privileged access to the council, now the boot was on the other foot and it was Noailles who was out in the cold. Nor had things begun well. While Renard appeared to enjoy the privilege of private meetings with Mary, Noailles had been ignored. According to Renard, he had not been present at Mary's triumphal entry into London, and may then have had - though we have only Renard's, highly dubious, word for it - the embarrassment of being turned away from an audience with the new queen because the letters of credence with which he had been furnished were addressed not to Mary but to Jane.[21]

More serious for Noailles than personal embarrassment was the real danger that France would now be surrounded by hostile powers. Although there was a recently-signed treaty of friendship with England, this might count for little if Charles was to use his influence with Mary. Admittedly, France had Scotland on its side to restrain English ambitions, but how much longer could the Scots remain independent if the Empire gave military backing for an English invasion of its northern neighbour? And given France's believed support for Jane, Noailles might even become *persona non grata* at the English court, or at best have his influence severely reduced. How the tables had turned.

However, at the end of July, things seemed to take a turn for the better. Formal letters did arrive from Henri, and Noailles was able to present them and kiss Mary's hand. For a short time, relations seemed to improve. The constable's offer to 'protect' Calais from Charles had been seen by the commander of the garrison as an attempt to take it over, and he had rebuffed it in fairly blunt language. This might have caused a diplomatic incident, but Noailles was relieved to hear, during a dinner with Gardiner and Paget, that the English had not taken offence and had laughed off the incident, claiming difficulties with translation.[22] The councillors appeared to warmly welcome him, and affirmed that they wanted peace with France, and had no intention of favouring Charles over Henri.

Yet this would prove a mere lull, for there was a greater danger approaching, one that was to cause severe difficulties for English-French relations, and oblige Noailles to exceed his diplomatic remit and even resort to plotting against the English government. It would also involve the Princess Elizabeth in suspected treason, and nearly result in the overthrow of Mary herself. For, in October 1553, the question of the queen's marriage began to come to a head.

8

The Wooing of Mary

Whereas the first half of 1553 was dominated by the matter of the king's health, the second was equally in thrall to the issue of the queen's marriage. So important was this question that it was to colour the whole of her reign, and lead to widescale popular resentment, major political turmoil including splits within the council, the intervention of Parliament, the threat of war from France, and a rebellion which nearly toppled her regime. What might, today, seem like a largely personal matter, and one little affecting the future of the realm, was nothing of the sort in Tudor England. There, it carried the utmost importance. For what was being chosen was not so much a husband; it was the next king.

And there was precedent. When Jane became queen, the French ambassador had referred less to her than to 'King' Guilford, as did some Spanish diplomats, although Scheyfve and Renard, it must be said, could hardly bring themselves to refer to either of them. Guilford, it is reported, was even treated, and viewed himself, as king, despite the refusal of Jane to allow him the honour, taking a seat at the head of the council table and having himself referred to as 'Your Excellency'.[1]

Exactly how much governing this king should do had not yet been worked out - there was no real precedent for that – but, legally, a husband had control over his wife's possessions and affairs. Mary was certainly the queen in name, and could be regarded as head of state, but who would actually make the important decisions? Her husband would doubtless expect to be crowned king, and be referred to as such, and, as Mary was a 'weak woman' (etc.), it must be presumed that his influence and direction would be considerable.

For foreign powers this matter was equally important. In fact, possibly more significant even than Mary becoming queen. Henri might have no-one suitable from his own family, but if he could ensure that the husband would be an Englishman, or at least someone of neutral persuasion, that might cancel out the disaster of Mary's accession. Likewise, Renard saw marriage to an English candidate as problematical, while a Habsburg, or allied Catholic prince, would strengthen the Imperial hold over England. Given the fact that such matters were not just for diplomacy, but also the queen's heart, the situation was ripe for intrigue, and worse.

The matter of Mary's marrying was also a legal issue, for it had been laid down in Henry's will that she must have the approval of the Privy Council in her choice of partner. Mary had shown precious little interest in marrying anyone, and the council had made only sporadic attempts to have her wed. In 1550 there had been brief interest from the son of the king of Portugal, and from the duke of Brandenburg, but these had come to nothing. The matter was not seen as a priority, since there seemed little chance of Mary succeeding to the throne, and relations between her and the council soon broke down over the issue of the Mass. However, once she had come to power, the council automatically became involved, both from the point of view of fulfilling Henry's will, and in effectively selecting its next boss. The only person who did not seem interested at all in the issue was Mary herself, but that could change.

*

As early as April 1553, three months *before* Mary's accession, Scheyfve had reported a rumour that the council might be considering marrying her to Philip of Spain, son of Charles V.[2] This comment can be seen as little more than idle gossip, and it was included in a list of speculative unions that included Edward being married to a daughter of Charles's brother, Ferdinand. Scheyfve made nothing further of it at the time. He was accustomed to transmit every piece of tittle-tattle that he picked up around court – as, indeed, he had been instructed to do – and it is possible that he saw little significance in it. Philip was a widower, and therefore back on the market, and a prime catch irrespective of his religion. More important was the future of Edward, who was approaching marriageable age and who was also highly eligible. However, it is equally possible that the envoy was planting a seed in his master's mind and, in view of the precarious nature of Edward's health, saw in Mary a possible diplomatic tie linking England more closely with the Empire. Scheyfve, and Renard after him, and equally Noailles, did not see themselves simply as observers reporting events, but as active players in the game.

In late June, when there had seemed to be a suggestion of a conspiracy to deprive Mary of her throne, Charles V had instructed his ambassadors to make it clear to the council that he would be happy to see her marry an Englishman, thereby attempting to neutralize some of the worries that he would foist a Catholic Habsburg on the country. This seemed at least to sway Mason and Petre, who came to see Scheyfve during the succession crisis, and may have had a similar effect on other councillors.

But this was not, of course, what Charles really wanted, as he himself made clear in his instructions of 23 June, hoping that once Mary had become queen, and things had calmed down, we may 'arrive at a better solution'.[3] However, he was not prepared to wait very long, for on 22 July, just three days after Mary had been proclaimed queen in London, he wrote urging her to choose a husband, so that she could be assisted 'in matters that are not of ladies' capacity'[4] – which meant, presumably, ruling a country. That same day, Renard informed Charles that there were rumours that Mary might marry Courtenay.[5]

This young, inexperienced, noble was clearly of no use to Charles; he had a better candidate in mind. His own son, Philip, heir to many of his huge dominions, was clearly ripe for a second marriage. At the end of July, he wrote to him, delicately pointing out that as he, Charles, had previously been betrothed to Mary there was a chance that he might be asked again. He, however, had no wish to take on another country so he might suggest Philip as a candidate. Although there was currently the possibility of Philip marrying the Portuguese *infanta*, if this came to nothing, perhaps Philip might consider Mary instead.[6]

At the same time, Mary assured Renard, who she had asked to come secretly at night through the oratory entrance to meet her, that, although 'as a private individual she would never have desired it, but preferred to end her days in chastity', she would be guided by Charles.[7] She had correctly assumed that his message to the council that he would support an English candidate was merely a ruse to get her on the throne, and so she would accept whoever he chose.

This statement clearly reveals that Mary had not understood the gravity of the matter, and it is a key to why she persisted with what would turn out to be an unhappy and potentially disastrous course. To many in English ruling circles, and to many of her subjects, this was one of the most important decisions she would have to make. This was the choice of England's next king, and the line of inheritance thereafter. To insouciantly abdicate responsibility for the decision to the head of a foreign power suggested that she had neither fully grasped the issue, nor gauged the mood of her people.

Indeed, this very issue caused fault lines to emerge within the council. Gardiner and Paget were split over this far more than they were over any other matter, including religion. Although Gardiner strongly wished to bring England back to Catholic beliefs, Paget, not being particularly concerned with questions of faith, was more relaxed, but in terms of the marriage, both were at loggerheads. Despite his Catholicism, which would seem to encourage a less narrowly nationalistic outlook, Gardiner saw the need for an Englishman to occupy the throne, while Paget, a specialist in foreign affairs, saw the benefits to England's international position in having closer links to the Empire.

Not that Paget was an entirely disinterested observer. He had quickly understood that the Imperial embassy was as much a centre of power in the new regime as the council, and he wasted no time in allying himself with Renard, who he knew was trusted by Mary. This enabled him to quickly win the ear of the sovereign, with whom he often seems to have enjoyed a more positive relationship than Gardiner, despite the latter's religious affiliations. Although Gardiner occupied the most prestigious position of lord chancellor, he was not to win this particular argument.

Partly this was because he lacked a suitable candidate. Choosing a wife for a monarch from within the realm was easy enough, but selecting a male who could be king was far harder. For a start, he would have to be from the nobility, and he would have to have the confidence of his peers. Given the febrile atmosphere of the Tudor court, in which plotting, scheming and backstabbing were everyday activities, these two, apparently straightforward, criteria ruled out just about everyone. The only name that Gardiner could come up with was Courtenay, who he had befriended in the Tower, and who enjoyed a third quality which was that, having spent the previous six years in prison, nobody knew much about him, and therefore nobody had a particular reason, yet, to dislike him.

At the beginning of August, Renard reported that Paget had told him, apropos of nothing, that a marriage with Philip would be 'the finest match in the world'.[8] Renard pretended that he had never considered the idea. Charles, through his minister Granvelle, was insisting that the suggestion should first come from Mary before he chipped in with his advice, but he nevertheless instructed his envoy to mention Philip if the subject came up, and not to dissuade her too vehemently from Courtenay in case she ended up marrying him.[9] At any rate, the queen at the moment did not seem particularly interested in marriage to anyone, and laughed several times when Renard mentioned it. Shortly after, however, she seemed to have reconsidered, and admitted that perhaps she should marry for the good of the country. She asked that Charles start proceedings with the Council 'as it did not behove a lady to be the first to make overtures of marriage'.[10]

Although all these conversations were supposed to be secret, Noailles had already guessed what was going on, for at the start of August he had informed Henri that Charles's ambassadors were proposing Philip.[11] He had been given this information by a helpful noble at court, and at this stage neither he nor Henri, who in his reply made no mention of it, seem to have taken it particularly seriously. However, the following month, he had firmer information to impart, not only what the Imperial ambassadors were up to behind the scenes, but also garbled details of a marriage agreement, told, or sold, to him by Sir John Leigh, a courtier who was to become one of his most trusted informants. It would, he assured his master, result in 'a perpetual war with your majesty, the Scots and her own subjects'.[12]

Henri was fatally slow to react to such concerns. In his reply, he issued vague instructions to Noailles to let him know everything that was going on, and to 'do all that you can to break and disrupt these schemes', and then turned to matters more after his heart, namely the progress of his armies in the war against Charles.[13] Throughout the course of the marriage saga, he would consistently fail to give his ambassador clear instructions on how to behave. Any initiatives came from Noailles, who was hamstrung by lack of adequate backing from home, and this left the field open to Charles to carry on much as he pleased.

Perhaps there was not much more the French king could have done. He was already at war with the emperor, so there were few additional threats he could use, and if he went too far there was a danger of provoking Mary into joining Charles against him. His one possibility was to present an alternative candidate, but he seems to have focussed attention on Courtenay who, it quickly became clear, was entirely unsuitable, and useful only as a disruptive agent. For the moment, he could only sit and fume, and hope that Noailles might have some luck in stirring things up among the English.

Although late into the lists, Noailles suddenly became more energetic. On the three days following his warning to Henri, and without waiting for further instructions, he had a secret meeting – like Renard, through the garden gate at night – with a friend of Courtenay to try to get him to build up a following in Parliament to oppose the match, and then with Soranzo, the Venetian ambassador, who he seems to have made into an ally, and, on 9 September, a talk with Gardiner to spell out his concerns. The chancellor, however, despite his known support for Courtenay, did not seem willing to join with any French intrigues, though he did reassure the ambassador that Mary was much too sensible to provoke France into war against her.[14]

Later that month, Noailles tried to provoke some reaction at home by producing a rumour that Philip was going to pass through England shortly, and what would happen if 'they find themselves one evening in bed together…?'.[15] This unlikely scenario did not seem to cause much concern at Fontainebleau, so instead he turned his efforts on the English council, warning its members of the dangers of joining with the Habsburgs, and threatening that any such alliance would end the friendship between France and England. One result of this may have been the sudden proposal by Gardiner for England to negotiate a peace between Henri and Charles. This was not a random suggestion, for Wotton, the English ambassador in France, was also ordered to put forward the idea. Periodically, England had offered this service, and it was inevitably rejected by Henri, but the fact that it was revived at this moment suggests that the council was aware of, and concerned by,

French fears. However much England may have been moving into the Imperial orbit, the very last thing the government wanted was to antagonise France.

Interestingly, in view of later events, Noailles also reported rumours of a planned rising by the men of Kent, and a plan to murder Gardiner[16] – a plot also noted by Renard. The chancellor was said to be sufficiently alarmed to go about his business clothed in a chainmail shirt. Noailles also made efforts to blacken the reputation of the Spanish, which may have included distributing anti-Spanish propaganda throughout the city. He understood, with more evident concern than Henri, that Philip, as the successor to Charles of both Spain and the Low Countries, was a highly dangerous option since, with these territories, and England, France would be almost completely surrounded.

Aware of the activities of the French ambassador, though probably not their substance, Renard chose to use some scare tactics of his own. He had long been insinuating to Mary that Courtenay was being backed by the French, but he now raised the spectre that they might be trying to marry him to Elizabeth, as some of the rumours around court were suggesting. Doubtless he was hoping this might spur her on to take some action against them.[17] In fact, Noailles was showing remarkably little appetite for Courtenay, despite acknowledging that he was one of the favourite English candidates.

Not that either of them needed to worry. Courtenay had spent much of his youth imprisoned in the Tower, and now decided to make up for lost time. He was obviously not interested in Mary, although the prospect of the crown may have appealed, and he turned his attention, in the disapproving opinion of one French writer, to fallen women and easy and shameful pleasures.[18] Despite his elevation to earl of Devonshire, he preferred these low delights, and very soon gained a reputation which, despite his distant royal blood, was to make him unsuitable as a match for either woman.

If it had not been such a serious issue, this whole episode might have provided fine material for a farce. Paget, a free thinker, was behind Philip, a narrowly counter-reformation conservative, while Gardiner, a strong Catholic, backed Courtenay, who wasn't particularly concerned with religion at all. Neither Courtenay nor Philip had the least desire to marry

Mary, and she had no particular wish to marry anyone. Throughout the autumn and winter of 1553, all stuck doggedly to their positions – except perhaps for Mary who, although dreading the prospect of actually having marital relations, did start to feel that she should take a husband – slowly bringing the situation to a point which nearly resulted in the defeat of all of them. Renard's apparently prominent role in the proceedings might be down to the fact that he wrote the most about it, or due to his being the only one who seemed to have a clear and rational idea of what he was trying to achieve.

Given the lack of a realistic alternative, the field was now open for the promotion of Philip as the prospective partner. On 3 October, Renard took the unusual step of writing to him informing him of Mary's coronation, and also explaining the difficulties of finding a suitable partner for her.[19] He pointed out that the English preferred Courtenay, and that they wanted someone who knew the language, who wanted to live in the country and who was a suitable age for the queen. None of these requirements, obviously, applied to Philip. He also stressed that the English feared a foreigner who might 'draw money out of the kingdom and spend it elsewhere, or change their form of government and promulgate new laws; give office to foreigners and set them to govern the country, or draw the English into war, through the alliance, and set the land in confusion'. Despite the dismissive tone, this was clearly an attempt to pique Philip's interest, and to give him guarded advice on how he should proceed if ever he found himself in this situation.

If he was simply playing devil's advocate, he was not the only one. On 4 October, he was visited by Paget, who also dwelt on just these drawbacks. He informed Renard that the council was discussing the issue, and had whittled down a shortlist of Philip, Dom Luis of Portugal, and the duke of Savoy. Paget noted that the latter passed all of these tests, though the following day, when the two met again – Renard, as appeared to be his custom, entering secretly by the back door – Paget only mentioned Philip. He said that the council was surprised that Charles had said nothing on the matter, and urged him to send letters to named councillors, encouraging them to select a husband for Mary.[20]

Paget's subtle behaviour seems a clear indication that the council was seriously divided over the issue. Council records make no mention at all of the matter, and so we have, once again, to go by what subsequently happened in order to get an idea of what was going on around the table. Confusingly, behind the serious matter at hand, there was also a subtext. Coming so soon at the start of the reign, such an issue gave councillors a chance to establish positions and develop factions. To some, it was an excuse to clip the wings of the overmighty Gardiner, whose closeness to Mary in religious matters threatened to make him pre-eminent in the council. The significance of these discussions is that, according to the acts of succession, Mary could not marry at all without the approval of the council, a proviso intended to ensure that she did not go against the interests of the realm. What Henry had not envisaged was that the council should be so divided over the issue that it might even threaten the stability of the realm.

To be fair to him, Paget's motives were not solely to regain the position of power that he had lost under Northumberland, but also a genuine desire to better England's international situation. He had considerable diplomatic experience, and had already been lead negotiator in two agreements with France. These meetings had inspired a deep-rooted dislike for that country, but, biased though he may have been, he was one of the few in government who had a realistic understanding of European affairs and of England's place within them. However, it is not clear at this stage how many of the council were aware of what he was doing, and whether he was really representing the views of a distinct faction, or just ploughing his own furrow.

Meanwhile, Mary still had to be persuaded. On 7 October, Renard surreptitiously handed her the message of 20 September from Charles in which he had pushed Philip's suit, and had argued that this would be in the best interests of England and would enable it to reclaim possessions in France[21] – a somewhat risky suggestion since it would obviously involve England in the war. Renard assured her that Philip would not meddle in English affairs, though he must have realised that this was an undertaking that Charles had little or no ability to honour.

Mary initially showed, or affected to show, reluctance.[22] In a meeting three days later, she pointed out the likely opposition from the council, and from the people, and said that with all his territories Philip would not be able to spend much time in the country, which would make him unpopular. She was concerned about his relative youth - at 26 he was eleven years younger than her - and the possibility that he might be 'amorous', which she did not care for. She agreed that he should play no part in the running of the kingdom, though she would, according to the divine commandment, 'do nothing against his will' – a contradiction that could, and would, prove tricky. One by one, Renard diplomatically, though not entirely honestly, refuted her arguments. Mary asked that Charles write to the council to set the ball rolling, and, once again, declared that she would be guided by his choice and not by the council's – an unpatriotic, and somewhat alarming, statement.

On 13 October, Paget managed to have a long conversation with Mary, in which he not only pushed for the marriage, but also a full-blown defensive alliance with the Empire - more far-reaching than the present agreement to send limited forces, or money, if the other were attacked. Always distrustful of French intentions, he was worried by its alliance with Scotland, and considered that an Imperial match would bring 'security and repose'. He assured her that some of the council thought similarly.[23]

Immediately he had departed, the queen scribbled a short note to Renard, signed 'Your good friend, Mary', asking him to come to see her that evening in private. Paget's visit, and his claim that he had council support, had apparently had an effect on her, for she now seemed much more interested in the idea of marriage, asking what Philip's character was like and whether she could see him before she made up her mind. To overcome any doubts she might still harbour, Renard wrote her a surprisingly indiscreet memorial on how she should counter arguments against the choice of Philip, full of insulting opinion about the English character, describing them as 'thoughtless' and 'vindictive', almost as if she were not queen of England herself.[24]

In fact, despite Charles's assurances that any suggestion must come from Mary first, and his apparent deference to her as queen, both he and Renard, and to a large extent Paget, too, seemed to be less interested in Mary's wishes, than in concluding a matter of Imperial, diplomatic business between themselves. This might have been appropriate when dealing with the betrothal of a minor, but it hardly befitted the adult queen of England. Mary does not emerge in these, admittedly partisan, reports as being much in control of the situation, or of laying down the law as she saw it. Although the final choice was hers, there doesn't seem to have been much initiative on her part in the making of it.

Attention now turned to winning over the council. On 27 October, Gardiner, who by now had received one of Charles's personal letters encouraging Mary to marry, had a meeting with Renard to discuss the issue. Arundel, Paget and a few other councillors were also present. Renard, presumably trying not to catch Paget's eye, explained (untruthfully) that Charles had not yet made any mention of a marriage to Mary, and his letter, which did not mention a candidate by name, was simply designed to open discussions. At the end of the meeting, Renard had a private conversation with Rochester, perhaps the most trusted of Mary's household, and handed over another of Charles's letters. Rochester was a supporter of Courtenay, and he sounded highly flattered to be in receipt of the emperor's attention.[25] The following day Renard handed a letter to Arundel, who expressed the same reaction, and promised Petre he had one for him, too. All these men seemed to be in Gardiner's camp, and so the letters were aimed less in gratitude than as an attempt to get them to change sides. Unless they were particularly incurious, they must have had some idea of why Charles should be taking such an interest in Mary's marital situation, and why he should have selected them, rather than other councillors, as recipients of his letters.

On 29 October, Renard was summoned to Mary's private chamber, where she was in a state of high emotion, claiming she had been unable to work for two days with worry over the marriage issue. In a bizarre scene, she insisted that she and the ambassador kneel before the Holy Sacrament, which was there on a table, and pray. She then revealed that she had finally resolved to marry Philip 'and her mind, once made up, would never change'.[26] She then began worrying about all the details of the voyage, and whether Philip would be able to travel safely at this time of year, sounding more like an excited schoolgirl than the middle-aged queen of England. The next day, Renard wrote to inform Philip of the situation, advising him to practise his French and Latin, and to come as soon as possible. Wisely, he chose not to enlighten him as to the possible terms of the agreement.

Now that she had made up her mind, the battle seemed pretty much won, for it had never been easy to get her to change it. When a deputation of councillors, headed by Gardiner, came to persuade her not to take Philip, but Courtenay instead, she gave them short shrift. And when she asked Renard for Charles to send details of the terms of alliance, she mentioned to him a list of the matters that she thought should go into it, adding that she would not confirm her choice of Philip until she had seen them. Since this list contained items that had not been discussed before, such as a ban on money being taken out of the kingdom, and that the council should have full powers in Philip's absence, it seems that Paget's influence was at hand.[27]

Charles, however, was unwilling to draw up the terms himself, for he foresaw another problem; Philip himself. Although the matters mentioned were acceptable to the emperor, it was on his son that they would fall, and they were, not to put too fine a point on it, humiliating. Philip was the heir to half of Charles's empire, and would, in time, become the most powerful man in Europe. This agreement would shackle him to a second-rate power, over which he would have minimal control, and which would oblige him to take orders from, horror of horrors, a mere woman. Calls to filial and political obedience would only go so far; Charles would have some persuading to do, and it would be that much more difficult if it appeared that the terms had been drawn up by him.

Meanwhile, despite the apparent gratitude with which Charles's letters had been received, Gardiner and Courtenay, unaware that Mary had finally made up her mind, were not yet prepared to give up the struggle. They now tried the unusual tactic of trying to get Parliament, which was currently sitting, to voice its opposition to a foreign match. Noailles had been urging Courtenay for some time to build support among its members, and it is quite possible that he was in some way involved in this initiative. Parliament authorised a delegation to go and speak to Mary, to urge her not to marry outside the kingdom, but the queen, claiming illness, declined initially to receive it.

On 5 November, Gardiner met with Renard and they had another 'diplomatic' conversation in which the ambassador forgot to mention that Mary had already made up her mind, and the former avowed that he had not tried to persuade Mary either way.[28] Both agreed that it should be

Mary's choice, which obviously gave Renard a considerable advantage. Despite his claimed neutrality, Gardiner then launched into a long list of reasons why it should not be a foreigner, stressing the point that, whatever the terms of any marriage treaty, a foreigner could not be guaranteed to abide by it.

Clarification for Gardiner was to come almost immediately, though it was not what he wanted to hear. Going straight from his meeting with Renard to Westminster, he was told point blank by Mary that she would never marry an Englishman. She did not mention Philip by name, and Renard in his despatch described Mary as having been 'instructed',[29] which could mean that she was saying only as much as he had recommended.

Renard and Paget now hurriedly concocted a scheme, or more properly a charade, to convince the council that it was not being sidelined, and that no agreement over Mary's choice of husband had yet been reached. The ambassador would ask in a formal audience for a reply to Charles's general letter about marriage. Mary would then agree to the principle of marriage, after which Renard would indicate Charles's formal proposal of himself, or Philip. Mary would then consult the six members of her inner council, after sounding out some of them in private, before giving her assent. In this way, it would all appear above board, and she could gain the consent of the council as laid down in Henry's will.

The plan was duly carried out on 8 October. The previous day, Renard had told Gardiner that a proposal was coming from Charles. Gardiner seemed to take it well, though he asked for a delay because of possible difficulties with Parliament, which was right in the middle of a tricky debate over the religious changes. He feared that if the Spanish match became public it might hold up, or even scupper the bill. Mary was reported to be very angry with him, after Paget had helpfully informed her of his attitude, and on the following day he seemed mollified, revealing that the religious bill had been successful, and apparently not opposing the decision of those councillors present to accept the proposal.[30]

Although Mary had gained some form of acceptance from the council, securing the, possibly reluctant, agreement of only five out of nearly fifty sworn councillors was hardly following the spirit of Henry's will. It meant that all the others would have a free hand to argue against the marriage, and it put its legality on shaky ground. Paget and Renard had won, for the time being, but they were laying themselves open to problems later on.

On 15 November, the delegation from Parliament finally came to meet the queen. It consisted of members of the Privy Council, and of both houses, and was led by the speaker of the Commons. They carried a petition, urging her to marry quickly, so that she could produce an heir to guarantee the succession, and, above all, to marry an Englishman. Mary had done her best to put off this meeting, but now that she had made up her mind she felt in a stronger position. The speaker launched into a long discourse - 'so confused, so long-winded and prolific of irrelevant arguments', according to Mary, that she had to sit down - pointing out all the problems that would arise from marrying a foreigner.[31] He referred to the people not liking it, something that particularly irritated Mary as Gardiner was forever using the same argument. She listened politely, but with increasing frustration.

After a while she could stand it no longer. Interrupting, and ignoring tradition which demanded that the chancellor, Gardiner, reply to such addresses on behalf of the monarch, she launched into a robust defence of her position. She berated the delegation for approaching her on this matter which, she said, was none of their business, and unprecedented, and declared that she would be guided by God and no-one else. After the speaker, and most of the delegation, had retired, somewhat abashed, there was a moment of humour when Arundel turned to Gardiner and told him, laughing, that now he was out of a job since the queen had taken on his role.

Gardiner doubtless did not see the funny side since he was now, at least temporarily, out of favour. Paget had made it clear to Mary that the chancellor was behind the idea of Parliament approaching her, and the next time he tried to speak up for Courtenay, the queen rather acidly retorted that she should not be swayed in her choice of partner simply because he was someone Gardiner had made friends with in prison.[32]

Renard gleefully reported that Gardiner had been in tears and had begged the queen for forgiveness. He may well have made this up, but the episode does reveal an interesting aspect of where power in the kingdom really lay. Gardiner and Paget were both strong, manipulative characters, while Mary is often portrayed as weak and indecisive, at the mercy of these two powerful men. It doesn't always look that way, however. Both men knew full well that, however uncertain she might appear at times, the true arbiter of their fate was the queen. The situation in which there was division on the council could actually work to her advantage, as it was to her that both had to turn for a decision. A council headed by one strong figure would have created a very different dynamic, and one in which Mary might have been controlled, as Jane would likely have been by Northumberland. It would, perhaps, be going too far to credit Mary with the Machiavellian tactic of deliberately pitting one against the other, nevertheless this factionalism occasionally could play nicely into her hands.

In the light of subsequent events, it is hard to forgive Mary for not listening more closely to what Parliament, as the representative of the people, had to say, even though the situation was unprecedented. No-one knew if Parliament even had the right to interfere in the question of the monarch's marriage. Inasmuch as it was an affair of the heart, she may have had a point, but the matter was far more important than that, and was quite clearly of national interest. She seemed perfectly happy to allow Charles to decide for her, while denying the right of the national Parliament to put forward its suggestion. The manner in which she had allowed herself to be sucked in by Renard and Charles into being a tool of Imperial diplomacy showed a lack of judgement, and even irresponsibility. How her people, heavily nationalistic and jealous of England's sovereignty, would react remained to be seen.

However, it is also worth considering, in defence of Mary, that if she were to marry within the realm who this other person might be. Gardiner's promotion of Courtenay seemed to be based on friendship, and perhaps some arrangement made between the pair of them while they were prisoners in the Tower. He could hardly have chosen anyone less suitable to bear the title of king; even Mary could see that. She needed someone to support her, who would be respected, and who would bring some gravitas to the role. Courtenay promised to fail miserably on all these counts. The fact that neither Gardiner, nor Noailles, nor Parliament could come up with any other name simply left the field open to those favouring Philip.

Yet there was another potential candidate, and one who under other circumstances might have been a serious choice for Mary's hand: Cardinal Reginald Pole. In 1553, Pole was fifty-three years old - too old some might say - a strong and enthusiastic Catholic favouring a return to papal supremacy, and, despite his cardinal's status, unordained and so therefore able to marry. He was also of royal blood. He had fallen out with Henry over royal supremacy and had been exiled to Rome, but he was now appointed papal legate and was ready and eager to return. This was made impossible by Charles who prevented him from leaving the Low Countries, ostensibly because his enthusiasm for a counter-reformation in England might turn the people against Gardiner's more cautious approach, but also, one suspects, because he might have been a serious obstacle to Charles's plans for Philip. The other big advantage was that he would have been acceptable to France, although Noailles was more interested in the disruption he would cause in England, and in the personal annoyance to Gardiner whose power he would doubtless challenge.[33] Given that, for these reasons, Pole's suit was not going to be proposed either within the council, or by Charles, the possibility of this match, in hindsight perhaps a better solution, was never seriously considered.

*

On 28th November, Charles sent his ambassador the terms of the marriage treaty, together with a long explanation of what they meant and how they should be presented.[34] Throughout his missive runs a thread of wisdom, awareness and compromise, and also a willingness to take on board Paget's concerns and to attempt to allay them. Considering the opposition that this treaty was to arouse within the hearts of some Englishmen and women, it is worth looking in detail at its terms, an activity which few at the time appear to have indulged in.

The marriage, Charles stressed, would not only link England to Spain, which he was well aware was a sticking point, but also to the Low Countries, England's largest trading partner. Furthermore, the son of this marriage would inherit both England and the Low Countries (though not Spain, which would remain in the line of Philip's first son, Don Carlos), thereby binding these two states in a union which could only be beneficial to both. Even a daughter could inherit both if her marriage were approved by the Spanish king. Thus, this wealthy and important territory was essentially going to be given to England for free.

Nor was England going to be tied to Spain against its will. Once the marriage ended, either through divorce or Mary's death, Philip was to have no claim whatsoever to the kingdom, and must return home. He would not be allowed to remove any artillery, money or anything else, including any heirs, nor would he be allowed to appoint non-Englishmen to offices or benefices. Charles also promised, though it was not written into the treaty, that Philip would not bring 'objectionable Spaniards' into his service, as this would annoy the English nobility. In terms of binding England to fight with the Empire against France, Charles stressed that the treaty of mutual assistance which already existed would remain, and England would not be forced to go to war. And to cap it all, Charles would pay Mary a substantial annual sum.

The impetus for the terms of the treaty, if one follows through the diplomatic correspondence, appears to have come from the English side, and this inevitably meant Paget, who had already distinguished himself in diplomatic negotiation and whose reputation was clearly known to Charles. Superficially, the treaty seemed overwhelmingly in England's favour. Philip would be a support for Mary, while having no real power himself, and the treaty would end the in-fighting within the government which was distracting it from other, more essential, business. It would give added protection against any French invasion, and against French piracy in the Channel, and it would strengthen ties with England's main trading partner.

In fact, the terms seem so advantageous to England one wonders why Charles agreed to them. Perhaps it was his gout that was befuddling his mind that he should hand over one of the jewels in his crown – the Low Countries – to another power. On closer examination, however, we can see that the treaty also gave him everything he needed. The last thing he wanted was to add another, inevitably hostile, country to his ramshackle empire. By handing it to Philip in this way, he would not have the headache of ruling it, but would still reap the advantages of it being within his orbit. At the very least he would have a neutral power on the other side of the Channel, and, who knows, in the future it might even become a more active ally. He had already decided to split his empire after his death into more manageable portions between his brother, Ferdinand, king of the Romans, and Philip, and now he was subdividing it further, but still within the Habsburg sphere of influence. In theory, the treaty was a match made in heaven, a perfect meeting of interests, though not all agreed: Philip was so angry when he saw the terms, that would reduce him to a virtual cipher under the orders of a woman, that he drew up a secret document absolving himself from any intention of being bound by it.

Nor was he the only one who was unhappy. In England, the treaty was greeted with fury in some quarters. Yes, there were benefits, if one cared to peruse and try to understand the terms, but these were only on paper, and could be broken as quickly as they were written – a point that one member of Parliament was bold enough to raise, and which was echoed by Henri II.[35] And, once Philip was installed, who would be there to ensure that he actually stuck to them, particularly if he didn't like them in the first place? No matter how sugared the pill, England was going to have a foreign king, and it was going to be an overweening Spaniard, who would doubtless flood the country with his own people. The nobility would be out of their jobs, the Inquisition would be brought in, and the nation would inevitably be forced into a war with France.

Ever since, it has been taken for granted that Mary's marriage to Philip was 'a bad thing', and that she must have been wilfully foolish to have embarked on it. Hindsight shows that Philip *did* involve England in a war with France, which led to the loss of Calais, and that he *did* play more of a part in English affairs than the treaty envisaged. But this was not the whole story, and certainly not from her point of view. For Mary had a project – to turn the country back to Catholicism – and for that she needed help. Not the sort that a wayward, irreligious, liability of a husband such as Courtenay could give her, but that of a prince, powerful in his own right, who shared the same beliefs as her. Allying herself with the most powerful man in Europe would give the country protection while her objectives were being carried out, and would add strength to her position.

It would also provide stability within the realm, something that most people really did hanker after. Englishmen might not like Philip, but they would, as they mainly did, respect his strength. Only in retrospect, and only with her early death and inability to produce an heir, does Mary's project appear misguided, and thus her marriage along with it; at the time, it seemed to her perfectly logical, and a risk well worth taking.

However, the manner in which she had achieved her aims was highly questionable. She had ignored and then schemed against her own council, insulted Parliament, and gone against the apparent will of her people. She had done all this while depending on the advice and guidance of a foreign power. Within six months of coming to the throne she seemed to have fulfilled the worst misgivings that Northumberland had used as a justification for trying to disinherit her. Whatever the real benefits to her or the country of the match, this did not bode well for the future.

Nor did it bring immediate relief. Mary's rule would not be secure until she had a husband on the throne beside her. The next few months, before Philip arrived, would be critical, and it was vital that he come as quickly as possible. But he didn't. He delayed, despite the attempts of Charles and Mary to speed him up. Partly this was because of the weather at this time of year, and the risks of sailing up the Channel where he would be in danger from pirates and the French, and partly he was hampered by lack of money for equipping his fleet and the followers he would bring to England, but mainly it seems that he was in the throes of an immense sulk, aimed against his father who had put him in this, admittedly invidious, position.

On 30 November, Charles, crippled with gout in his hands, dictated a letter to Philip insisting he make preparations for handing over power in Spain to some trusted advisors so that he could sail as soon as possible for England. He was to bring with him 'a full million in gold' for purposes that were unspecified, though he referred, somewhat worryingly, to 'some campaign in which you may be present'.[36] Philip should choose only reliable people to accompany him, that is people who would act with tact and discretion so as not to alienate the English, and he emphasised the need to show friendliness and cordiality in order to earn 'popularity and goodwill'. All this sounded good advice, but for it to be useful Philip had to move quickly. There were already signs of opposition in England, and France could not be guaranteed to stand by and do nothing.

Philip of Spain, copy of original by Titian
(Copy of the painting mentioned below)

Meanwhile, a portrait of Philip by the Spanish court painter, Titian, had arrived, and Mary was delighted. She even told Renard that she had fallen a little in love. The painter had clearly done an excellent job – the famous Habsburg jaw was not as pronounced as in some contemporary pictures, and the result was an image of a serious and handsome young man. The only warning sign, perhaps, was the fleshiness of the lips, which might hint at the voluptuousness for which the prince was already renowned – 'youthfulness', as his father delicately termed it[37] – which Mary had already declared she was not wont to share. Comparisons of this portrait with those of the queen herself at the same time, show clearly the difference in age, and, dare one say, looks. Once again, Philip was getting the raw end of the deal. Even Renard, eager to portray Mary in the best possible light, could only describe her as 'more than middling fair'.[38]

While the country waited for Philip to arrive, problems were building up for Mary. One issue that the marriage treaty did not resolve was the succession, if she and Philip should have no children. Given her age – thirty-seven - this was a distinct possibility. The problem was that, by the same statute that gave Mary the throne, Elizabeth was due to succeed her. But Elizabeth was a Protestant, despite her apparent conversion which seems to have fooled no-one, and Mary distrusted her and was convinced, probably correctly, that she was plotting against the marriage which could see her being effectively excluded from the line of succession.

Paget was not helping Mary's state of mind by feeding her rumours that Elizabeth had been observed meeting in secret with a French priest, and when this coincided with a request from Noailles for the granting of a general passport to allow any Frenchman to travel through England to Scotland, the council became suspicious and turned him down. Renard recommended putting Elizabeth in the Tower. He had noticed suspicious activity around London, including meetings between Frenchmen and 'heretics', as well as the laying up of weapons. Ever-sensitive of opposition to his plans for the kingdom, Renard was as eager as his predecessor to raise the spectre of French intrigue, and if he could link Elizabeth to this in any way, so much the better. His opinion of the English did not help his mood, describing them as 'treacherous, inconstant, false, malicious and easily to be roused that little trust is to be placed in them'.[39]

Mary, herself, was becoming jittery, too. Throughout the kingdom there were various unsettling incidents. A gun was fired at a priest in a village church; two other priests were murdered; a shout of 'treason' was made as Mary entered her chapel at Westminster; people refused to allow Mass to be said in churches in Norfolk and Kent; and a dog with shaven head and a rope around its neck, with 'scandalous writing' attached suggesting that priests and bishops should be hanged, was thrown into her presence chamber. A number of people were arrested for claiming that King Edward was still alive. All these signs hinted at rebellion. At this moment, Elizabeth, who had been kept in a virtual state of house arrest, asked permission to retire to another of her properties near St Albans. She was granted permission, but only after she had been given a good talking-to by Paget, Arundel and Renard. If only Philip would hurry up and sail.

One bit of good news was that, on 7 December, the full council approved the marriage treaty proposals. It appears to have been a lengthy and lively discussion, but the upshot was that with a few minor modifications – all of which Charles was later able to accept – the terms were agreed and the marriage could go ahead. Paget and Renard excitedly talked of where Philip would land and what arrangements should be made for his arrival. They wanted the marriage performed between the two parties in person, before any plots could take hold. On 12 December, Charles dispatched a delegation of three nobles, led by Count d'Egmont, carefully ensuring there were no Spaniards among them, as special ambassadors to conclude the treaty.

Braving the Channel in winter, and escorted by English warships, they arrived in the country on 27 December, feeling somewhat worse for wear from seasickness. However, they were pleased with their reception at Dover, and shortly travelled to Canterbury. On 2 January they arrived at the Tower and then entered London, where they were formally welcomed by, of all people, Courtenay. In their report to Charles, they noted that a great crowd of people had come to see them 'who seemed to us to rejoice at our coming',[40] though the anonymous author of the *Chronicle of Queen Jane* wrote that 'the people nothing rejoicing held their heads down sorrowfully'.[41] The chronicle also asserted that the previous day the retinue had been pelted with snowballs.

Nevertheless, on 12 January 1554 (still 1553 in the official record), the marriage treaty between England and the Empire was formally signed, according to the terms previously agreed. Philip was not present, so there was no wedding, but in diplomatic terms the marriage was concluded. It wasn't all good news, however. Philip had agreed to authorise his representatives to swear to observe the articles, but it was revealed that he, personally, could never agree to them.[42] The worries of the doubters seemed justified; what looked so good on paper might turn out to be worthless. England would be at the mercy of the whims of a foreign prince.

9

Revolt and Resolution

The marriage treaty had been signed; England had a powerful ally in the Empire; a husband had been found to support the new queen, and he should be arriving soon; the Privy Council appeared to be behind her; Parliament had begun the process of restoring Catholicism, and had legitimized her accession. The start of the new year (or end of the old one if one goes by Tudor chronology) should have been full of promise for Mary. But it wasn't.

No reign is ever problem-free. There are always issues raising their heads to disrupt the smooth course of pre-determined plans, but the difficulties facing Mary at the start of 1554, although half-hidden, were considerable. No way could she feel safe on her throne until these had been resolved.

For a start, Philip was not there. Furthermore, there seemed little sign that he would come in the near future. He was angry. He had not been consulted about the terms of the marriage treaty, refused to consider himself bound by them, and greatly resented the fact that he would have to leave his comfortable existence in Spain, to come to a country whose language he did not speak, whose customs he did not understand - and what little he did know of them he abhorred - to cohabit with an older, plain and neurotic woman, to whom he would be obliged to defer. He felt no obligation, and certainly no willingness, to make the potentially dangerous sea journey anytime soon.

Nor did she enjoy the unquestioned loyalty of her subjects. Parliament may have acceded to some of her wishes regarding religion, but this had been a struggle, and she had failed to have the question of supremacy dealt with, or even to resolve adequately the question of how to deal with married priests or the enforcement of attendance at Mass. Given their unhappiness over the marriage treaty, next time she called them the Lords and Commons might be even less accommodating.

Her Privy Council, despite outward signs of loyalty, was also divided and faction-ridden. Gardiner had reluctantly supported the marriage, but there was no question that he was unconvinced, and that he was still at loggerheads with Paget, on whom she found herself depending. She needed their support and guidance to make important decisions, but they could not decide themselves on the best way forward.

France was also causing problems. Despite all her efforts to allay its fears, and insist – and she had done this several times with Noailles – that the marriage did not alter the effects of the treaties made previously, Henri had taken great offence at what he seemed to see as England taking sides in his conflict with the emperor. And what was worse, he seemed to be plotting behind the scenes, together with the Venetians, against her.

And, if Paget and Renard were to be believed, with Elizabeth, too. Her sister was definitely not to be trusted. Even though she had recently asked for Mary to send her all the accoutrements needed for Mass, there were strong doubts as to whether this was genuine. After all, this was the second time she had done this. Elizabeth clearly wanted her throne, and how could she ever have faith in the daughter of that she-devil, Anne Boleyn.

And then there were her people, those who owed her loyalty and should be supporting her. But Paget and Renard were filling her ears continually with rumours of plots and conspiracies, all aimed, it seemed, against the things she held most dear, and over which she should never have to compromise: her religion, and her right to choose whoever she wanted for a husband.

These rumours of revolt had been circulating for some months, though they seemed to take their time to get through to Mary, despite Renard's best efforts. However, on 17 December, she was alarmed enough to contact the ambassador and tell him of her concerns. The ladies of her court were beginning to fret, and this had induced in her a state of 'melancholy and sadness to the point of illness'.[1] She had summoned the council to her chamber, and voiced her worries, urging them to show unity and to support her. They - already, or shortly to be, generously rewarded by the emperor - had apparently fallen over themselves in their protestations of loyalty towards her and the realm, but she was only 'somewhat consoled'. There were also signs of suspicious activity in France - the fitting out of warships, and a message from Wotton, her ambassador, that the French king could not tolerate the marriage treaty. In reply, the council had ordered English ships to be armed, and forts in Scotland and Ireland put on alert.

Within the council there had been a certain amount of re-arranging of positions and attitudes now that the marriage was a done deal. Rochester, who had stood by Mary through all the dark days of Edward's reign, now sought out Renard and complained that he was being cold-shouldered by the queen, presumably due to his support for Courtenay. He assured the ambassador, evidently aware that this was the quickest route to the queen's attention, that he had not realised the depths of her affection for Philip, and that he was now completely loyal to her choice. Others were also changing their minds, though for more political reasons. Gardiner was now speaking out loudly in favour of the match, and even the duke of Suffolk, Renard mistakenly believed, was 'pleased'.[2]

On 23 December, Noailles requested an audience with Mary to ask what safeguards she had to ensure that the terms of the marriage treaty would be kept.[3] He made it clear that Henri was worried and didn't believe that England would be able to continue with its policy of neutrality. He hinted that the king would welcome any efforts by Mary to broker peace between the two warring sides. How sincere this offer was, or whether he was just trying to find out English intentions, as Paget, who relayed all this in writing to Renard, believed, is unclear, but there was no doubt that Henri was genuinely alarmed. Wotton had said that he was so upset that he was unable even to get his words out to frame a reply. In this state he might try anything.[4]

Not that Paget's own behaviour was entirely above suspicion. He seems to have regarded himself as almost an unpaid (and shortly to be well-paid) member of the Imperial service, as much as of the English council, but he now took it upon himself to promote the idea of an Elizabeth-Courtenay marriage, allegedly to please the nobility and forestall opposition to Mary's own match. This may have fooled Renard, but not Charles, who noted that this particular union would be a source of opposition, not support, and insisted that the idea be dropped.[5] A generally skilful reader of men's souls, he attributed Paget's motives as fear for the succession if Mary should die childless, and he doubtless understood the personal interest that Paget had in such a situation.

While this may have been an accurate interpretation of Paget's motive, it may also have underestimated his deviousness. Given the conclusion of the marriage negotiations, the French had little option but to continue with their two-headed tactics of badgering the queen and council for declarations of peace between their two countries, and underhand plotting to try and disrupt the match, including attempts to encourage Cardinal Pole to come immediately to England. Noailles took the opportunity to bribe Paget with fine French wine, in the hope of him performing the same 'services' for Henri as he had done for Charles,[6] a gift that Paget happily accepted, perhaps assuming that being corrupted by both sides allowed him to disclaim partiality in the affair. His promotion of the Courtenay-Elizabeth match at the same time might not have been entirely unrelated.

On 7 January 1554, Count d'Egmont, Charles's special ambassador, wrote to Philip to bring him up to date with the situation in England. The nobility, he reported, were 'much more gracious' than he ever expected, but the people were 'uncertain' and 'fickle', and he had advised the queen to keep troops in readiness in case of trouble. To forestall such trouble, it was vital that Philip should come as soon as possible.[7] This was not the first, nor the last, time that the prince had been encouraged to hurry, but he still seemed unwilling to move. He also appeared reluctant to send his formal assent to the marriage. Mary would have been happy if he had even deigned to write to her. This was a problem, because rumours of plots were not altogether unfounded. On the same day, amid talk on the streets of London that he had already seized Exeter, Sir Peter Carew was summoned to the council to explain his behaviour, with a view to throwing him in the Tower.

Carew did not wait around. After a failed attempt to raise Exeter, he managed to flee to France - no easy undertaking - which suggested that there might indeed be a problem. And there was; perhaps the biggest that Mary would have to face. For Carew was part of a much larger conspiracy, and one that was to come close to removing her from the throne. As early as 29 November 1553, nine men had met in secret in a

London tavern to plot an uprising to prevent the Spanish marriage. Worryingly, these were men of some stature. The ringleader appeared to be William Thomas, a former clerk to the Privy Council, and others included Carew; Sir James Croft, a former lord deputy of Ireland; William Pickering, formerly ambassador to France; and Sir Thomas Wyatt, a prominent Kent landowner.

The plan was four-pronged. Carew would raise the West Country, starting with Exeter; the duke of Suffolk would take the Midlands, Croft the Welsh border, while Wyatt would form a force in Kent and march on London. How much Courtenay and Elizabeth were also involved is not clear, but reports from Renard show that he was convinced of it, or at least wished to convince others. It seems at this stage that Courtenay was at least aware of what was going on, since it was he – on 21 January, under interrogation by Gardiner - who gave sufficient information for the conspiracy to be revealed, but it is doubtful that he was told much more than to sit tight and await events. He was a useful figurehead, but far too indiscreet and incompetent to trust with details, or give a role to. As for Elizabeth, anything is possible.

For the plotters, the final straw may well have been rumours of an attempt by the government to neutralise Courtenay by giving him a prestigious mission as a special ambassador to Charles. This would keep him safely out of the country, and give him something useful to do. This was certainly what Renard and Charles were proposing, but the purpose may have been misunderstood. On 18 December, Noailles had reported that up to 50 young nobles, including Courtenay, were to be sent to Charles as hostages to guarantee Philip's safety when he came to England.[8] This rumour – which is not supported by any evidence in Imperial diplomatic correspondence - would certainly have been enough to provoke an uprising among just the class of people who might be expected to supply their sons.

The ostensible aim of the plot was simply to prevent the Spaniards from arriving and taking over the kingdom, which is why the revolt was to begin in the West Country, where Philip was expected to land, and why it was timed for Palm Sunday – 18 March 1554 - a date close to when he might arrive. Wyatt's proclamation at Maidstone, on 25 January, referred only to protecting England from being overrun by strangers. At some stage, however, matters became more serious, and by the end of December, Noailles was informed that the plot might also involve the assassination of Mary.[9]

For once, Renard's dire warnings of French involvement in the conspiracy were not his usual blend of hysteria and paranoia. Noailles and Henri were significant collaborators in this one, albeit, true to form, just enough to blacken their reputation, though not enough to be of any practical use. Acting on his orders to 'disrupt' the marriage, and encouraged by no small legion of spies, reward-seekers, patriots, and casual traitors who flocked to his gate, Noailles was not only aware of what was going on, but keen to help. He had a poor view of Courtenay, considering that his 'youth and inexperience' would ruin the plot, but, significantly, he had already spoken to him a fortnight before the plotters began meeting, and dissuaded him from fleeing to France, an action that seems to suggest some French involvement even at this early stage.[10]

Requests for French help were initially modest - the rebels wanted no more than for French ships to block the Channel to prevent Philip from landing. They certainly didn't want French soldiers, as that would have as bad an effect on the people as Spanish ones.[11] Henri was happy enough with this, and told Noailles that French ports would also be open to rebel ships, if required.[12] Renard reported signs of suspicious activity along the French coast, including the fitting out of large numbers of warships, and assumed that these would be for some sort of invasion of England. In the second week of January, D'Oysel, the French ambassador to Scotland, spent a few days in London, with instructions to join Noailles in assisting the revolt.[13] In late December, the rebels made a request for arms, munitions and money. A courier was even sent to the French court, and returned with 5000 gold crowns and orders for Noailles to fully support the rebels, but by this time the revolt was already over.

French policy over this whole affair was conflicted by the same type of factionalism evident in the English council. Two groups vied for the ear of the king: the Guises, who favoured a more aggressive course, which included active support for the rebels; and that led by the constable, who was more concerned with maintaining good long-term relations with England. In a despatch of 23 November, the Guises had offered Noailles – in extremely guarded language – a more or less free hand to help the rebels if they looked like succeeding,[14] and it is probable that D'Oysel was instructed by them and that he was more proactive in the affair than Noailles. The result was confusion, with no useful aid being offered to the rebellion, but with the enduring suspicion that France was deeply involved.

Courtenay's arrest and interrogation meant that the uprising began before the rebels were fully prepared, but the council, too, was in a state of confusion and unreadiness. Gardiner was now highly embarrassed, if not compromised, by the behaviour of his champion for Mary's hand, and the slowness with which the government now acted may have been due to his reluctance to further implicate him. He also failed to inform Renard about the plot for a further two days, which drew the ire of the queen. Paget and Arundel were, conveniently perhaps, absent from the council due to illness, and there seemed no-one willing to act with resolution against the rising.

While the flight of Carew put an end to trouble in the west, Wyatt and Suffolk stuck to their plans and attempted to go ahead with the plot in their areas. On 25 January, Wyatt raised his standard at Maidstone in Kent, and shortly after took over the castle and town of Rochester. Men, for whatever reasons, began to flock to him. Although, as with any rebellion, individual motives were many and varied, the headline aim of resisting foreigners struck a chord with those who lived along the route from the channel ports, and who were told that they would shortly see bands of armed Spaniards, numbering a hundred or more, who had already arrived at Dover, moving up through their county.[15]

The earl of Huntingdon was sent after Suffolk, while the duke of Norfolk was dispatched to deal with the more serious trouble in Kent. In London, the Tower was speedily filled with provisions and artillery in case of a siege. The guards on the gates of the city were reinforced and the mayor and aldermen took it in turns to ride around checking their alertness. The Imperial envoys – still in London following the signing of the marriage agreement – urged Charles to do something, especially in view of continued French preparations for some unknown action. They were also worried that their route to Dover would be cut by the rebels and they would be trapped in the country. The council had not told them anything of what was going on, nor had it offered them any protection. Not that they were the only ones to feel let down; Mary had requested a bodyguard almost a week ago, and as yet not a single soldier had been provided for her.[16]

Thomas Wyatt, by Hans Holbein

Charles decided that it would be inappropriate to send troops to help Mary, as their good behaviour could not be guaranteed, and enemies of the match would be sure to highlight any misdemeanours. He also claimed that he had no money to help her, though he was prepared to send ships to patrol the Channel to prevent any attempts by France to further exploit the situation. He also urged that Courtenay should immediately be sent to his court in Brussels, both to get him out of the country, and so that he could be persuaded to act more loyally towards Mary. Yet he was full of detailed advice on how Mary should behave which sounded more like he, rather than the queen, was in charge of the situation.[17]

Nevertheless, he could hardly hide the fact that this was the second time in under a year that he had abandoned his cousin to her fate. Perhaps this revealed the weakness of the Empire, already engaged in a war which was taking up most of its military and financial resources, but more likely it showed England's real significance, or lack of it, in his strategic thinking. The country could be useful – hence his involvement in the marriage negotiations, which gained him a prize at no personal cost – but it was not *that* important. Even with Philip installed, he judged it unlikely that he would get much useful help. Of course, there was the danger that the French might get involved, but past history showed that the possibility of the two countries joining against him would be an exceedingly remote one, and if France did intervene, then he could take further measures at the appropriate time. For now, it was simply not worth the risk.

Fortunately for him, this did not seem to upset Mary unduly. As in July, as support seemed to ebb from her and her position became weaker, she, personally, became stronger. And why not? Her whole life seemed to have been spent under attack; it was almost her default position. With her back against the wall, the old stubbornness kicked in, and she came out fighting again. After all, she was Henry's daughter, and she had a God-given right to the throne, and, moreover, God had already shown his support once, so why should He abandon her now?

She was certainly going to need help from somewhere, for the situation was rapidly deteriorating. On 26 January, with Wyatt encamped in Rochester Castle, the duke of Norfolk, approaching the town with the royal army, sent in a herald to offer a pardon to all those who would change sides. This resulted in only one defection – the rebels claiming they had done nothing to require pardoning – and, as Norfolk ordered his troops forward, the 500 Londoners – the Whitecoats - who had been hurriedly raised to deal with the revolt, under their captain, Brett, who gave a rousing speech assuring them that the Spaniards would 'ravish our wives before our faces, and deflower our daughters in our presence',[18] opted to change sides, and with cries of 'we are all Englishmen'[19] poured down to join the rebels.

Norfolk was obliged to flee, ignominiously, leaving behind his cannon. The return of his dishevelled and humiliated men to London was a serious blow to Mary and her council, 'and no less joyous to the Londoners, and most part of all others',[20] according to one chronicler. Despite the patriotic slogans of the Whitecoats, it is perhaps not irrelevant to note that four of Brett's officers were in the pay of the French ambassador.[21]

Alarmed by this turn of events, and in order to delay Wyatt's advance, Mary sent an envoy offering to listen to his demands, provided that they were related solely to the issue of the marriage. She had little interest in his response, for she was certainly not going to change her mind, but if the rebels were to advance immediately, they would find the royal forces

Kent

unprepared. Wyatt's reply to the offer was to adopt a harder line. With a large force, and with the capital apparently at his mercy, he demanded control of the queen, the council and the Tower, and a stop to religious changes. It was now clear that the rebels were inspired as much by the desire to prevent the move to Catholicism, and to change the government that was enforcing it, as to safeguard the country from the Spanish peril. These demands Mary could never accept, and they undoubtedly helped to strengthen her resolve. Wyatt had effectively given her little choice.

Nevertheless, she was unwilling to spill English blood if it could be avoided, understanding, perhaps, the terrible beginning this would give to her marriage with Philip. Urged by some of her lords to deal speedily with the rebels, before they even reached Blackheath, she refused, either in the hope that the rebellion might simply peter out, or because she did not trust the loyalty of her captains following the debacle at Rochester. It was a risky decision, since it put her on the defensive and handed the initiative to the rebels.

Wyatt then marched his men to Greenwich, where they waited for three days. London was in panic, with everyone who had armour being ordered to don it and come to the defence of the city. John Stow reported that the elderly Ralph Rokeby, sergeant-at-law, put on his armour under his legal robes and turned up at Whitehall to defend the queen armed with a bow and sheaf of arrows, and that even Dr. Weston, the queen's chaplain administered Mass wearing armour under his vestments.[22] On 1 February, the queen tried to forestall matters by issuing another general pardon to all save a few of the ringleaders, offering a reward of a hundred pounds in land for the capture of Wyatt. In the afternoon she rode from Westminster into the city, to the Guildhall, where members of the guilds were assembled dressed in their liveries. There on a stage, under a canopy of rich cloth, she addressed her people.

Mary was obviously in a position of considerable danger. The Privy Council seemed overwhelmed by the situation, and largely incapable of organizing her defence – any practical measures seemed to be being taken by the City authorities alone. There were suggestions that she should flee to the country, or to the Tower. But she would do neither. Whatever else could be said about her, Mary did not lack physical courage. She was determined to stay and brave it out. The speech she made that afternoon in the Guildhall was possibly the most impressive and moving, and the most important, of her reign. It is always Elizabeth who is credited with being the consummate actress, but Mary could also put on a show when she chose.

She began by reminding them of the demands of the rebels, which were aimed as much against them as her, and pointed out that it would be their goods that would be despoiled if Wyatt and his bands were allowed to enter the city. She was, she said, wedded to the realm, as she had promised at her coronation – and here she showed the ring that she had put on at the time of her oath, and which had never since left her finger. She had a perfect right, as the daughter of Henry, to be their sovereign, and she loved her subjects, and her country, as a mother loves a child.

Touching the marriage, she assured her listeners that it had the support of the council, and was altogether in the interests of all her subjects. She had never sought to wed, and would happily remain a virgin, but in the interests of the country she wished to leave them a successor, which she trusted would give them cause to rejoice. If she thought that in any way this might damage the kingdom she would never go through with it, nor would she do so if Parliament was opposed. She ended by urging them to have courage and stand firm, 'And now good Subjects, pluck up your hearts, and like true men, stand fast against these rebels, both our enemies and yours, and fear them not: for I assure you, I fear them nothing at all'.[23] When she had finished, Gardiner, standing next to her, cried out how fortunate the country was to have such a wise and learned prince.

The speech was recorded by Foxe, no supporter of Mary, who remarked that she spoke without notes. It was a bravura performance – a mixture of steel cloaked in maternal care – and, according to Wriothesley, it made those present 'weep for joy'.[24] Those who considered it more carefully, however, might have been bemused by her suggestion that she would abandon the match if Parliament was opposed. Since she, and all those present, would have known for sure that Parliament *was* opposed, either she was dissembling, or she never said this at all. As she was, given the current situation, very possibly arguing for her life, perhaps she can be forgiven this exaggeration, and to give her credit, she did later put the treaty before Parliament and receive its consent.

Afterwards, Mary went not to the relative safety of the Tower, but back to her far more vulnerable palace at Westminster. The palace lay outside the city, on the road the rebels would have to take to get to London. By putting herself in very obvious danger, she was to prove an inspiration to those on whose loyalty she counted for her survival. The following day, a thousand men were mustered in armour to defend the city under the command of William Howard, the lord admiral. The earl of Pembroke was appointed to take charge of the army in the field.

Not everyone showed the same fortitude, however. The Imperial ambassadors, Renard excluded, had already decided that an abrupt departure was called for. Leaving behind their horses and servants, and taking rapid leave of the queen and council, they hastily fled back to the Low Countries. Once again, Charles's representatives, sent to look after Mary and arrange her affairs, had abandoned her in the face of danger. Their argument that their presence may have made matters worse was little more than an excuse; their belief that their lives would be in danger if Wyatt was to enter London perhaps carried more weight.

Nor was Mary going to get any help from her future husband. Philip was being inundated with letters from Charles, his chief minister – Cardinal Granvelle - Renard, the regent of the Netherlands, and several other Spanish grandees urging him to come quickly to England, otherwise it would soon be taken over and he would lose his kingdom. But to no avail. Philip mentioned the difficulties of raising money and equipping the over-large fleet which he wished to escort him, but the truth is he was simply unconcerned with what happened in England. He would have quite enough countries to administer when he became king of Spain, and he didn't particularly want the addition of a fractious, Protestant-leaning, nation that was bound to cause him trouble.

After his rest at Greenwich, Wyatt moved his army up to Southwark, at the far end of London Bridge, and right opposite the city. The mayor had ordered the gates of the bridge to be closed, and the drawbridge cut. As the rebels approached, some salvoes of artillery were fired from the Tower, though they missed their target. Wyatt, who now had about 2000 men, entered Southwark peacefully, and moved two of his captured cannon up against the bridge. Just across the river, orders went out for shops and windows to be boarded up, and house owners to stand by their doors in armour.

Wyatt issued instructions that there should be no looting, especially since some of the locals had chosen to join his forces. There was one exception, however. Gardiner's house, unfortunately for him, happened to lie in Southwark, and the rebels took great delight in ransacking it, consuming the considerable quantities of food, removing the doors, and tearing up the books in his library so that men waded 'up to the knees' in the leaves of paper.[25]

On 6 February, recognizing that he would not be able to get across London Bridge, Wyatt moved his force along the south side of the river to Kingston, where the next bridge was located. He had been speeded on his way by renewed artillery barrages from the Tower, which caused some damage to churches and houses in Southwark, and caused a delegation of householders to beg him to leave before they were all killed. It is said that gunners at the Tower had asked permission to pummel the village with fire, and bring down the houses on the heads of the rebels, but Mary had refused.

Why he delayed three days in Southwark is a mystery. It doesn't seem that he was gaining reinforcements, and there was an urgent need for movement while Mary's forces were still unprepared. He may have been hoping for an uprising within London, and there is also the possibility that he may have been waiting for signs of help from France. One writer at the time, no friend of Wyatt, suggested that he was losing confidence, and considering returning to Kent, and perhaps even fleeing abroad, and that it was Brett, the London captain, who urged him forward.[26]

But the delays, both in Southwark and Greenwich, amounting to nearly a week in total, were costly. Supplying his army was a problem, especially if it entailed not trying the tolerance of the local inhabitants, and some of his men began to desert. Most important of these was Sir William Cobham, one of his lieutenants, who slipped across London Bridge at midnight, and met with the earl of Pembroke, presumably giving intelligence about the rebel dispositions, before being escorted to the Tower. His defection can hardly have improved Wyatt's confidence.

If he had been waiting for signs of support from London, the delays actually worked against him. The atmosphere in the city as his forces approached was more akin to dread than sympathy. Either as a result of deliberate propaganda or, more likely, desperation, the messages put out by the council portraying Wyatt and his men as an invading army who threatened their lives and livelihoods struck home. Locked inside the walls, with armed men rushing to and fro, and ordered to stand by their doors, ordinary Londoners do not seem to have viewed Wyatt as a liberator. Merchants and shopkeepers were annoyed by the disruption to trade, and ordinary people were assailed by a sense of uncertainty and fear, which only increased as the days wore on.

One chronicler summed up the atmosphere during that time: 'aged men were astounded, many women wept for fear; children and maids ran into their houses, shutting the doors for fear; much noise and tumult was everywhere; so terrible and fearful at the first was Wyatt and his armies coming to the most part of the citizens, who were seldom or never wont before to hear or have any such invasions to their city.'[27]

The rebels reached Kingston at about 4 o'clock in the afternoon of the 6th, but found that the bridge had been deliberately broken, and on the other side there was a small force of some 200 men ready to stop any attempt to cross. These they dispersed easily enough with cannon, but there still remained the problem of how to cross the river - the council having decreed, under pain of death, that all boats should be moored on the north bank. At nightfall, some sailors were able to swim across the Thames – an exceptionally dangerous undertaking – and loose some barges that were tied up on the other side. With these, and by repairing the bridge, Wyatt was able to transport his whole army and ordnance across before midnight.

They then marched towards London, intending to be at Westminster by daybreak. However, within five miles of the city, the carriage of one of his heavy guns broke, and he stopped to try and repair it. Although he appears to have had other cannon available, Wyatt became fixated by the need to rescue this one, to the evident frustration of his followers, many of whom, already nervous, and made more worried by the inexplicable delay, began to desert. Among them was George Harper, his right-hand man, who went straight to Westminster to tell the council exactly what Wyatt was planning, and where he now was.

The previous afternoon, a herald had gone around the streets of the city ordering all horsemen, men at arms, and footsoldiers to assemble at St James' Field by 5 o'clock the next morning. Ten or twelve cartloads of weapons and ammunition were moved to St Paul's to be ready for the coming showdown. Now, news came that Wyatt had crossed the river, and that his arrival was imminent. The court was said to be 'wonderfully affryghted'.[28] The herald was sent out again to tell the soldiers to assemble instead at Charing Cross under the orders of the earl of Pembroke.

Wyatt's men were disheartened to hear that they would be opposed outside the city. They had been travelling for two days without sleep, and with very little food, and were tired and hungry. He rested his men at Knightsbridge while there was 'no small ado' in the city, and the Tower girded itself for the expected attack. By 10 o'clock on 7 February – Ash Wednesday - Pembroke had his men drawn up – the horsemen on higher ground at St James's, and the footsoldiers in the rear near Charing Cross (now Trafalgar Square). Wyatt now made the fatal mistake of splitting his forces. Stationing his ordnance on higher ground, he then advanced

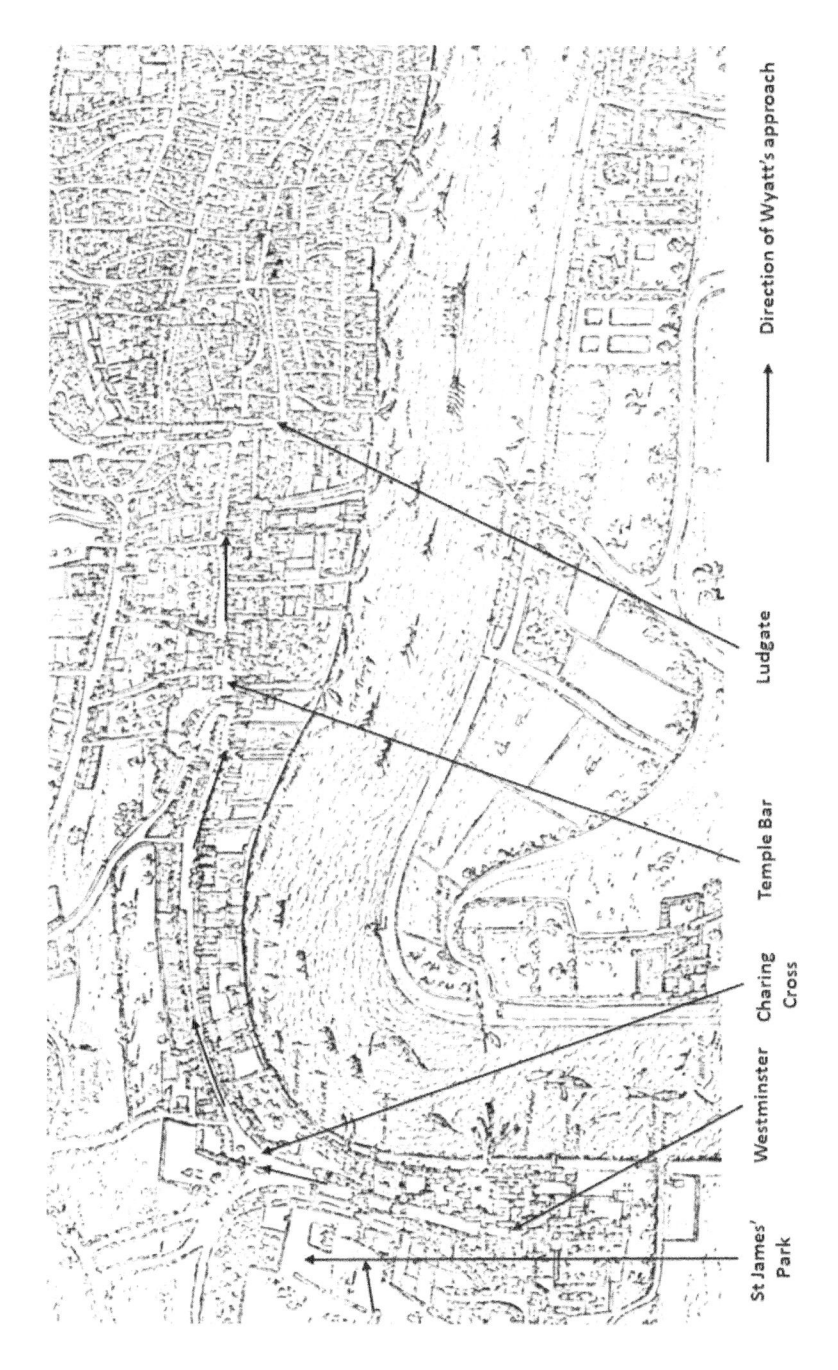

Wyatt's advance on London, February 1554

with one column down towards St James's Palace, with another turning towards the court at Westminster.

Pembroke's horsemen held firm until most of Wyatt's column had passed, then rushed down and cut off the tail. It is not clear whether this was a strategic manoeuvre, or whether it was due to an initial reluctance of the soldiers to attack – one report averred that Pembroke had had to remove his helmet and ride along the lines personally chivvying his men into action.[29] The cannon on both sides then opened fire, Wyatt's shot falling clear, but Pembroke's causing casualties. As Wyatt moved his men along the wall towards Charing Cross, the queen's footsoldiers fell on them, but were soon forced back.

At Charing Cross, the palace guard was drawn up under the command of the lord chamberlain, Sir John Gage. These, too, after firing a few shots retreated in disarray to the safety of the palace and shut the gates, their leader ignominiously falling into the mud in the rush. This caused more panic and confusion in the court, where it was believed that Pembroke had defected to the rebels. Ladies ran about shrieking, while servants hastily bolted doors and windows. The rebels were too few to break into the grounds, but they contented themselves with firing arrows at the windows, one of which struck a lawyer through the nose. The defenders were mainly a motley collection of household servants, and those hurriedly pressed into service, including some senior judges, who would be ill-equipped to deal with a full-on assault.

But among them were the Gentlemen Pensioners, one of whom - Edward Underhill, whom we have already come across being imprisoned for his scurrilous ballad - wrote a vivid account of events which shows the confusion and lack of order among those defending the queen. The day before, he had tried to join up with his old comrades but had been rejected for being a 'heretyke'.[30] Now he arrived again at the court, dressed in armour, and simply joined in without being challenged.

The terrified Gage, and three other judges, who were supposedly responsible for guarding the gates, tried to break into the Hall for greater safety but were resisted by the Pensioners. These were better trained and made of sterner stuff, and they asked Mary for permission to open the gates and disperse the rebels outside. The queen, leaning from her window by the gatehouse, gave her consent, on the condition that they did not go far since they were the only ones she could trust to defend her. By the time they opened the gates, the rebels seemed to have dispersed, and they spent the next hour doing little more than marching up and down.

Some of the council, including Gardiner, were still urging Mary to flee - to Windsor or the countryside - but she refused. Renard later took credit for this decision, assuring her that if she fled this would hand the initiative to the rebels. Whether inspired by this advice, or by her usual stubbornness, she had decided to stay. Now her fate depended on Wyatt's next moves, and the resolve of her palace guard.

Wyatt, meanwhile, moved his men along Temple Bar, through Fleet Street, to the Bel Sauvage Inn next to Ludgate. While marching along the Strand, they had come across a company of some 300 of the lord treasurer's men who passed them by on the other side of the street without firing a shot. They also passed armed householders standing at their doors, who simply watched them go by. Some of his men were shouting that the queen had pardoned them, and when Wyatt rapped on the closed doors of the Ludgate he announced that he should be allowed to enter as Mary had granted his requests. Some historians have seen this lack of involvement by the militias as evidence of a basic sympathy for the rebels, though those with military experience may prefer a less sinister explanation: soldiers generally have little desire to start a fight in which they may well get killed, and their commanders, aware that the rebels had already bypassed the main defences, may not have had the confidence to engage them.

Unfortunately for Wyatt, on the other side of the gate stood Howard, the commander of the City's defences, who knew exactly what Mary had decreed, and he refused to open up, loudly proclaiming Wyatt a traitor. Wyatt rested a few minutes at a stall just outside the inn, and then, realizing that he could not get through or over the wall, and understanding that the citizens of London were not going to rise up in his support, led his men back towards Charing Cross. At Temple Bar, he was met by Pembroke's horsemen, and there was a brief skirmish, resulting in some forty deaths.

At that moment, a herald appeared and called on Wyatt to surrender for the good of his followers, suggesting that if he did so he might find the queen in a merciful mood. Obviously exhausted and dispirited, and seeing that the game was up and the queen's soldiers were resolute, he offered to surrender to a gentleman. A gentleman was duly found – three of them, in fact – and the ringleaders – Wyatt, Thomas Cobham (son of Sir William) and William Knevet – mounted on the backs of their horses and were ridden into the city. And in this anticlimactic way, the revolt ground to a halt. Altogether, some seventy men from both sides had been killed in the fighting.

Back at court, a jubilant Mary received the Pensioners, who she allowed to kiss her hand, and to whom she promised many things, though, as Underhill sourly remarked, 'few or none of us got anything'.[31] The ringleaders were brought by water to the Tower. As they were led in, they were threatened and jostled by the officials there, who insulted them, calling them traitors. Over the next few days, they were joined by a distinguished band of others, including Courtenay, the duke of Suffolk, and, sometime later, the Princess Elizabeth.

Suffolk's role in the plot turned out to be more of a distraction than a real threat. Tasked with the job of raising the Midlands, a fair amount of which was in the hands of his extended family, he failed even in this. Warned, on 25 January, that he was about to be summoned to court, he and his brothers, John and Thomas, rode off towards Lutterworth and the family seat at Bradgate Park. Ironically, the reason for his summons may well have been that the council was going to offer him a command *against* the rebels, but given that information about his involvement was beginning to come to light this may have been just a trick.[32] He called for the towns of Leicester and Northampton to rise up, but received little or no support. On the 29th, he made for Coventry, with 150 men, and urged the town to join him. It refused even to open its gates.

By this time, the earl of Huntingdon was closing in, and the duke retreated to another of his houses at Astley Park, where he dismissed his men, and the brothers decided to split up and make their own ways to safety. There he was found, a couple of days later, attempting to hide in a hollow tree, betrayed by his own park keeper, and by his dog which kept up a furious barking beside it. His brother, John, was found nearby, under a pile of hay. His other brother, Thomas, nearly made it, but his servant left behind a bag of money at an inn and, on going back to fetch it, was arrested, along with his master.

Suffolk's main achievement in this farcical escapade was to ensure the death of his daughter. It does not seem likely that his motive was to restore Jane to the throne, indeed it is far from obvious what his motives were – perhaps to restore Protestantism, perhaps to prevent the marriage, perhaps just rancour at the way he felt he had been marginalized by Mary and her council, or, more likely, he had just been talked into it to give some authority to the enterprise. Only one contemporary chronicle – Bishop Cooper's - records that he was doing it in favour of his daughter.[33] Yet, as early as 28 January, Mary and her council had sent out a proclamation claiming that Suffolk was intending to bring back Jane.[34]

This notice effectively signed Jane's death warrant, and it is possible that it may have been issued whether Suffolk had stated this intention or not. If Mary was to be overthrown, and it seemed that this probably was the motive of the plotters, then she would have to be replaced by someone. Yet it was blindingly obvious to all that this would not have been Jane. However much she had royal blood, and that she had been queen before, and that she was wedded to the new religion, she was a broken thing. She was Northumberland's creature, and he was gone, and no-one wanted him back in any form.

The name that could not be mentioned was, of course, Elizabeth's. If it had been written on this proclamation – and it should have been since her name was referred to by the plotters - then it would have committed Mary to executing her. It would also have informed the whole country that there was a struggle for the throne between the two sisters, which might have given people an attractive alternative, and a good reason to support the rebellion. This could easily have led to civil war. How much safer to blame the uprising on one who was already under sentence of death.

It also, perhaps, showed the influence of Gardiner. He had every reason to want attention turned away from Elizabeth and Courtenay, since he was so obviously, and embarrassingly, linked to the latter. It was he who had insisted on investigating Courtenay alone, and he had been coy in his revelation of what Courtenay had told him. Either way, it certainly seemed to serve everyone's purpose to lay the blame at Jane's door.

Despite her subsequent reputation, Mary was a reluctant killer, at least within her own circle. She had no wish, personally, to see Jane dead, and she was well aware, as were the council and the Imperial ambassador, that Jane was an innocent scapegoat. But at the time that the decision to execute her was made – probably on 8 February - Wyatt's revolt had just ended, and Mary had to be seen to take some action. She was being assailed by Renard, who wanted all obstacles to his plans done away with, and by the council, to some of whom Jane was an embarrassment and a constant reminder of things they would rather forget, and the only logical alternative would have been to execute her own half-sister.

Mary's decision was not nice, but it was politically expedient. She could not be seen to be a weak woman, afraid or too-sensitive to take such a step, otherwise she would be prey to continuous challenges to her authority, and those who had supported her up to now would wonder whether it was worth it. Executing Elizabeth would carry a risk, but Jane was a safe option; no-one would mourn her. Sad to say that, while all her life she had been at the mercy of those who used her to achieve their own ends, even in death Jane was probably a proxy for someone else.

Mary's mercy did not extend to the rebels, either. Gallows were set up at key points in London to mete out immediate, and exemplary, justice, and about 50 of Wyatt's men were hanged. Other ringleaders were sentenced to death and removed to Kent so that the punishments could be witnessed by those who had joined them. However, in a staged display of grace, Mary had several hundred of the rebels paraded before her at Westminster, with halters around their necks, so that she could be seen to pardon them. The mixture of ruthlessness and mercy showed political acumen, and a warning that she was not to be taken lightly.

It is, perhaps, significant that none of the chroniclers appeared to see anything extreme in Mary's treatment of the rebels. Nor did it immediately result in any further revolts. In fact, it is probably fair to say that it was welcomed by most of the country. If there were doubts about the ability of a woman to rule, they would be mainly over whether she had the strength to maintain order, and the courage to punish when necessary. Severity was not an issue. People could put up with a strict monarch, just as long as the rules were clear and the law-abiding were able to get on with their lives.

Not that Mary was prepared to put up with any sympathy for the rebels from ordinary citizens. In April, Sir Nicholas Throckmorton was arraigned for high treason for his role in the plot. During the trial he ran rings around his accusers, who could present no evidence other than hearsay, or depositions from untrustworthy sources, and who refused him the chance to call witnesses in his defence. The jury consequently found him not guilty, a verdict they stuck to, despite threats from the court. Throckmorton was spared execution, though he wasn't immediately released, but the jury were arbitrarily sentenced to six months imprisonment, and subsequently released only on payment of swingeing fines, or a confession that they had acted in bad faith.[35] Apart from being an interesting vignette of Tudor justice, the acquittal was significant, also, in showing a degree of opposition to the government among even middle-class Londoners, and it marked an end to further trials.

Another curious episode, which might reveal latent support for the rebels, and which was deemed sufficiently interesting, or significant, to be reported by both Renard and Noailles, was the staging of a mock battle between 'Wyatt' and 'the queen', involving as many as 300 lads in a meadow at some undisclosed location. Such contests were not uncommon, and usually involved the 'French' against the 'English', but on this occasion things got out of hand, several participants were injured, and the boy playing the part of Philip of Spain was taken prisoner and mock-hanged, a process that nearly led to his (real) death. Noailles reported that the queen was not amused, and the leaders were whipped and briefly imprisoned.[36]

In fact, Mary's vengeance did not extend to as many of the original ringleaders as Renard was hoping. William Thomas, who had pressed for her assassination was, understandably, executed, but apart from him, only Suffolk, his brother, Thomas, and Brett, Knevett and Wyatt from among the most prominent, suffered the same fate. Carew might well have joined them, but he was in France and, for the time being, safe. Once the dust had settled, those in power realized that there would be little profit in further persecution - Mary and Paget, because they wanted to pretend that opposition to the Spanish match was small-scale; Gardiner both because of his own involvement, and a reluctance to draw attention to the anti-Catholic aspects of the revolt; and others on the council because of their somewhat ambivalent behaviour during the uprising.

Within days of the end of the rebellion, Mary's government felt confident enough to issue a proclamation expelling all foreigners, with the exception of diplomats and a few merchants, a move designed primarily against radical Protestants, who constituted a potentially dangerous fifth column within the country, and who were a ready source of opposition to her religious and marital plans. This did not, of course, affect the 'strangers' who were most in people's thoughts – Philip and his entourage – but it did make her position more secure, and did please some of the mercantile class who had been facing competition from such people.

Mary had good reason to feel more confident, for although it would prove to be the most serious challenge to her authority during her reign, what was perhaps most significant about the conspiracy is not so much what happened, as what did *not* happen. Wyatt seemed to have come close to achieving his aims, though it is not entirely clear if even he knew exactly what these were, and he had given the government a scare. Indeed, if he had concentrated his forces against the court at Westminster, where Mary was, rather than split them and attempt, somewhat pointlessly, to enter London, he might have done more than this. But he didn't, and his rebellion fizzled out with almost ludicrous ease. It has achieved notoriety because he briefly came so close to the centre of power, but that was as far as its significance goes.

For what the revolt showed was not so much wide-scale opposition to the Spanish match, and perhaps to Mary, too, but widespread indifference. Wyatt is estimated to have had between 2-3000 followers; Kett, in 1549, may have had as many as 20,000, and the Pilgrimage of Grace in 1536 more than 30,000. The conspiracy was meant to involve most of southern England and the Midlands, and yet only relatively few from one or two counties joined it. The West Country, so often seen as a focus of revolt, remained peaceful, and Suffolk's efforts to rouse the Midlands failed completely. Far from proving that Mary had made a terrible mistake in contracting marriage with Philip, the failure of the revolt actually showed that she had got away with it.

But perhaps she was lucky, too. There is evidence of disaffection in the counties of Surrey, Sussex, and Hampshire, which was successfully suppressed by loyalist gentry. Nor do we know to what extent the failure of other areas to support the Kent rebels was down to opportunism, a lack of communication, or a genuine unwillingness to upset the peace. The Spanish match was undeniably unpopular, and the plot to prevent it undeniably threatening; thankfully for Mary, its execution was more of a damp squib.

Yet the uprising is significant enough to demand some examination of its causes. It is worth noting that Charles V had always expected some sort of rebellion, and had long been aware of an English antipathy towards foreigners. He, along with his ambassador, had often highlighted this as a feature of the English character, implying a sort of innate racism. However, one should not over-egg this. Any student of diplomatic correspondence, from any period of history, and almost any country, will be well aware of an almost genetic intolerance among ambassadors towards the people of whichever country they happen to be accredited to. Furthermore, to suggest that the English were more jealous of their national integrity than, say, the French, or even the Spanish, is simply incorrect.

However, jealousies between people exist, and those between people of different countries are particularly marked, yet the antagonism towards Spain did seem exceptional. To a certain extent, this defies rational explanation. England and Spain had never yet come to blows, and the two countries hitherto had had precious little to do with each other. Katherine of Aragon was Spanish, and she had been popular and respected, and even her opposition to Henry's attempts to divorce her had done little to diminish this. Mary, herself, was half-Spanish, and she had recently been installed by popular acclaim in preference to a candidate of impeccable English stock. It was the French who were England's traditional enemy, and there was any number of very good reasons for disliking them.

For the Spanish to supplant the French there had to be better reasons, and they can mostly be found in the new situation caused by the match. The Spanish had already gained a negative reputation in Europe due to their military power, the size of their world empire, and the extraordinary wealth that this brought them. Their involvement in the Low Countries, with whom England had a special commercial relationship, made stronger by Protestant religious links, was unpopular, and the Spanish themselves were seen as haughty and condescending in character, something even Charles V recognized. The thought of one such becoming king, and flooding the country with his followers, however peaceful their intentions, was likely to cause worry and resentment.

Merchants feared that there would be competition with Spanish merchants coming to set up businesses in London and in the Low Countries. Craftsmen held similar views. Nobles feared that Philip would try to bring his own men into the council, and that Spanish grandees might act as rivals in the highly competitive Tudor social scene. Many feared that Philip might act too quickly in restoring Catholicism, and those who had acquired monastery land were particularly nervous. Others who had dealings with the Low Countries would have been well aware that Philip had spent time there, and that he had not been popular.

Of course, all this assumes that the Spanish match was the main cause of the uprising. However, the supposed desire of some of the plotters to bring the Protestant, Elizabeth, to the throne, the fact that many of the plotters were Protestant themselves, and the new demands issued by Wyatt when he was within sight of London, strongly suggest that religion may have been a more important reason. Hatred of the Spanish, which was easily whipped up through placards and fliers, and which appealed to a wide range of people through its catch-all message, was more likely the excuse. Simply trying to persuade Mary to change her choice of husband does not seem to have been the real, or at least the only, aim of the plot.

There is still dispute among historians as to whether the revolt was mainly about religion, or the marriage. In part, this is academic since the two went hand in hand. Philip represented hard-line Catholicism, and so the marriage was inevitably connected with religion. However, even among Catholics there was a division of opinion. Some were content to put the clock back only as far as the later days of Henry, while others favoured the full restoration of papal authority – a point of view that it was supposed Philip represented. We can suppose that some of those apparent Catholics who joined the rebellion were moderates, for whom the religious changes envisaged by Mary were as unacceptable as they were to Protestants.

However, to try and find a defining cause for Wyatt's – indeed, probably any – rebellion is a thankless, and probably pointless, task. They simply don't work that way. Wyatt did trumpet the anti-Spanish aspect, and urged one follower to keep quiet about the religious motivation in case that reduced his appeal.[37] At one point he demanded the replacement of Gardiner, even though he was the councillor most opposed to the Spanish match, thus highlighting apparent contradictions and confusion over his intentions.

However, it is important to distinguish between the *reasons* for the revolt, and its *aims*. Wyatt and his fellow conspirators were clearly upset about the marriage and the changes to religion, but it soon became obvious that their aims went far deeper than simply trying to persuade Mary to change course. Unless he had been seriously inattentive over the previous six months, he should have been well aware that Mary was not going to change her mind over religion, and highly unlikely to renounce her marriage partner. Pressure was not going to work, and it is clear from his subsequent demands that he understood this and was actually intent on regime change. Mary would have to go, which meant Elizabeth, a Protestant, would be installed as the next queen, probably with Courtenay as her husband, thus resolving both of the likely causes of the revolt.

Since the main motives – concern over the Spanish marriage, and the changes in religion – would seem to affect just about everyone in the kingdom to some degree, the question then has to be asked as to why so few people actually joined the revolt. One striking factor is the almost complete absence of the nobility – with the exception of the duke of Suffolk, whose significance to political affairs was minimal. Nobles not only lent prestige, and a degree of validity to an uprising, but they also brought with them a great number of followers – their manred (apart from the duke of Suffolk, of course, whose failure to manage even this, apparently simple, task, says much about him). The reasons must be found in the individual circumstances of each peer, but in this case it is clear that none of them saw cause enough to upset the status quo. This was highly significant. A century before, nobles would have been all too willing to join, or lead, a rebellion to defend, or enhance, their interests.

Now, they preferred peace. This showed just how much had been achieved by the Tudors. Twice in the space of a year, with different degrees of involvement, the most powerful people in the land had supported the legitimate queen. As a sign of future stability, this was highly encouraging.

The revolt was mainly led by those from the gentry class. Their reasons for rebelling tended to be the same as the nobility. Almost all those who planned the rebellion basically did it to maintain their power and influence, or at least to prevent it declining. They feared for their positions if Mary should bring in Catholics and/or Spaniards to replace them. Putting Elizabeth on the throne would prevent this. The leading conspirators were those actively involved in the political scene, who felt themselves affected in a way that the nobles, largely relegated to their estates, no longer did.

But even here, it is important to note how few were prepared to risk everything by joining the revolt. This may have been down to poor planning, and the fact that the revolt began before the conspirators were ready, and before they had time to mobilise more nation-wide support. As previously mentioned, there were signs that some in neighbouring counties might have joined in, but in the West Country and Midlands, despite active efforts by the plotters to involve them, the gentry, as a class, did not rise up. The fact that they did, or some did, in Kent was probably down to the fact that Wyatt was one of those most actively involved, who could call on his network of family and friends and those owing him favours, and possibly because Kent lay along the route between London and the Channel ports where anti-Spanish propaganda was most effective.

As for the commoners, there is no doubt that the majority of them would have much preferred Mary to marry an Englishman, and many were possibly genuinely nervous about the consequences, but for them it was hardly an issue worth rebelling over. Remembering that rebellion meant risking life, the motives for doing so had to be cast-iron, and the consequences had to promise something better than life as it was. With Kett's rebellion, the main issue was over land, and that was something that could be a matter of life and death. But who Mary chose to marry, and what the official religion of the country should be, clearly weren't.

There are many reasons why people rebel, both then and now. Beliefs inspire a few, but only a few, and only so far. What anyone can relate to is a perceived threat to one's existence, and this is what inspired most of the Tudor rebellions, no matter how much religious or political demands may have been high on the list of complaints. Most Englishmen accepted the changes of religion with almost no resort to arms (with the obvious exception of the Pilgrimage of Grace which, it can be argued, was more to do with the dissolution of the monasteries, which *did* affect their existence, and the 1549 uprising in the West Country in which religion may have been only a headline reason), but price rises, harvest failures, and land grabs resulting from enclosures were issues that threatened their way of life and their very survival. By 1553-4 there had been two years of good harvests, the coinage had been stabilized and prices significantly reduced, and Mary had remitted the subsidy. In short, life was better than it had been for some time.

For most, the issue of the Spanish match was a conceptual rather than an existential one. It was a luxury concern, of interest to those who had the time and leisure to consider it, and who might possibly be damaged by the arrival of Spaniards. Those lower down the scale – the ploughman, the miner – would hardly be affected, and thus the question was of little importance to them. The very low numbers of those who actively took part in the rebellion are testament to this. Wyatt's rebellion was never a great popular uprising; it was the frustrated reaction of a few malcontents who happened to get further than they should have done.

And this could perhaps be seen in the attitude of Londoners. The Kentishmen had been sure that the citizens would open their doors and welcome them in, but this never happened. As in the time of Queen Jane, Londoners just stood back and watched events unfold. It seems unlikely that this was because they were passionate supporters of Mary. This was the place closest to the centre of government, where people were most aware of what was going on. They would be the ones who would have to put up with the Spaniards lording it over them. They were the people most affected by the teachings of the Protestant refugees and were least likely to approve of Mary's proposed religious changes. So why did they not open the gates to Wyatt?

Their reaction, or lack of one, may partly have been due to the fact that because they were closest to government, they were the most tightly, and easily, controlled. Mary had effectively ordered the city to be put under martial law, and this would have put a dampener on any public support for the rebels. She had also been in the habit of hanging people who spoke against her, and against the marriage, so, to some extent, Londoners had been effectively cowed. Admittedly, the London contingent under Brett had defected readily enough at Rochester, and this might show that the citizens would have shown more support if Wyatt had actually entered the city, but at least they were not sufficiently roused to have tried to open the gates for him.

But it is more likely that the lack of support for Wyatt was due to self-interest. Londoners feared a mob of country people invading their city – they would doubtless have heard what had happened to Gardiner's house – and, above all, they feared the inevitable instability that would arise if Mary was overthrown. They could cope with religious changes; more important was a peaceful country where their shops and businesses would be safe and they would be allowed to prosper. This is not to say that London, and the rest of the country, would welcome Philip; it would just get on with its business, keep its collective head down, and hope for the best.

It is not irrelevant to note that not a single member of the council actively joined the rebellion. Despite the picture of a body riven with dissension over the issue, all came together to protect the regime – a very different picture from its behaviour during Northumberland's coup. If any of them doubted the religious project, or Mary's abilities, this was the perfect opportunity to show their hand, but, either out of fear, or self-interest, or loyalty, none did. Since these councillors would be the very ones most concerned if Mary really was as weak and indecisive as is popularly believed, then they would doubtless have acted, as their predecessors did with Somerset. Their inactivity has to be seen, in part, as an endorsement of the queen.

Perhaps this is not so surprising. Both of the leading lights in the council had good reasons to back Mary. Paget, of course, was firmly behind the Spanish match, and although he was probably loyal to none but himself, this attitude did ensure that he was in the queen's favour, and more so for a time than Gardiner. The latter, despite being indirectly implicated in the plot, and temporarily outmanoeuvred by Paget, depended on Mary for the success of the mission that he shared with her. The last thing that he, or any of the Catholics on the council, wanted, whatever they might think of her privately, was for Mary to be replaced by Elizabeth.

Nevertheless, there has remained a cloud over the behaviour of the lord chancellor. Stephen Gardiner had long opposed the Spanish match, believing it to be divisive, unpatriotic, and a hindrance to the acceptance of the Catholic revival. He was also close to Courtenay. Although head of the government, he was dilatory in organizing Mary's military defence, dishonest about what he had learned from Courtenay, and suspiciously half-hearted in his treatment of those believed to be involved. There are even suggestions that during the crisis he was marginalized by the other councillors, perhaps because they did not fully trust him. Unquestionably, he did not want the revolt to succeed, but it has been suggested that he may have wanted it to develop just enough to scare Mary into abandoning the marriage which, along with his other aims, would also deal a blow to Paget.[38] Probably, this motive is a little too subtle; the truth is most likely that his embarrassment over his known links with Courtenay threw him into confusion and temporary paralysis.

Wyatt's revolt is usually seen as one of the defining moments of Mary's reign, showing that her choice of husband was universally unpopular, and therefore flawed. But, as shown by events before and after, it was not defining at all. It did not alter Mary's resolution to marry Philip; it did not bring about changes in policy and personnel within the government; it did not alter her project to restore England to the true faith, and it did not lead to significant further opposition, at least not in the short term. It could be argued that it caused Mary to have the marriage treaty debated in the April session of Parliament, but she had promised this anyway in her Guildhall speech, and it was clearly part of her *modus operandi* to have all contentious issues decided in Parliament so she could shelter behind its legality.

What it *did* help define, however, was the historical view of Mary. To those who wanted to see it in this way, it showed the hostility of true Englishmen to Catholicism and the 'selling' of the realm to foreigners.

Certainly, these elements were present, but when one steps back, it is clear that such concerns were far from universal. Most true Englishmen were not sufficiently aroused by either of these issues to join in the rebellion. But subsequent Protestant, and nationalist, orthodoxy has chosen not to look at the bigger picture, and simply used the rebellion to show the wrongness of Mary's policies and, fundamentally, of her.

Yet this ignores one salient detail. This was not the first time Mary had faced a revolt; she had already had to cope with Northumberland's attempt to usurp her. And, interestingly, the purported issues were almost the same. The council's propaganda in July had laid emphasis on the fear of Mary contracting a foreign marriage and 'selling' the realm to strangers. It hadn't worked then, either. For all the huffing and puffing by some at the time, and by the majority of historians since, Mary's decision to marry a Spaniard was clearly not as unpopular, or disastrous a mistake, as is fondly imagined. Twice, in the space of seven months, Englishmen had been offered the opportunity to defend their country against foreigners, and twice they had declined. In fact, on the first occasion, the only significant activity had been *in support* of her. Mary is often criticized for either ignoring, or not understanding, the deep-seated fear of foreigners in positions of power in the country; but the abject failure, and limited appeal, of both revolts may suggest that she had gauged the situation rather better than her critics.

Perhaps the most telling comment on the failure of Wyatt's rebellion, however, is that put forward by historian, David Loades, who suggests that the country had simply outgrown rebellion as a means of effecting political change.[39] Under the Tudors, England had become a more peaceful, better administered, and generally more sophisticated society. The power of the nobility had been curbed, the merchant and middle class had risen in importance, and, more significantly, Parliament had begun to find its voice. He sees the snub delivered by Mary to the parliamentary delegation over the marriage issue as a turning point; never again would a monarch get away with treating the mouthpiece of the people with such contempt. Of course, rebellion from commoners, mainly over social and economic issues, would always be a possibility, but those who traditionally were prone to challenge monarchical power – the aristocracy and gentry – had found, in Parliament, a less disruptive way of pressing for change. And, of course, the next major challenge to a monarch's authority would come from Parliament itself.

10

Aftermath

The story ends, as it began, with an execution. Or, to be more exact, three executions. And these are the important ones. Not the historically unimportant dismemberings and suffocations of Wyatt and his accomplices, but significant ones. *Royal* ones.

First, there was unfinished business to be dealt with. Jane and Guilford were the easy options. Already under sentence of death, they could be safely dispatched, with no need for a further trial which might take minds inconveniently back to the issues of Mary's accession. This was just a matter of belatedly carrying out a previous court order.

The executions were ordered on 9 February – probably; we don't know exactly - and they were to be immediate. But Mary found yet further cause for delay, to the frustration of Renard and some of her council – particularly Gardiner, who preached an inflammatory sermon on the topic on 8 February - who were baying for blood. This time, the reason was Jane's avowed and unrepentant Protestantism. Reminded of her success with Northumberland's last-minute conversion, Mary now tried to change Jane's mind before she sent her to eternal damnation. Partly, she was aware of the propaganda value of persuading Jane to convert, but there was also a completely genuine concern for her soul, a belief that later enabled Mary to view the burnings carried out in her name with equanimity. Mary was not trying to prolong the agony; she really believed she was trying to help.

She sent her own chaplain, John Feckenham, to try to bring her back to the fold. It was an apparently astute choice. Feckenham was no firebrand, but an intelligent and evidently kind man. Their conversations, perhaps written by Jane herself, or perhaps imagined by reformers, were later published by Foxe, and suggest that Jane could put up a robust and academic defence of her faith. Feckenham did not really try terribly hard to convert her, and Jane clearly was not prepared to trade her beliefs for her life, either because she had seen that this was not the offer, or, more likely, because she was as committed to her cause as Mary. Interestingly, Jane, so determined when she put her mind to it, put up no resistance to Feckenham being the priest present with her on the scaffold, so the two must have struck up some sort of rapport.

She had already shown the strength of her feelings with an uncharacteristically blistering attack on Thomas Harding, her former tutor, who had earlier renounced his beliefs. He was, she wrote to him, 'the deformed imp of the devil', and described his soul as 'the stinking and filthy kennel of Satan',[1] language which later upset some of her biographers who preferred a more saintly image. Mary was clearly going to get no concessions from Jane.

This fairly pointless exercise put an extra three days on the lives of Jane and Guilford, though they must have been tense ones. They did at least give both the chance to see Jane's father, the duke of Suffolk, and undoubted cause of their situation, brought to the Tower. This gave both the opportunity to inscribe poignant, filial, messages to him in her prayer book, and for Jane to write a respectful, but meaningful, letter of farewell to him in which she alluded to his responsibility for her condition. Typically austere, she refused her husband's request for a last meeting, denying him even this small pleasure, much as she had denied him others in the course of their brief relationship.

On Monday 12 February, at about 10 o'clock in the morning, Guilford was led from the Tower towards the scaffold on Tower Hill. He was remarkably cheerful, and shook hands with several fellow inmates, asking them to pray for him, before his short walk to the execution site. He had no priest with him, and is reported to have made a short speech before the blow was struck. No record of his words has survived. Considering that this was supposed to be the opportunity to admit his crimes, he must have been hard-pressed to find something to say. Of all the people who suffered death as a result of the plot to disinherit Mary, he, surely, was the least deserving of his fate.

Jane may, or may not, have seen his bloodstained body, unceremoniously flung into a cart, trundle back into the Tower courtyard, before it was her turn. Either because of her, fairly slight, royal connection, or because Mary feared disruption if her beheading was public, she had been granted the benefit of a private execution within the Tower grounds. The downside was that she would have heard, and possibly even seen, the scaffold being constructed, which can have done little for her peace of mind. Despite, or perhaps because of, her tender years – she was still only 17 - she showed remarkable composure throughout the ordeal, her serene mask slipping only at the end, when, blindfolded, she couldn't find the block and cried out in despair, a moment brilliantly captured in the epic painting by Delaroche.

She had already written to Mary, admitting responsibility for moving the country against her, but denying that she had been the instigator of the plot, and she repeated this in her final speech: 'The fact, in deed, against the queen's highness was unlawful, and the consenting thereunto by me: but touching the procurement and desire thereof by me or on my [be]half, I do wash my hands in innocence...'[3] The speech was published and widely disseminated throughout Europe. In it, she re-affirmed her faith and asserted that she died 'a true Christian woman',[2] thus establishing her position in the canon of Protestant martyrs.

The Execution of Lady Jane Grey, by Paul Delaroche

Encapsulating this notion is the nineteenth-century painting by Paul Delaroche in the National Gallery in London. It is a large canvas, and depicts the moment of Jane's execution. As a work of art, it is extraordinary – stunning, even – and presents an image that, once seen, is hard to forget. As a historical record it is wrong in almost every respect – location, dress, personnel, apparatus, physiognomy (probably; we still have no recognised portrait) –apart from one; the *image* it presents of her is spot on. For it is clear from the lighting, the white (almost bridal) dress, and the iconography, that Jane is an innocent victim, a child sacrifice. And despite the valiant efforts of some recent writers to portray her almost as a feminist icon, capable of making her own decisions, that is, sadly, exactly what she was.

The next, and significantly more deserving, to go was her father. It is very difficult to find anything positive to say about Henry, duke of Suffolk, a problem equally taxing for his contemporaries. As an enthusiastic supporter of Northumberland, he had given oxygen to the original conspiracy, and having, thanks to the energetic pleading of his wife, escaped without even so much as an arraignment, he had shown his gratitude by involving himself in a further plot against Mary. To be as fair as one can to him, his main weakness was stupidity, rather than malice. Almost completely devoid of common sense, or political perspective, he could be talked into just about anything - a great advantage for Wyatt, who could be seen to have the backing of the second highest noble in the land.

This was evident at his trial, where he attempted the unusual defence that for a peer of the realm to have raised troops to prevent foreigners coming into the country could not be evidence of treason.[4] He turned to the sergeants standing near him to ask their opinion, to which they were, understandably, bemused. Condemned to die, he tried, belatedly, to put the blame on his brother, Thomas, who had encouraged him not to report to the council when ordered. He also took the opportunity to suggest that the purpose of the plot was to put the crown on Courtenay's head, thereby helpfully implicating him as well.

True to form, he even managed to lower his reputation still further at his execution. In the faint chance of a last-minute conversion, Mary had provided him with a Catholic priest, who attempted to mount the steps to the scaffold at the same time. Henry tried to block him, and the other pulled him down so that an undignified scuffle ensued at the foot of the steps. He lost even this battle, and Weston was with him on the scaffold at the end. Suffolk redeemed himself thereafter, even managing to attend to a bystander who shouted out that the duke owed him money, before patiently giving up his life to the executioner.

Throughout the rest of February, and into March, prisoners kept arriving at the Tower, and leaving for the scaffold. Wyatt met his end on Tower Hill on 11 April, fortunately avoiding the gruesome quartering until after his death. At his trial he had vehemently denied any plot to kill Mary; that had been the suggestion of William Thomas, and Wyatt had actually armed himself with a cudgel in order to beat Thomas to death for the very idea. His – Wyatt's – aim had been merely to prevent Spaniards from entering the country, a claim that was somewhat discredited by some of his utterances during the revolt. In his speech on the scaffold, he denied the involvement of Elizabeth and Courtenay in the conspiracy.

Despite this, Elizabeth was still in a dangerous position. At the close of the revolt she was declaring herself ill, but the council had sent doctors to establish whether this was genuine. Renard lost no time in pouring poison about her into Mary's ear, and recommending that she and Courtenay be executed.[5] The latter had already been denounced by Suffolk, but there was no good evidence yet against her. In the meantime, to blacken her name still further, Renard made much of a rumour that she had become pregnant due to loose living.[6]

On 23 February, Elizabeth was brought to Westminster, dressed all in white, and carried in a litter whose curtains she insisted remain open so that the crowds could see her face. She was accompanied by a considerable escort, including her own men, so was presumably not yet a prisoner, though there were guards on her door. Some letters, sent to Henri by the French ambassador, had been intercepted, which apparently contained evidence that the plotters would put her on the throne in place of Mary. This was alarming, but not necessarily incriminating: proof would still have to be found that Elizabeth was actively involved in securing such a result.

Meanwhile, plans were made to put her and Courtenay on trial, although these proceeded without much enthusiasm, according to Renard because the process was in the hands of Gardiner, who was reluctant to carry it through. Gardiner felt himself severely compromised by the revolt, and Courtenay's links to it. Most incriminating was Noailles' intercepted despatch, including a copy of the letter from Elizabeth to Mary, which mentioned his interrogation of Courtenay, which he had been reluctant to disclose. The original document had fortuitously gone missing, which helped, eventually, to exonerate him, as well as Elizabeth and Courtenay.

Nevertheless, on 18 March, Elizabeth was finally consigned to the Tower, entering, ominously enough, through the Traitor's Gate. There she remained until mid-May, her life hanging in the balance while Mary heard arguments for and against her execution. A lack of will, on Mary's part, and a lack of evidence from those who wished her ill, decided that the princess would be spared for the time being, and she was transferred to her home at Woodstock under house arrest, as was Courtenay to Fotheringhay castle.

This could be seen as evidence of Mary being too lenient, or fearful, to take this final step, but equally it could be interpreted as a sign of strength. Mary now felt more comfortable. The last remnants of Jane's conspiracy had been dealt with, and Wyatt's revolt had fizzled out of its own accord. The country clearly had no appetite for further upheaval. In April, Parliament ratified the marriage treaty, which ensured, in theory, the support of the people for the Spanish match. The stability could be seen in the fact that on 19 July, over six months after he had first agreed to marry the queen, Philip of Spain finally considered it safe enough to arrive in England.

Mary, at last, could start to feel secure in her inheritance.

Conclusion

Why was 1553 so Turbulent?

In November 1558, Mary died peacefully in her bed; her half-sister, Elizabeth, succeeded, unopposed, to the throne; and Philip, by now king of Spain, dutifully obeyed the terms of the marriage treaty and never set foot in England again, leaving it pretty much alone for the next three decades. This may sound a somewhat bland epitaph for Mary's reign, but in many ways it is remarkable. Few, at the close of 1553, could confidently have predicted these outcomes.

1553 had been an exceptionally turbulent year, but it was by no means a disastrous one, either for Mary or the country. Neither of the revolts which greeted her on her accession were revolutions. Neither involved large swathes of the population. In fact, compared to the uprisings of 1536 or 1549, both were small-scale, even though both came closer to toppling the government, and one, it could be argued, actually did. Northumberland's plot was little more than a botched palace coup, while Wyatt's, although part of a much larger, planned, conspiracy, in practice only involved a small number from a single county. Both challenges to Mary were from the elites, not the populace, the latter interested only inasmuch as they were obliged to be.

However, with the possible exception of Charles II, no monarch since, and few before, have experienced such difficulties in coming to power as Mary Tudor. Despite being the rightful heir to Edward by act of Parliament, the will of her father, and by dint of tradition, common law and the obvious desire of the people, she nevertheless faced two revolts within six months, both with the ultimate aim of denying her her rightful inheritance. The question must be asked as to why this should have been.

Before examining possible reasons, there may be doubts as to whether the two major challenges to her position – Northumberland's and Wyatt's

– can really be classed as part of the same process. Few historians have seen them as linked, other than by temporal proximity and the fact that both involved Mary. Apart from this, they seemed, superficially, to be very different. Northumberland was apparently just trying to seize power for himself through the guise of Jane Grey, while Wyatt was trying to alter the direction the country was taking with the Spanish marriage.

Yet both have so many points in common that it becomes clear that they were, in fact, two parts of one whole. Only by understanding this can we properly explain either, and properly understand the struggle that Mary faced to establish herself as England's first crowned queen. For both were inspired by concerns over the character of Mary herself, her unmarried status, the religious direction of the country, and, like it or not, her gender.

*

Mary's proposed marriage to Philip of Spain was the headline cause of the December conspiracy, but it was also, though less obviously, a major reason for the July plot, too. The danger that Mary might marry unsuitably was first recognised by Henry VIII, which is why he made the point of stipulating in his will that the council must approve any such union. He had been happy enough to contract her to both the Habsburgs and the French while she was still a child, and therefore, in no danger of actually acceding to the throne, but he had done nothing to tie up this loose end by seeing her appropriately wed before his death, possibly because he thought her bastardy would prevent her from securing a significant match, and partly because he put faith in Edward surviving to have heirs. The same problem, with the same outcome, and for the same reasons, existed during Edward's reign.

By May 1553, however, her accession had become a real possibility. It is generally supposed that her unmarried status was a mere detail, and that it was Northumberland's ambition which was the only pertinent reason for disinheriting Mary, but this needs closer scrutiny. While not excluding the duke's personal motives, a direct line can nevertheless be traced from Henry's will, through the July plot, and the December conspiracy, and beyond, even into the reign of Elizabeth, that emphasised the vulnerability of an unmarried ruling queen, and her kingdom, to a foreign takeover. This was seen as a very real menace.

It is mentioned as a reason in Edward's letters patent that formed his will, and in Jane' proclamation, and hinted at in the July instructions to the lords lieutenant to apprehend Mary. It could clearly not be the headline reason because there was no legal basis in excluding Mary just for what she possibly *might* do, but the fact that it was mentioned at all, besides being a good propaganda point, shows the seriousness of the issue. It might also explain why Northumberland's council continued to oppose Mary even after Edward's death.

That this was such an issue could be explained by the emphasis on English nationalism that Henry had inspired. Over the previous century, ever since the end of the Hundred Years War, England had become more insular and had mostly withdrawn from European affairs, with only the occasional, largely meaningless, expedition undertaken for motives of dynastic propaganda. It had also withdrawn from the 'family' of Catholic nations, and, as yet, not joined with other Protestant ones. As an island, separated from others, it began to feel itself more inviolate, more English, and this had aroused a growth in nationalist feeling. The idea of handing control of the kingdom to foreigners had become unthinkable.

Mary's links with Charles V, through the Imperial ambassadors, were no secret, nor was it forgotten that she was half-Spanish. It was known that Philip of Spain's first wife had died some nine years previously and that, although he had a son, no ruler was going to rely on just one, and he would soon be looking for a suitable match. It did not take an enormous flight of imagination to recognise a possible link, and we can be sure that Northumberland and the council would have been well aware of it. There was not just the fear that England might be put in the hands of Spaniards, and might even become effectively a province of Spain, but also that Philip would insist on the restoration of the Catholic religion.

*

Mary's Catholicism, and her determination to enforce it, was another common thread in both revolts. Although it may seem that Northumberland was personally motivated by ambition, or fear (of

Mary), rather than religion, it should be remembered that the plot to disinherit her almost certainly began with Edward, and his reason was quite clearly religious. The move to Protestantism was his mission, the idea that defined his reign, even his existence, and Mary's stolid opposition, and the threat that she would destroy everything he had achieved, was behind the first draft of the 'devise'. Northumberland went along with this because it suited him to do so, and because, at that time, he did perhaps also feel a pride in what he had achieved in terms of the Reformation. It seems highly unlikely that Edward would have consented to, or initiated, the exclusion of Mary if she had not been such a determined Catholic.

But we must again be careful to distinguish between religion and faith as a causative factor. The move towards Protestantism had only seriously begun six years previously; before that, Englishmen had experienced nearly a millennium of Catholic rites and belief, enough time for it to become engrained into the national consciousness. Most of those on the council had lived the great majority of their lives as Catholics, so it is hard to believe that the prospect of reversion was, *by itself*, a significant cause for them to disbar Mary. And the fact that so few ordinary people joined either revolt suggests that religion, in terms of faith, was not a significant factor for them, either.

But what was a key factor, in both revolts, was the *political* implications of a religious change. It wasn't that Mary was a Catholic, so much as the fact that she would inevitably choose Catholics to occupy positions of power, which would mean that those who currently held those roles would lose out. No-one seriously expected a massacre of Protestants if Mary was to succeed in July, but they did expect to lose position and status. These were serious enough considerations for councillors to try and oppose Mary's accession, though not serious enough to risk life for when things started to get tough.

In the December conspiracy, a similar situation can be seen. An obvious example is the duke of Suffolk who had lost his position on the council under Mary, and clearly wanted it back. The other leading plotters were also Protestant, and formerly in positions of influence that they were unlikely to regain while Mary was on the throne. In both revolts, religion by itself was not the main motive – if it had been then the people would more likely have become involved and there could have been a continental-style war of religion – but the fact that the uprisings were mainly a matter for the elite shows that it was politics rather than doctrine that was behind the religious slogans.

Yet there were some genuine worries over religion. Philip and Spaniards were not just ordinary Catholics, they were champions of the Counter-reformation. A Spanish king did not promise an era of religious tolerance, and Mary had already made it clear that she intended to restore papal authority, which would doubtless include the Inquisition, and this was far beyond what ordinary Englishmen could accept. If Mary had not been so *determinedly* Catholic, and committed to a project for which she would need a powerful ally alongside her, she would have been able to listen more closely to the howls of protest that greeted her choice of spouse.

*

Given the near uniqueness of Mary's difficulties in establishing herself as monarch, we also have to consider what might be unique about *her*, and this is almost certainly to be discovered as much in who she was, as in what she stood for.

There was nothing intrinsically unsuitable about Mary as a person. Despite her ill-health and occasional dark moods, she was more personable than her grandfather, more level-headed than her father, more grown-up than Edward, and less histrionic than her sister. Those who knew her, liked her. Given the process, or lack of it, by which English monarchs are invested, the position has attracted its fair share of oddballs, and Mary was some way from being the oddest.

Yet she was not without flaws. The most obvious – those that were noticed by commentators at the time, and so inevitably coloured contemporary views of her - were doubtless the most damaging, namely her weakness and her stubbornness. That these were diametrically opposed did not even things out but simply compounded the problem. The fact that she was often indecisive could be a serious failing when it came to controlling a council that was factionally divided in the first place. This could be seen in her initial agonising over the choice of a husband, which exacerbated splits within the council, and may have caused her to look outside of it for advice.

But this needs to be qualified. Since none of the councillors defected to the rebels, it cannot be seen, outwardly, as a significant issue during Wyatt's rebellion, and nor can it have been during Northumberland's since she was not yet queen. So, no-one was exasperated enough purely by her indecisiveness to rebel. However, it is still a factor, since indecisiveness is taken as a sign of weakness and provides the *opportunity* to rebel. The rifts in the council helped convince the plotters in December that their rebellion would be successful, and that Mary's government would not be united or determined enough to resist them.

Her stubbornness is more relevant to both revolts. Northumberland, and Edward, had seen, over the issue of the Mass, that Mary was not willing to back down, and it needed the arrest of her chaplains to even get her to compromise by being discreet about it. She was clearly not going to be someone who he, or the council as a whole, could bend to their will, and given her views on religion, and the worries over who she might choose as a husband, this stubbornness and inability to compromise, made her appear unsuitable, and were key causes of the decision to disbar her. Exactly the same could be said of the reasons for the December conspiracy; the only way to get her to compromise, or change, was to use force. Parliament, and the majority of her councillors, had tried to talk her out of the Spanish match, as had what went for public opinion, but all had failed. What was left?

*

And this provides another explanation for why there were rebellions in 1553, and indeed why there seem to have been so many during Tudor times: there simply was no alternative. There are clues in the statements made by both Northumberland and Suffolk at their trials. The former had asked whether it could be treason for someone to follow orders given under the royal seal, and the latter had enquired of his judges whether treason could be applied to rebelling to stop foreigners entering the country. From our twenty-first-century perspective, both can be seen as clear cases of 'trying it on', but it is quite possible that they were absolutely serious. Northumberland certainly had some legal justification, and maybe even Suffolk had a point.

Nowadays, armed action against a government is legally, and usually morally, indefensible, and the justification is that, at least in a democracy, there are so many other ways that opposition can be voiced. But in Tudor times, there was no other outlet apart from rebellion. Parliament was summoned, and dismissed, at the will of the monarch, and during its sessions could only be moderately disruptive; the council was chosen either by its own president, or by the monarch, so there was no hope for an opponent of the government to get policy changed; and there was strict censorship.

For Northumberland and Wyatt there really was no alternative to rebellion. Attempts at compromise had been suggested by Charles in May – that Mary allow the new religion to remain, that she marry an Englishman, and that she keep the present government - but, given Mary's character, no-one believed she would agree, and even he was not sincere. Since there was no possibility of compromise, what alternative was there for Northumberland but to take the law into his own hands? Suffolk doubtless felt the same in early 1554 – how else was England going to be protected from being taken over by foreigners, when Mary was ignoring all opposition to the match? The fact that both revolts failed showed that Tudor society had, for the most part, settled down, but that they happened at all showed that frustrations were building, the same frustrations that were to lead to much more serious trouble a century later.

*

And Mary was a woman. There can be little point in ignoring the fact that both rebellions took place at the start of the reign of England's first ruling queen. The fact that the replacement monarch in each case was also a woman is certainly a mitigating factor, but it should not completely disguise the importance of gender as an explanation. This is not to say that either rebellion was planned simply *because* she was a woman. Not even the Tudors were that misogynistic. Rather, the rebels took action because, as she was a woman, they again sensed an opportunity, a possible weakness. When, after Wyatt's rebellion they saw clearly that there wasn't a weakness, they gave up. In a sense, Renard was right all along; she ought to have been more ruthless after Northumberland's revolt, and proved that, even as a woman, she had what was needed to keep the peace.

So would Northumberland, and Edward, have formulated their plan if Mary had been a man? It is not unthinkable. Male monarchs were as vulnerable to revolt and deposition as women, but there was something in the way that Northumberland operated - almost as if Mary wouldn't protest – with an innate sexism bordering on contempt, that convinced him that he could get away with it; that she didn't need to be closely monitored; that if she left Hunsdon it could only be to flee, not to fight. Even on the scaffold, he acted as though Mary couldn't possibly be so unsentimental as to go through with his execution, that being a woman she would show mercy at the last moment. Wyatt may have been similarly fooled, convinced by the merciful way she had treated the earlier plotters that he, too, could get away with it. His surrender had been expedited by being told that Mary might be merciful if he gave up immediately. We don't know whether he believed it, but the mere fact that such an, apparently ludicrous, statement was even made might show a general belief that Mary, being female, was 'soft'.

Tudor society may not have been overtly misogynistic, but it was certainly not a level playing field when it came to the status of women. Even the law considered married women to be essentially the property of their husbands, daughters of their fathers, and only widows having significant property rights of their own. As for the rights of queens, this was an unknown, and it would depend on the attitudes of those in positions of power how Mary would be regarded.

In terms of attitude, it is possible to distinguish between the industrious and the idle classes. With the former, there was a greater sense of equality. In a peasant household, women had to contribute, and were thus valued for their work. With those higher up the social scale, where women's roles were often more decorative than functional, the distinction was starker. Northumberland, Wyatt and their ilk, were not brought up to see women as fulfilling an equally significant role. The important jobs of fighting and politics were the preserve of men; women produced children, and that was about it. The idea of women being precious, delicate, and over-emotional creatures was not one that held much sway in a labourer's cottage, but in an upper-class mansion it was more prevalent. This might be further explanation for why those active in both rebellions were people of a higher social class.

So, if Northumberland so disrespected women, how come he chose Jane? Well, for exactly these reasons. There was no suitable male available, and so, if he was forced to choose a woman, let it be one who he could easily manipulate. He assumed that Mary would not be so easy to control – he had experience of her stubbornness over the issue of Mass – so he selected someone who he thought he could. This might also explain why he passed over her mother, whose age and experience made her a less easy prospect. His treatment of, and attitude towards, Jane was appalling, only equalled by her father's, and can only really be explained by a degree of misogynistic contempt that was innately typical of his class.

*

And then there is Northumberland's own role in these events. It has become almost a truism that he, and he alone, was responsible for the July plot, and that it was solely due to his ambition. Although more recent historians have tried to 'whiten' the legend, by focusing more on his achievements prior to 1553, it still seems received wisdom that he conducted the coup for personal rather than national reasons. There is, actually, surprisingly little evidence to support this belief. The Imperial ambassadors lost no opportunity to accuse him of selfish ambition, even before 1553, and Renard, interestingly, was still warning Mary against a 'Northumberland party' shortly before Wyatt's rebellion. But they had a political motive for doing so, firstly because he was bringing in a Protestant reformation, and then because he was preventing a Catholic from becoming queen. Later, privy councillors, and Montagu and Jane, were eager to exonerate themselves by piling all the blame onto him, but none of these sources offer anything like conclusive evidence. The saying 'well, they would say that, wouldn't they?' is clearly applicable here.

Even later historians – Stow and Holinshed – who were writing during the reign of Elizabeth had every reason to damn Northumberland's character, since he had been intent on excluding her, too. Those writers who followed were happy to continue this tradition - so much more interesting than simply portraying him as someone trying to do the right thing for his country.

While there can hardly be any doubt as to Northumberland's involvement in the plot, questions still remain as to his motives, and even whether it was his idea in the first place. Up until July 1553, his record had been one of complete loyalty to the Tudor dynasty, and his ambition had been limited to whatever was possible and allowable for a commoner. For someone who is accused of treating Edward like a puppet, he had shown unusual diligence in extracting him from the bubble in which Somerset had abandoned him, allowing him to partake in manly sports and educating him in the practicalities of kingship. It might also be said that for someone who was merely a selfish adventurer, he had spent an unusual amount of time and energy throughout his career into making England a more prosperous country, and the lives of Englishmen more pleasant.

It is also worth mentioning that just about everything he may have feared for his country with the accession of Mary actually came to pass – the forcible return to Catholicism, involving burnings and general repression; the marriage to a foreigner resulting in a rebellion; and England being involved in a war in which it had no interest. And, with religion become such an issue due to the chopping and changing, the consequent period of Elizabethan repression of Catholics, too. Counterfactually, England might have been a more united and happier country if the 'evil' duke had won.

And was it all his idea, anyway? We know Edward wrote the first version of the 'devise', and experts are fairly sure that the changes that made Jane queen were also in the king's hand. Was this really at the instigation of Northumberland? Possibly, but there is no evidence. The only real clues we have come from his career, in which he loyally served the orders of his sovereigns – the loyal ass, as he described himself. Of course, the plot made perfect sense to him, and he undoubtedly enabled it, but perhaps we should see him as someone following orders, rather than as one acting purely for his own benefit.

If we can allow ourselves the iconoclastic thought that maybe he was acting in July 1553 for the good of the country, rather than just himself, we might see that his decision to abandon his march on Mary was caused as much by a desire to avoid bloodshed, and the spectre of civil war, as by cowardice. Likewise, his determination to be guided by council orders, rather than acting on his own initiative, might also be seen as symptomatic of that respect and loyalty that he had exhibited throughout his career.

We know of three occasions when he and Jane, his 'surrogate' monarch, had disagreements. The first in which he persuaded her to become queen against her will, when he won the argument. The next was when, now queen, Jane refused to make Guilford king, and the third was when she overruled his choice of Suffolk to lead the expedition against Mary, and on both these occasions he deferred to the will of his sovereign. As he had throughout his career, the loyal servant, loyally obedient to the wishes of the Crown, and, like his father, paying for that loyalty with his life.

*

That Wyatt's rebellion subsequently happened, and that the issues were so similar to those in July, shows that there were more profound reasons for unrest during this one year than simply the ambition of one man. Yet all this must be kept in perspective. Tiny objects seen through a microscope appear enormous, and so do historical events viewed in microcosm. Close-up, the rebellions of Northumberland and Wyatt appear threatening, with the potential to change the course of history, and both came close to doing just that. Yet, seen from a distance, the events of 1553 created barely a ripple to disturb the course of the Tudor century. Their importance lies less in the fact that they happened, than in the fact that they failed.

There were, undoubtedly, important principles involved: legitimacy, as claimed by Mary, and on the other hand the desire to protect the country from a possible threat from foreigners in the form of Philip and the Pope. These were vital issues, but what was more significant was the reaction of the country to them. For better or worse, England decided, in

1553, to go for the stability offered by the Tudors, rather than the uncertain future that might result from rebellion.

Perhaps the most revealing moment of the year was the reaction of Sir John Harington, the Leicestershire landowner who, when asked by Richard Troughton where his allegiance lay, simply brought down a copy of the statute book and pointed, without comment, to the Act of Succession. His meaning was clear. No words were needed. England was now a law-abiding country, and the law must be followed. That was the achievement of the Tudors, and 1553 was the proof of it.

References

Preamble
1. Holinshed, *Chronicles*, vol.III, p.1033
2. *Ibid*, p.1034
3. *Ibid*
4. *Ibid,* p.1036
5. Nichols, *Literary Remains*, p.390
6. Wriothesley, *Chronicle*, p.67
7. *Ibid*, p.70
8. Nichols, *Greyfriars Chronicle*, p.74
9. Fuller, *Church History*, p.91

1. 1553: A Year of Promise?
1. Wriothesley, *Chronicle*, p.81
2. Nichols, *Diary of Henry Machyn*, p.30
3. Crankshaw, *Tudor Privy Council*, p.2
4. Hoak, *King's Council*, p.111
5. C[alendar of]S[tate]P[apers] (Spain), vol.11: Scheyfve to Queen Dowager, 20/1/53
6. Dietz, *Finances of Edward VI*, p.74
7. *Ibid*
8. *Ibid*, p.81
9. *Ibid*, p.85
10. Wordie, *Deflationary Factors*, p.39
11. Loach & Tittler, The Mid-Tudor Polity, p.108
12. Dietz, *op cit.*, p.88. He estimates a total cost of £1.35m over 5 years, including its capture; Wordie (*op cit*, p.56) estimates £600,000 to capture, and £400,000 over the next 4 years.
13. Loades, *John Dudley*, p.57
14. Jordan, *Edward VI*, p.507
15. Hoak, *op cit*, p.337, fn 81
16. Loades, *op cit*, p.59

2. The Problem with Mary
1. CSP (Spain), Scheyfve to the Emperor, 17/2/1553
2. CSP (Spain), Van der Delft to the Emperor, 14/1/1550

3	CSP (Spain), Van der Delft to the Emperor, 17/3/1550
4	CSP (Spain), Van der Delft to the Emperor, 2/5/1550
5	CSP (Spain), Edward VI to the Lady Mary, 28/1/1551
6	CSP (Spain), The Emperor to Scheyfve, 7/3/1551
7	*Ibid*
8	Nichols, *Literary Remains of Edward VI*, pp.308-9
9	CSP (Spain). Scheyfve to the Emperor, 6/4/51
10	CSP (Spain), the Queen Dowager to the Bishop of Arras, 5/10/1551
11	CSP (Spain), *fn* 4, pp.341-8, Aug 1551
12	CSP (Spain), the Ambassadors to Mary, 24/7/1553
13	Harbison, *Rival Ambassadors*, p.15
14	CSP (Spain), the Queen Dowager to the Emperor, 23/6/1552
15	CSP (Spain), Scheyfve to the Queen Dowager, 24/7/1552
16	CSP (Spain), Scheyfve to the bishop of Arras, 17/2/1553
17	CSP (Spain), Scheyfve to the Emperor, 25/7/1551
18	CSP (Spain), de Courrières to the Queen Dowager, 28/4/1552
19	Cooper, *Chronicle*, p.357
20	CSP (Spain), Scheyfve to the Queen Dowager, 10/9/1552
21	Ascham to Sturm, 4/4/1550 in: Giles, *Roger Ascham*, p. LXII

3. 'My devise for the Succession'
1	Raithby, *Statutes at Large*, p.494
2	Hoak, *Rewriting the History*, p.4
3	CSP (Spain), Scheyfve to the Emperor, 14/1/1552
4	Stow, *Annals*, p.1038
5	Nichols, *Chronicle of Queen Jane*, p.21

4. Preparing the Ground
1	CSP (Spain), Scheyfve advices, 28/4/1553
2	CSP (Spain), Scheyfve to the Emperor, 28/4/1553
3	CSP (Spain), Scheyfve to the Emperor, 30/5/1553
4	CSP (Spain), Scheyfve to the Emperor, 11/6/1553
5	Haynes, *State Papers*, p.150
6	CSP (Spain), Scheyfve to the Emperor, 30/5/1553
7	Vertot, *Ambassades* vol.2, p.3
8	*Ibid*, p.9
9	Beer, *Northumberland*, p.150
10	CSP (Spain), Scheyfve to the Emperor, 11/6/1553
11	Strype, *Life of John Cheke*, p.22

12   Fuller, *Church History*, pp.137-146 *passim*
13   *Ibid*, p.140
14   Strype, *Annals* vol.4, pp.485-9
15   Nichols, *Chronicle of Queen Jane*, pp.91-100
16   *Ibid*, p.90
17   CSP (Spain), Scheyfve to the Emperor, 15/6/1553
18   *Ibid*
19   Noailles to the Constable, 16/6/1553, in: Vertot, *op cit.* vol.2, p.31
20   Noailles to the King, 22/6/1553, in: Vertot, *op cit.*, p.39
21   CSP (Spain), Scheyfve to the Emperor, 19/6/1553
22   CSP (Spain), Scheyfve to the Emperor, 19/6/1553
23   CSP (Spain), the Emperor to various, 23/6/1553
24   CSP (Spain), the Emperor to the Ambassadors, 23/6/1553
25   CSP (Spain), Scheyfve to the Emperor, 24/6/1553
26   CSP (Spain), Courrières and Renard [special ambassadors] to The Emperor, 30/6/1553
27   CSP (Spain), Scheyfve to the Emperor, 4/7/1553
28   *Ibid*
29   Skidmore, *Edward VI*, p.258
30   CSP (Spain), Ambassadors (including Scheyfve) to the Emperor, 7/7/1553

5. The Rebellion against Mary

1   Tytler, *England under the reigns of Edward VI and Mary*, pp.192-5. Cecil's letter served its purpose, since he was to escape with his life, but it did not do enough to immediately rehabilitate him. The survival skills, and duplicity, that the experience taught him were, however, to be of great use in his subsequent rise to prominence under Elizabeth.
2   CSP (Spain), Sheyfve to the Emperor, 4/7/1553
3   Ives, *Lady Jane Grey*, p.172
4   *Ibid*
5   Wingfield, *Vita Mariae Reginae*, p.262; quoted in de Lisle, *The Sisters who would be Queen*, p.108
6   CSP (Venice), Soranzo to the Senate, 18/8/1554
7   Noailles to the King, 7/7/1553, in: Vertot, *op cit.* vol.2, p.50
8   Harbison, *Rival Ambassadors*, p.45
9   CSP (Spain), the Ambassadors to the Emperor, 7/7/1553
10   CSP (Spain), the Emperor to the Ambassadors, 11/7/1553
11   McIntosh, *Heads of Household*, ch.4, para.33

12	Strype, *Ecclesiastical Memorials* vol.3, pp.14-5
13	Haynes, *State Papers*, pp.117-9
14	The earliest reference to this story seems to have come from Commendone, the papal envoy to Mary, who arrived in London a month later.
15	At any rate, Mary seemed to be convinced that Jane knew nothing about it beforehand for she mentioned this in a conversation with the Imperial Ambassador as a reason not to execute her. CSP (Spain), the Ambassadors to the Emperor, 16/8/1553
16	Nichols, *Greyfriars Chronicle*, p.78
17	Howell, *State Trials*, pp.739-42
18	Nichols, *Chronicle of Queen Jane*, pp.116-121
19	Ives, *op cit.*, p.65
20	Ascham, *The Scholemaster*, pp. 201-2
21	Foxe, *Actes and Monuments*, (1570) Bk.10, pp.1605-6
22	*Ibid*, p.1606
23	Strype, *Memorials* vol.3 issue 1, pp.5-6
24	CSP (Spain), the Emperor to the ambassadors, 11/7/1553
25	CSP (Spain), the ambassadors to the Emperor, 12/7/1553
26	Stow, *Annals*, p.1030
27	Nichols, *Chronicle of Queen Jane*, p.8
28	The best analysis of events concerning the ships can be found in: J. D. Alsop, 'A Regime at Sea: The Navy and the 1553 Succession Crisis'
29	Haynes, *op cit.*, p.155
30	Nichols, *Chronicle of Queen Jane*, p.9
31	CSP (Spain), the Ambassadors to the Emperor, 22/7/1553
32	Stow, *op cit.*, p.1032-3
33	Howard, *Lady Jane Grey*, p.288

6. Mary the Queen

1	Whitelock, *Mary Tudor*, p.173
2	Madden, *Petition of Richard Troughton*, p.22
3	*Ibid*
4	Grafton, *An Abridgement*, ff.154r
5	Nichols, *Diary of Henry Machyn*, p.39
6	Noailles to the Constable, July 1553, in: Vertot, *Ambassades* vol.2, p.99
7	CSP (Spain), the Ambassadors to the Emperor, 6/8/1553
8	CSP (Venice), Soranzo to the Senate, 18/8/1554

9 Noailles to the King, 7/8/1553, in: Vertot, *op cit*.vol.2, p.104
10 Loach, *Parliament and the Crown*, pp.11-12
11 Ponet, *A Short Treatise*, p.101
12 CSP (Spain), Renard to the Bishop of Arras, 9/9/1553
13 CSP (Spain), the Ambassadors to Mary, 24/7/1553
14 CSP (Spain), the Ambassadors to the Emperor, 16/8/1553
15 *Acts of the Privy Council*, 28/11/1553, p.374
16 Stow, *Annals*, p.1038
17 CSP (Spain), the Emperor to the Ambassadors, 23/8/1553
18 Nichols, *Chronicle of Queen Jane*, p.16
19 *Ibid*, p.19
20 Loades, *John Dudley*, p.32
21 Foxe, *Actes and Monuments* (1570) Bk.10, p.1607. Foxe, however, being a protestant martyrologist, probably *would* suggest this anyway, and he provides no evidence to back up his assertion.
22 Cooper, *Chronicle*, ff.360r
23 Howard, *Lady Jane Grey*, p.322
24 Nichols, *Chronicle of Queen Jane*, p.25
25 *Ibid*, p.20
26 *Ibid*, p.22 *fn*
27 Tytler, *England under the Reigns of Edward VI and Mary*, p.155
28 Strype, *Ecclesiastical Memorials* vol.3 issue 1, p.41
29 Tytler, *op cit.*, pp.154-6

7. Establishing the New Regime
1 Stow, *Annals*, p.1037. Ironically, both the rescuers were burnt later in Mary's reign for refusing to renounce Protestantism.
2 Acts of the Privy Council, 13/8/1553, p.317
3 *Ibid*, 13/9/1553, p.345
4 Wriothesley, *Chronicle*, p.101
5 CSP (Venice), Soranzo to the Senate, 18/8/1554
6 *Acts of the Privy Council*, 15/9/1553, p.349
7 Nichols, *Diary of Henry Machyn*, p.48
8 Nichols, *Narratives*, pp.177-217
9 Cooper, *Chronicle*, ff.360r
10 Nichols, *Narratives*, pp.134-176
11 Guaras, *The Accession of Queen Mary*, p.132
12 CSP (Spain), the Ambassadors to the Emperor, 16/8/1553
13 *Ibid*

14	CSP (Spain), Renard to the Bishop of Arras, 9/9/1553
15	CSP (Spain), the Ambassadors to the Emperor, 23/9/1553
16	CSP (Spain), the Ambassadors to the Emperor, 19/9/1553
17	Nichols, *Chronicle of Queen Jane*, p.29
18	For an interesting discussion of these issues, see: Richards, 'Mary Tudor as Sole Quene', pp.900-3
19	Loach, *Parliament and the Crown*, p.77
20	Nichols, *Chronicle of Queen Jane*, p.26
21	CSP (Spain), the Ambassadors to the Emperor, 6/8/1553. Noailles makes no mention of such an issue, and Henri sent the necessary letters on 29 July (the King to Noailles, 29/7/1553 in: Vertot, *Ambassades* vol.2, p.95)
22	Noailles to the Constable, 7/8/1553, in: Vertot, *op cit.* vol.2, pp.105-7

8. The Wooing of Mary

1	CSP (Spain), the Ambassadors to the Emperor, 22/7/1553
2	CSP (Spain), Scheyfve 'Advices', 28/4/1553
3	CSP (Spain), the Emperor to the Ambassadors (Instructions), 23/6/1553
4	CSP (Spain), the Emperor to the Ambassadors, 22/7/1553
5	CSP (Spain), the Ambassadors to the Emperor, 22/7/1553
6	CSP (Spain), the Emperor to Prince Philip, 30/7/1553
7	CSP (Spain), the Ambassadors to the Emperor, 2/8/1553
8	CSP (Spain), Renard to the Bishop of Arras, 7/8/1553
9	CSP (Spain), the Bishop of Arras to Renard, 14/8/1553
10	CSP (Spain), the Ambassadors to the Emperor, 16/8/1553
11	Noailles to the King, 9/8/1553, in: Vertot, *Ambassades* vol.2, p.109
12	Noailles to the King, 7/9/1553, in: Vertot, *op cit.* vol.2, p.144
13	The King to Noailles, 16/9/1553, in: Vertot, *op cit.* vol.2, p.150
14	Noailles to the King, 22/9/1553, in: Vertot, *op cit.* vol.2, p.157
15	*Ibid*, p.159
16	Noailles to the King, 25/9/1553, in: Vertot, *op cit.* vol.2, p.167
17	CSP (Spain), Renard to the Bishop of Arras, 9/9/1553
18	Vertot, *op cit.* vol.1, p.249
19	CSP (Spain), Renard to Prince Philip, 3/10/1553
20	CSP (Spain), Renard to the Emperor, 5/10/1553
21	CSP (Spain), the Emperor to Renard, 20/9/1553
22	CSP (Spain), Renard to the Emperor, 12/10/1553
23	CSP (Spain), Renard to the Emperor, 15/10/1553

24	Renard to Mary, Memorial, in CSP (Spain), Renard to the Emperor, 15/10/1553
25	CSP (Spain), Renard to the Emperor, 28/10/1553
26	CSP (Spain), Renard to the Emperor, 31/10/1553
27	CSP (Spain), Renard to the Emperor, 23/10/1553
28	CSP (Spain), Renard to the Emperor, 6/11/1553
29	*Ibid*
30	CSP (Spain), Renard to the Emperor, 8/11/1553
31	CSP (Spain), Renard to the Emperor, 17/11/1553
32	CSP (Spain), Renard to the Emperor, 20/11/1553
33	Noailles to the King, 4/9/1553, in: Vertot, *op cit.* vol.2, p.135-6
34	CSP (Spain), the Emperor to Renard, 28/11/1553
35	Harbison, *Rival Ambassadors*, pp.103-4
36	CSP (Spain), the Emperor to Prince Philip, 30/11/1553
37	CSP (Spain), the Emperor to Renard, 28/11/1553
38	CSP (Spain), the Ambassadors to the Emperor, 6/8/1553
39	CSP (Spain), Renard to the Emperor, 12/12/1553
40	CSP (Spain), the Ambassadors to the Emperor, 7/1/1554
41	Nichols, *Chronicle of Queen Jane*, p.34
42	CSP (Spain), a writing *ad cautelam*, 4/1/1554

9. Revolt and Resolution

1	CSP (Spain), Renard to the Emperor, 17/12/1553
2	CSP (Spain), Renard to the Emperor, 20/12/1553
3	CSP (Spain), Paget to Renard, 23/12/1553
4	Wotton to the Council, 23/12/1553, in: Tytler, *England under the Reigns of Edward VI and Mary*, p.266
5	CSP (Spain), the Emperor to Renard, 24/12/1553
6	Paget to Renard in: CSP (Spain), Renard to the Emperor, 29/12/1553
7	CSP (Spain), Egmont to Prince Philip, 7/1/1554
8	Noailles to the King, 18/12/1553, in: Vertot, *Ambassades* vol.2, p.322
9	Harbison, *Rival Ambassadors*, p.117. It was William Thomas who suggested killing Mary, though Wyatt at his trial denied that this was an aim of the conspiracy (Howell, *State Trials*, p.863)
10	Noailles to the King, 14/11/1553, in: Vertot, *op cit.* vol.2, pp.253-4
11	Howell, *State Trials*, p.883

12	Harbison, *Rival Ambassadors*, p.119
13	*Ibid*, p.120
14	The Guises to Noailles, 23/11/1553, in Vertot, *op cit.* vol.2, p.263-4
15	Pollard, *Tudor Tracts*, p.212-3
16	CSP (Spain), the Ambassadors to the Emperor, 31/1/1554
17	CSP (Spain), the Emperor to the Ambassadors, 31/1/1554
18	Nichols, *Chronicle of Queen Jane*, p.38
19	Pollard, *op cit*, p.230
20	Nichols, *Chronicle of Queen Jane*, p.39
21	Harbison, *French Intrigue*, p.548
22	Nichols, *Chronicle of Queen Jane*, p.40-1 *fn*(d)
23	Foxe, *Actes and Monuments*, (1570) Bk.10, p.1618
24	Wriothesley, *Chronicle*, p.109
25	Stow, *Annals*, p.1047
26	Pollard, *op cit.*, p. 246
27	Nichols, *Chronicle of Queen Jane*, p.43
28	*Ibid*, p.48
29	Samson, *Marriage of Queen Mary*, p.118
30	Nichols, *Narratives*, p.162
31	*Ibid*, p.168
32	Loades, *Two Tudor Conspiracies*, p.25
33	Cooper, *Chronicle*, p.362
34	Nichols, *Chronicle of Queen Jane*, p.185
35	Howell, *State Trials*, pp.901-2
36	Noailles to the Constable, 12/3/1554, in: Vertot, *Ambassades* vol.3, p.129-30
37	Pollard, *op cit*, p.210
38	Robison, *Wyatt's Rebellion in Surrey*, p.780
39	Loades, *Two Tudor Conspiracies*, p.242

10. Aftermath

1	Foxe, *Actes and Monuments* (1563), p.920, in: Ives, *A Tudor Mystery*, p.22
2	Nichols, *Chronicle of Queen Jane*, p.56
3	*Ibid*, p.57
4	*Ibid*, p.60
5	CSP (Spain), Renard to the Emperor, 12/2/1554
6	CSP (Spain), Renard to Prince Philip, 19/2/1554. This reputation had followed Elizabeth around, beginning with the sensational revelations at the trial of Thomas Seymour, brother

of the Duke of Somerset, of the flirtations between the two of them.

Bibliography

Archival (online) Sources
Acts of the Privy Council of England Volume 4, 1552-1554, ed. John Roche Dasent (London, 1892) British History Online http://www.british-history.ac.uk/acts-privy-council/vol4

Calendar of State Papers, Spain, Volume 11, 1553, ed. Royall Tyler (London, 1916), British History Online http://www.british-history.ac.uk/cal-state-papers/spain/vol11

Calendar of State Papers, Spain, Volume 12, 1554, ed. Royall Tyler (London, 1949), British History Online http://www.british-history.ac.uk/cal-state-papers/spain/vol12

Calendar of State Papers Relating to English Affairs in the Archives of Venice, Volume 5, 1534-1554, ed. Rawdon Brown (London, 1873), pp. 531-567. British History Online http://www.british-history.ac.uk/cal-state-papers/venice/vol5/pp531-567

Published Sources
Alford, S., *Edward VI* (Penguin, 2014)

---- *Kingship and Politics in the Reign of Edward VI* (Cambridge, 2004)

Alsop, J.D., 'The Revenue Commission of 1552', *Historical Journal*, 22 (1979), pp. 511-33

---- 'A Regime at Sea: the navy and the 1553 succession crisis', *Albion*, 24 (1992), pp. 577-90

---- 'The Act for the Queen's Regal Power, 1554', *Parliamentary History*, vol.13 (1994), pp. 261-76

Ascham, R., *The Scholemaster* (London, 1570)

Baker, R., *A Chronicle of the Kings of England* (London, 1670)

Beer, B.L., *Northumberland: the political career of John Dudley, Earl of Warwick and Duke of Northumberland* (Kent, Ohio, Kent State University Press, 1973)

---- 'The Myth of the Wicked Duke and the Historical John Dudley', *Albion*, 11 (1979), pp. 1-14

Bindoff, S.T., 'A Kingdom at Stake 1553', *History Today*, 3 (1953), pp. 642-8

Braddock, R.C., 'The Character and Composition of the Duke of Northumberland's Army', *Albion*, vol. 6 (1974), pp. 342-356

---- 'The Duke of Northumberland's Army Reconsidered', *Albion*, vol.19 (1987), pp. 13-17

Bryson, A., 'Edward VI's 'speciall men': crown and locality in mid Tudor England', *Historical Research*, vol. 82/216 (2009) pp. 229–251

Buckley, H., 'Sir Thomas Gresham and the Foreign Exchanges', *The Economic Journal*, vol.34 (1924), pp. 589-601

Burnet, G., *History of the Reformation of the Church of England*, vol.5, ed. N. Pocock (Oxford, 1865)

Cooper, T., *Coopers Chronicle* (London, 1560)

Crankshaw, D.J., The Tudor Privy Council, c. 1540–1603 (*State Papers Online 1509–1714*, Cengage Learning EMEA Ltd., 2009)

De Lisle, L., *The Sisters who would be Queen* (London, 2008)

Dietz, F.C., *Finances of Edward VI and Mary,* Smith College Studies in History vol.3 n°2 (Northampton, Mass, 1918)

Ellis, H., *Original Letters, illustrative of English History*, vol.2 (2°) (London, 1825)

Elton, G.R., 'Parliament in the Sixteenth Century: Functions and Fortunes', *The Historical Journal*, vol. 22 (1979), pp. 255-278

Feuillerat, J. (ed.), *Documents relating to the revels at court in the time of King Edward VI and Queen Mary* (Louvain, 1914)

Florio, M., *Historia de la vita e de la morte de l'illustriss. signora Giovanna Graia* (1607)

Foxe, J., *Actes and Monuments* (The Unabridged Acts and Monuments Online or TAMO (HRI Online Publications, Sheffield, 2011). Available from: http//www.johnfoxe.org)

Fuller, T., *Church History of Britain*, vol.4 (Oxford, 1845)

Furdell, E.L., *The Royal Doctors, 1485-1714: medical personnel at the Tudor and Stuart courts* (Rochester, NY, 2001)

Gammon, S.R., *Statesman and Schemer. William, First Lord Paget – Tudor Minister* (Newton Abbot, 1973)

Giles, J.A. (ed.), *The Whole Works of Roger Ascham*, vol.1 pt.1 (London, 1865)

Grafton, R., *An Abridgement of the Chronicles of England* (London, 1564)

---- *A Chronicle at Large*, vol.2 (London, 1809)

Guaras, Antonio de, *The Accession of Queen Mary*, ed. R. Garnett (London, 1892)

Guy, J., *Tudor England* (Oxford, 1992)

Hakluyt, R., *The principal navigations, voyages, traffiques and discoveries of the English nation* (Edinburgh, 1886)

Harbison, E.H., *Rival Ambassadors at the Court of Queen Mary* (ACLS Humanities E-Book, 2008)

---- 'French Intrigue at the Court of Queen Mary', *The American Historical Review*, vol. 45 (1940), pp. 533-551

Haynes, S., *A Collection of State Papers* (London, 1740)

Hayward, J., *The Life and Raigne of King Edward the Sixt* (London, 1630)

Heard, N., *Edward VI and Mary: a mid-Tudor crisis?* (London, 1991)

Historical Manuscripts Commission, *Calendar of the Manuscripts of the Most Hon. the Marquis of Salisbury, K.G.*, pt.1 (London 1883)

Hoak, D.E., *The King's Council in the Reign of Edward VI* (Cambridge, 1976)

---- 'The Succession Crisis of 1553 and Mary's Rise to Power', in *Catholic Renewal and Protestant Resistance in Marian England,* eds. Evendon, E. & Westbrook, V. (London, 2016)

---- 'Re-writing the History of Tudor Politics and Government: the regimes of Somerset and Northumberland' *The Journal of the Rutgers University Libraries*, vol.40 (1978), pp. 4-13

Holinshed, R., *Chronicles*, ed. H. Ellis (6 vols; London, 1807-8)

Howard, G., *Lady Jane Grey, and Her Times* (London, 1822)

Howell, T.B. (ed.), *A Complete Collection of State Trials*, vol.1 (London, 1816)

Ives, E., *Lady Jane Grey: a Tudor mystery* (Chichester, 2011)

---- 'Henry VIII's Will-A Forensic Conundrum', *The Historical Journal*, vol. 35 (1992), pp. 779-804

Jack, S.M., 'Northumberland, Queen Jane and the Financing of the 1553 Coup', *Parergon*, 6 (1988), pp. 137-48

Jordan, W.K., *Edward VI: the threshold of power. The dominance of the Duke of Northumberland* (London, 1970)

Kewes, P., 'The 1553 Succession Crisis Reconsidered', *Historical Research*, vol.90/249 (2017), pp. 465-85

Knox, J., *The First Blast of the Trumpet against the monstrous regiment of Women*, ed. E. Arber (London, 1878)

Loach, J., *Parliament and the Crown in the Reign of Mary Tudor* (Oxford, 1986)

---- *Parliament under the Tudors* (Oxford, 1991)

Loach, J. and Tittler, R. (eds), *The Mid-Tudor Polity c.1540-1560* (London, 1989)

Loades, D., *John Dudley, Duke of Northumberland, 1504-1553* (Oxford, 1996)

---- *Mary Tudor* (Stroud, 2012)

---- *The Mid-Tudor Crisis, 1545-1565* (London, 1992)

---- *Two Tudor Conspiracies* (Cambridge, 1965)

Madden, F., 'Petition of Richard Troughton, Bailiff of South Witham, Lincolnshire, to the Privy Council in the Reign of Queen Mary', *Archaeologia*, vol.23 (1830)

McIntosh, J.L., *From Heads of Household to Heads of State: The Pre-accession Households of Mary and Elizabeth Tudor, 1516-1558* (Columbia, 2008)

MacCulloch, D., 'Kett's Rebellion in Context: A Rejoinder', *Past and Present*, vol.93 (1981), pp. 165-73

Nichols, J.G. (ed.), 'The diary of Henry Machyn, citizen and merchant-taylor of London, from 1550-1563', *Camden Miscellany* (Camden Society, 1st ser., 42; London 1848).

---- (ed.), 'The chronicle of Queen Jane and two years of Queen Mary, and especially of the rebellion of Sir Thomas Wyat', *Camden Miscellany* (Camden Society, 1st ser., 48; London, 1850).

---- (ed.), 'Chronicle of the Grey Friars of London', *Camden Miscellany* (Camden Society, 1st ser., 53; London, 1851).

----(ed.), *Narratives of the days of the Reformation* (Camden Society, 1st ser., 77; 1859).

---- *The Literary remains of King Edward VI* (Roxburghe Club, vol.2; 1857)

Outhwaite, R.B., 'The Trials of Foreign Borrowing: The English Crown and the Antwerp Money Market in the Mid-Sixteenth Century', *The Economic History Review*, vol.19 (1966), pp. 289-305

Pollard, A.F., *The History of England, from the accession of Edward VI to the death of Elizabeth (1547-1603)* (London, 1923)

Pollard, A.F. (ed.), *Tudor Tracts* (New York, 1903)

Pollnitz, A., *Princely Education in Early Modern Britain* (Cambridge, 2015)

Ponet, J., *A Shorte Treatise of Politike Power* (https://archive.org/details/AShorteTreatiseOfPolitikePower)

Raithby, J., *The Statutes at Large of England and of Great Britain*, vol.3 (London, 1811)

Rapin de Thoyras, M., *Acta Regia* (London, 1733)

Richards, J.M., *Mary Tudor* (London, 2008)

---- 'Mary Tudor as 'Sole Quene'?: Gendering Tudor Monarchy', *The Historical Journal*, vol. 40 (1997), pp. 895-924

---- '"To Promote a Woman to Beare Rule": Talking of Queens in Mid-Tudor England', *The Sixteenth Century Journal*, vol. 28 (1997), pp. 101-121

Robinson, H., (ed.), *Original Letters relative to the English Reformation, Parker Society* (2 vols; Cambridge, University Press, 1846)

Robison, W.B., 'The National and Local Significance of Wyatt's Rebellion in Surrey', *The Historical Journal*, vol. 30 (1987), pp. 769-790

Ruding, R., *Annals of the Coinage of Great Britain and its Dependencies* (London, 1840)

Skidmore, C., *Edward VI: the lost king of England* (London, 2008)

Stone, J.M., *The History of Mary I. Queen of England* (London, 1901)

Stow, J., *Annals of England to 1603* (https://archive.org/details/annalsofenglandt00stow)

Strype, J., *Annals of the Reformation*, vol.4 (Oxford, 1824)

---- *Ecclesiastical Memorials* (3 vols; Oxford, 1822)

---- *The life of the learned Sir John Cheke, first instructor, afterwards secretary of state to king Edward VI* (Oxford, 1821)

Tawney, R.H. & Power, E. (eds.), *Tudor Economic Documents*, vol.2 (London, 1924)

Thorp, M.R., 'Religion and the Wyatt Rebellion of 1554', *Church History*, vol. 47 (1978), pp. 363-380

Tighe, W.J., 'The Gentlemen Pensioners, the Duke of Northumberland, and the Attempted Coup of July 1553', *Albion*, vol.19 (1987), pp. 1-11

Tytler, P.F., *England under the reigns of Edward VI and Mary*, vol.2 (London, 1839)

Vertot, *Ambassades de Messieurs de Noailles en Angleterre* (5 vols; Leyden, 1763)

Whitelock, A., *Mary Tudor: England's first queen* (London, 2009)

---- 'A Woman in a Man's World: Mary I and political intimacy, 1553–1558', *Women's History Review*, 16:3, pp. 323-334,

Whitelock, A. & MacCulloch, D., 'Princess Mary's Household and the Succession Crisis, July 1553', *The Historical Journal*, 50, 2 (2007), pp. 265–287

Wordie, J.R., 'Deflationary Factors in the Tudor Price Rise', *Past & Present*, 154 (1997), pp. 32-70

Wriothesley, C., *A Chronicle of England during the reigns of the Tudors from 1485 to 1559*, vol.2, ed. Hamilton, W.D. (Camden Society, London, 1877)

Unpublished theses
Samson, A.W., 'The marriage of Philip of Habsburg and Mary Tudor and anti-Spanish sentiment in England: political economies and culture, 1553-1557', PhD dissertation, Queen Mary College, University of London (1999)

Index

42 Articles, 55
Act of Supremacy, 52
Act of Uniformity, 54, 180
Alford, Roger, 104
Ascham, Roger, 63, 82, 127-8
Aylmer, John, 127-8
Barne, George, 26
Berwick, 33
Boisdauphin, 91, 97-8
Boleyn, Anne, 43, 74, 174, 207
Bonner, Edward, 52, 167-8
Boulogne, 16, 19, 33-6, 57, 100
Bourne, Gilbert, 167
Brett, Alexander, 214, 219, 227, 234
Calais, 35, 41, 57, 136, 182, 200
Carew, Peter, 209-212, 227
Cecil, William, Lord Burghley, 30, 36, 59, 90, 95, 98, 100, 104-105, 114, 117, 132, 166, 258
Chancellor, Richard, 99
Chapuys, Eustace, 43-4
Charles V, 42-3, 246, 250; backs Mary over religion, 45-50; relations with England, 56-8; opposition to Northumberland, 88, 90, 96-8, 108-10; opposes Northumberland's coup, 117, 119, 129, 133-34, 136-7, 140, 143, 147; helps Mary establish control, 156-8, 161, 168-9, 173, 176, 179, 181-2; and Spanish marriage, 184-204, 208-9; and Wyatt's revolt, 210-4, 217-8, 229-30
Cheke, Sir John, 63, 80, 83, 100-1, 114
Cheyne, Thomas, 141, 152
Cleves, Anne of, 150, 177
Clifford, Margaret, 69-70
Clinton, Edward, 119, 135, 141
Cobham, Lord, 133-4, 137
Cobham, Sir William, 219, 224
Commendone, 90, 124, 259
Cooper, Thomas, 61, 163, 225
Counter-Reformation, 150, 168, 189, 198, 248
Courtenay, Edward, Earl of Devonshire, 149, 204; as marriage candidate, 175, 185-200, 208-9; and links to Wyatt's conspiracy, 210-13, 224-5, 231, 235, 241-3
Cox, Dr., 14, 63
Cranmer, Thomas, 53-4, 103, 158, 168-70
Croft, Sir James, 210
Cromwell, Thomas, 27, 44, 154
D'Egmont, 204, 209
D'Oysel, 211-2
Darnley, Henry, 86
Delaroche, Paul, 240-1
Devise, 65-88 passim, 90-4, 100-6, 114, 140, 172, 177, 247, 253
Dudley, Andrew, 161-2
Dudley, Edmund, 16
Dudley, Guilford, 140, 183, 254; and marriage to Jane, 83, 92, 129-30; trial and execution, 158, 173, 238-9
Dudley, Henry, 136
Dudley, John (s), 161
Dudley, John, duke of Northumberland, 4, 8-9, 59, 61, 90-1, 98, 152, 154-6,

169, 171-4, 179-81, 191, 197, 201, 241; early career, 16-24; 35; opinions of, 24, 113-4, 117-8, 164-6, 244-7, 249-54; coup against Somerset, 22-23, 46, 50; and Privy Council, 26-8, 30-1, 113-5, 234; economic policy, 34-7, 57; and Parliament, 37-40; and Mary, 45-7, 51, 55-6, 107-10, 121, 236, 238; and Reformation, 53; foreign policy, 35, 57-8; and relations with Edward VI, 62-4; and devise, 65-89, 100, 104; and Guilford-Jane wedding, 92-3; and rumours of poisoning, 94-5; and relations with France, 93, 95-8, 119; and letters patent, 101-3, 106; and Jane Grey, 111, 124-5, 129-30, 131-2, 225; military campaign against Mary, 132-42, 146-8; trial and execution, 159-64

Dudley, Robert, 118, 131

Dussindale, Battle of, 19, 24

Edward VI, 3-5, 8-9, 28-9, 38, 57-8, 91, 110, 127, 150, 156, 176, 178-9, 181, 184, 204, 208, 245; and Somerset, 18, 21, 23-4; and Northumberland, 118, 253; social ideas, 34, 37; health, 26, 40, 45, 51, 55-6, 58-62, 91, 93-5, 97-100, 107, 109, 133; training for kingship, 42, 62-4, 129; and Mary, 44, 46-8, 50, 108, 145, 160, 169, 249; and religion, 52-3, 130, 151, 154, 180; and devise, 65-89, 92, 100-4, 165, 172, 247, 251, 253; and letters patent, 101-103, 105-6, 115, 137, 246; death, 111-3, 119, 122-5,132, 136, 143, 146, 148; burial, 157-8, 166

Elizabeth I, 3-5, 7-9, 41, 97, 100, 121, 125, 125-7, 137, 144, 148, 150-1, 177-8, 180, 216, 244-5, 252; and Mary, 43-4; and religion, 46, 54, 103-4, 253; and devise, 66, 71-75, 78-9, 85-7, 90, 90-1, 105; and suspicions of, 158, 173-5, 182, 203-4, 207; and marriage to Courtenay, 189, 208-9; and Wyatt's rebellion, 210, 224-6, 230-5, 242-3

Engagement, 103, 106, 109, 115

Feckenham, John, 238-9

Ferdinand, king of the Romans, 184, 200

Ferrers, Sir George, 26

Fitzalan, Henry, earl of Arundel, 20, 23, 49, 136-7, 142, 148, 152, 162-4, 193, 196, 204, 212

Fitzpatrick, Barnaby, 80

Foxe, John, 13; and 'book of martyrs', 165, 217, 238

Framlingham, 120, 135, 138-46, 152, 156

Gage, Sir John, 222

Gardiner, Stephen, bishop of Winchester, 52, 114; lord chancellor, 152-4, 162, 168, 171-2, 176, 178-9, 182; and Spanish marriage, 186-198; and Wyatt's revolt, 207-8, 210-12, 217-8, 223-27, 231, 234-5, 238, 243

Gates, Sir John, 21, 81, 101, 114,

156, 161-3
Gentlemen Pensioners, 138, 172, 222-4, 271
Granvelle, Cardinal Antoine Perrenot de, 187, 218
Greenwich, 26-7, 91, 99, 111, 113, 119, 122, 157, 216, 218-9
Gresham, Sir Thomas, 36, 181
Grey, Frances, duchess of Suffolk, 69-70, 76, 85-6, 106, 140, 173
Grey, Henry, duke of Suffolk, 23, 30, 77, 86, 92-3, 114, 134 141-2, 161, 208; and link to Wyatt's rebellion, 210-12, 224-8, 231, 239, 241-2, 247, 249-50, 254
Grey, Lady Jane, 3, 8, 16, 94, 97 117, 143-7, 149, 163, 182-3, 252, 254; and devise, 76-7, 79, 82-3, 85-7, 106; marriage, 92-3, 90; accession, 90-1, 107, 122-6; early life, 127-9; as queen, 129-30, 132-7, 139-42, 160; trial, 158, 173-4; execution, 225-6, 238-241
Grey, William, 135, 138
Grice, Gilbert, 138
Guilford, Sir Edward, 17
Hales, James, 103, 172
Harding, Thomas, 239
Hastings, Francis, earl of Huntingdon, 93, 114, 135, 212, 224
Henry VII, 5, 16, 165
Henry VIII, 4-5, 15-18, 27, 32, 35, 38, 51, 53, 56-7, 172, 181, 245; and succession, 70-2, 74, 84-5, 87-8 105, 122; and

Mary, 130, 132, 143; 168,
Herbert, William, earl of Pembroke, 23, 93, 114, 117, 137, 141-2, 147, 152; and defence of London against Wyatt, 217-23
Hoby, Sir Philip, 98
Holinshed, Raphael, 91, 252
House of Commons, 38-9, 84, 179-80, 196, 207
House of Lords, 38-9, 84, 207
Howard, Thomas, duke of Norfolk, 121, 149, 152, 159-60, 212, 214
Howard, William, 217, 223
Hungate, Thomas, 130-1
Ivan IV, 99
Jerningham, Francis, 138, 152, 156
Katherine of Aragon, 41-4, 74-5, 84, 180, 229
Kenninghall, 120, 131, 135
Kett, Robert, 19, 24, 138, 228, 232
Knevet, William, 224, 227
Knox, John, 53, 91
L'Aubespine, 93-100, 110, 134
Latimer, Hugh, 170
Leigh, Sir John, 187
Lennox, Margaret, 86
Machyn, Henry, 27, 91
Malet, Francis, 48
Mary I, 3-4, 7, 16, 40, 61, 244; reputation, 5, 150-1; fears over marriage partner, 8-9, 55-6, 97, 111, 245-6; religion, 44-51, 52, 55, 100-1, 116, 167-72, 246-8; economic and social policies, 34, 37, 180-1; upbringing, 41-44; and

devise, 65, 71-89, 90-1, 93-8; and letters patent, 101-6; and Charles V and Imperial envoys, 107-8, 109-11, 119-20, 133-4, 156-7, 175-6; fights for throne, 113, 117, 121-4, 126, 130-3, 135-42; reasons for victory, 144-7; entry into London, 148; character, 149, 239-43, 248-9, 250-2; forms Privy Council, 152-6; and Edward's burial, 157-8; deals with July plotters, 158-66, 173-4, 225-6, 238-42; and Elizabeth, 174-5, 242-3; coronation, 176-9; and Parliament, 176, 179-80, 196; and Noailles, 181-2; marriage negotiations, 183-205; and Wyatt's rebellion, 206-37, 242-3

Mary, Queen of Scots, 5, 86, 97, 133, 138

Mary, Regent of Netherlands, 48, 58, 218

Mason, Sir John, 133-4, 137, 142, 152, 185

Montagu, Sir Edward, 65, 83, 101-3, 114, 252

Morison, Richard, 48

Noailles, Antoine de, and Northumberland's plot, 91, 97-8, 107, 119; ingratiates himself with Mary, 148, 181-2; and Spanish marriage, 185-9, 194, 197-8, 203; and involvement in Wyatt's rebellion, 207-12, 227, 243

Northumberland, *see Dudley, John*

Paget, Sir William, as advisor to Somerset, 20, 23, 28, 35-6; rejoins council, 142, 152-4, 156, 179, 182; character, 154, 197; and Spanish marriage, 186-204; and Wyatt's rebellion, 207-9, 212, 227, 234-5

Palmer, Sir Thomas, 23, 161-4

Parliament, 6, 9, 17, 55, 60, 244, 249-50; and Northumberland, 31-2, 37-40; and succession, 71-5, 78-9, 84-8, 91-4, 100, 102, 106, 113, 132; and Mary, 143, 146-7, 168-9, 173, 176-80; and Spanish marriage, 183, 188, 194-7, 200-1, 206, 217, 235-7, 243-4

Parr, Queen Katherine, 8, 18, 128

Parr, William, earl of Northampton, 23-4, 30, 101, 114, 159, 161

Paulet, William, marquis of Winchester, 36, 114, 142, 152, 181

Petre, Sir William, 95, 98, 100, 102, 137, 152, 185, 193

Philip, Prince of Spain, 3, 130; and marriage, 56, 184-195, 198-204, 206-18, 227-30, 234-5, 243-8, 254

Pilgrimage of Grace, 44, 228, 233

Pole, Reginald, Cardinal, 169, 198, 209

Potter, Gilbert, 126, 144-5

Prayer Book, 54, 149, 153, 167-8, 180

Privy Council, and Mary's marriage, 9, 55-6, 72, 183-198, 201, 245-7; and Somerset's execution, 11, 13; and Northumberland, 16-25, 26, 37, 38-40, 77, 159-62, 254; functions and history, 27-30, 34;

and conflict with Mary, 45-51, 73-4; and religion, 52-5, 158, 167, 170-2; and Edward VI, 58, 63-4, 78, 82; and devise, 70, 83; and plot against Mary, 88, 91-3, 97, 100-12, 113-17, 119-125, 130-7, 139-42, 145-7; under Mary, 151-57, 166, 179, 203-4, 206-9, 248-9; and Wyatt's rebellion, 210-231, 234-6, 238, 242

Reformation, 6-7, 20, 29, 36, 45-6, 51-5, 77, 94, 97, 104, 162-3, 169, 171, 247, 252

Renaissance, 6-7, 32, 42, 127

Renard, Simon, 109; opposition to Jane, 119; helping Mary establish rule, 149, 155-8, 173-6, 181-2; and Spanish marriage, 183-97, 202-4; and Wyatt's rebellion, 207-8, 210-212, 217, 223, 226-7, 238, 242, 251, 252

Revenue Commission, 36

Ridley, Nicholas, 34, 125, 141, 167

Rochester, Robert, 47, 49, 152, 156, 193, 208

Scheyfve, Jean, 39, 58, 87; dispute over religion, 48-50; Edward VI's health, 58-9, 61, 92, 98, 110; and suspicions of plot, 92-8, 107-111, 119-20, 134; and Mary's marriage, 183-5

Seymour, Thomas, 128

Shelley, Richard, 140

Sidney, Sir Henry, 112

Six Articles, 53

Seymour, Edward, duke of Somerset, 18, 114-7, 128, 132, 136, 152, 154, 159, 161-2, 165, 169, 181; execution, 11-15, 16, 76; career, 18-22, 28-9, 33-5, 39, 50, 52, 55, 62; and dealings with Mary, 45-7, downfall, 20, 23-5

Soranzo, Giacomo, 118, 149, 171, 188

St André, Marshal, 63

Statute of Merton, 72

Stow, John, 91, 135, 141, 216, 252

Succession Acts, 9, 75, 102, 146, 255

Sweating Sickness, 59, 82

Thomas, William, 80, 210, 227, 242, 262

Throckmorton, Sir Nicholas, 227

Titian, 49, 202

Treaty of London, 42

Treaty of Utrecht, 57-8

Troughton, Richard, 145-6, 259

Tunstal, Bishop Cuthbert, 52-3, 168

Underhill, Edward, 166, 22227

Van der Delft, François, 46-7

Vives, Juan, 42

Willoughby, Sir Hugh, 99

Wolsey, Cardinal Thomas, 17, 154

Wotton, Nicholas, 45, 98, 188, 208

Wriothesley, Charles, 25-6, 171, 217

Wriothesley, Thomas, earl of Southampton, 20

Wyatt, Sir Thomas, 4, 8, 106, 171-2; and revolt against Mary, 210-236, 242-50; trial, 238-42, 254

Printed in Great Britain
by Amazon